FOOD CORPORATION OF INDIA

[FCI]

PRELIMINARY EXAMINATION

Manager (General / Depot / Movement / Accounts / Technical / Civil Engineering / Electrical Mechanical Engineering / Hindi)

10

PRACTICE SETS

Edited & Compiled by:

Diamond Power Learning Team

DIAMOND POWER LEARNING

Published by:

Diamond Power Learning

An imprint of

Diamond Pocket Books Pvt. Ltd.

Head Office:

X-30, Okhla Industrial Area, Phase–II,

New Delhi –110020

Tel : +9111-40712200

Website : www.diamondbook.in

E-mail : sales@dpb.in

Production : Pushpendra Sharma

Contents

PRACTICE SETS

1 Practice Set

Reasoning

Directions (Q. 1-5): Study the following information carefully and answer the questions given below:

Seven persons —A, B, C, D, E, F and G — are standing in a straight line facing north at equal distances but not necessarily in the same order. Each of them is a different professional *viz,* Actor, Reporter, Doctor, Engineer, Lawyer, Teacher and Painter but not necessarily in the same order. G is standing at the fifth position to the left of C. Reporter is standing at the third position to the right of G. F is standing at the fifth position to the right of A. E is standing second to the left of B. Engineer is standing at the second position to the left of D. Three persons are sitting between Engineer and Painter. Doctor is to the immediate left of Engineer. Lawyer is to the immediate right of teacher.

1. **How many persons are there to the left of Reporter?**
   (a) None (b) Four
   (c) Two (d) Three

2. **Which of the following pairs of persons are sitting at the extreme ends?**
   (a) A and Actor
   (b) Engineer and C
   (c) Doctor and F
   (d) F and Lawyer

3. **Who among the following is sitting exactly in the middle of the row?**
   (a) Doctor (b) F
   (c) Lawyer (d) B

4. **Who among the following is sitting second to the right of Teacher?**
   (a) Painter (b) B
   (c) A (d) Actor

5. **Who among the following are the immediate neighbours of Painter?**
   (a) Actor and Teacher
   (b) B and Lawyer
   (c) B and Engineer
   (d) Reporter and C

Directions (Q. 6-7): Study the following information carefully and answer the questions given below:

Point A is 11 metres to the north of point B. Point C is 11 metres to the east of point B. Point D is 5 metres to the north of point C. Point E is 7 metres to the west of the point D. Point F is 9 metres to the north of point E. Point G is 4 metres to the west of point F.

6. **Point D is in which direction with respect to point F?**
   (a) North-East (b) South-East
   (c) South (d) North-West

7. **Which of the following three points lie in a straight line?**
   (a) A, E and D (b) F, E and C
   (c) G, F and B (d) G, A and B

Directions (Q. 8-10): Study the following information carefully and answer the questions given below:

Among six persons — K, L, M, N, O and P— each lives on a different floor of a building having six floors numbered one to six (the ground floor is numbered 1, the floor above it is numbered 2 and so on and the topmost floor is numbered 6).

L lives on an even numbered floor. L lives on a floor immediately below K's floor and immediately above M's floor. P lives on a floor immediately above N's floor. P lives on an even numbered floor. O does not live on floor number 4.

8. **Who amongst the following live on the floors exactly between K and P?**
   (a) O and L (b) L and N
   (c) L and M (d) M and N

9. **On which floor does O live?**
   (a) 6th (b) 2nd
   (c) 3rd (d) 5th

10. **Who amongst the following does live on floor 5?**
    (a) O (b) M
    (c) N (d) K

Directions (Q. 11-15): Each of the questions below consists of a question and two statements numbered I and II given below it. You have to decide whether the data provided in the statements are sufficient to answer the question. Read both the statements and Give answer

(a) if the data in statement 1 alone are sufficient to answer the question, while the data in statement II alone are not sufficient to answer the question.
(b) if the data in statement II alone are sufficient to answer the question, while the data in statement I alone are not sufficient to answer the question.
(c) if the data in both the statements I and II together are necessary to answer the question.
(d) if the data, given in both the statements I and II together are not sufficient to answer the question.

11. **Is D the mother of S?**
    I. L is the husband of D. L has only three children.
    II. N is the brother of S and P. P is the daughter of L.

12. How many students are there in the class?

I. There are more than 20 but less than 27 students in the class.

II. There are more than 24 but less than 31 students in the class. When the students are divided into groups, each group contains five students.

13. Among J, K, L, M and N, each has different height. Who amongst them is the second tallest?

I. N is taller than M and K. K is shorter than M.

II. L is taller than N. J is not the tallest,

14. Five persons —A, B, C, D and E— are sitting in a circle facing the centre. Who is sitting to the immediate left of D?

I. C is sitting second to the left of A. B and D are immediate neighbours of each other.

II. D is sitting to the immediate left of B. E its not an immediate neighbour of D and B.

15. How is 'cost' written in a code language?

I. 'tell me the cost' is written as '@ 0 # 9' and 'cost was very high' is written as '& 6 # 1' in that code language.

II. 'some cost was discount' is written as '187 #' and 'some people like discount' is written as '875 %' in that code language.

Directions (Q. 16-20): In these questions, relationship between different elements is shown in the statements. These statements are followed by two conclusions. Mark answer

(a) if only conclusion I follows.

(b) if both conclusions I and II follow.

(c) if either conclusion I or II follows.

(d) if neither conclusion I nor II follows.

16. Statements:

$K > I^3 T^3 E; O < R < K$

Conclusions:

I. $R < E$

II. $O < T$

17. Statements:

$B > A > S < I > C > L < Y$

Conclusions:

I. $B > L$

II. $A > Y$

18. Statements:

$C < L < O = U = D > S > Y$

Conclusions:

I. $O > Y$

II. $C < D$

19. Statements:

$B > R > E > A > K; H > A > S$

Conclusions:

I. $H > K$

II. $S < B$

20. Statements: $J = A; C > K > S > A$

Conclusions:

I. $C > J$

II. $C = J$

Directions (Q. 21-24): In each of the questions/set of questions below are given two statements followed by two conclusions numbered I and II. You have to a sum is every thing in the statements to be true even if they seem to b e at variance from commonly known facts and then decide which of the two given conclusions logically follows from the information given in the statement. Give answer

(a) if only conclusion I follows.

(b) if only conclusion II follows.

(c) if either conclusion I or conclusion II follows.

(d) if neither conclusion I nor conclusion II follows.

21. Statements: All alphabets are numbers.

Some alphabets are letters.

Conclusions:

I. At least some letters are numbers.

II. No letter is a number.

22. Statements: Some squares are circles.

Some circles are triangles

Conclusions:

I. At least some triangles are squares.

II. No triangle is a square.

23. Statements: No office is a building.

All colleges are building.

Conclusions:

I. All buildings are colleges.

II. No college is an office.

24. Statements: Some wins are losses.

All trophies are losses.

Conclusions:

I. All trophies are wins.

II. All losses are trophies.

25. In the following question, select the related letters from the given alternatives.

NPBG : OQCH : : AJOT : ?

(a) BKPU (b) BUPK

(c) BHKP (d) HBKU

Directions (Q. 26-30): Study the following information carefully and answer the questions given below:

In a certain code language 'very large risk associated" is written as *'nu ta ro gi'*, 'risk is very low' is written as *'gise nu mi'*, 'is that also associated' is written as *'ta mipofu'*, 'inherent risk also damaging' is written as *'fu nu diyu'*

26. Which of the following is the code of 'damaging'?

(a) di (b) yu

(c) gi (d) either di or yu

27. Which of the following may represent 'risk is very large'?

(a) *gi mi nu ro* (b) *nu gi tase*

(c) *nu ro seyu* (d) *ro gi di nu*

28. Which of the following is the code of 'associated'?

(a) nu (b) po

(c) ta (d) fu

29. What would be the code for 'inherent large risk'?

(a) *yu ro nu*

(b) *di ro nu*

(c) *yu fu ro*

(d) Cannot be determined

30. Which of the following may represent *'low risk associated industry'*?
(a) *ta nu gi ro* (b) *ta hi nu se*
(c) *mi ta sefu* (d) *di gi tapo*

Directions (Q. 31-35): Study the following information carefully and answer the questions given below:

C E B A C D B C D A C E D E D C A B A D A C E D U B A N B D

31. How many such D's are there in the above arrangement each of which is immediately preceded by a consonant and also immediately followed by a vowel?
(a) None (b) One
(c) Two (d) Three

32. How many D's are there in the above arrangement?
(a) Four (b) Three
(c) Five (d) Six

33. If all the B's are deleted from the above arrangement, which of the following will be eleventh from the left end?
(a) D (b) C
(c) E (d) A

34. How many such A's are there in the above arrangement each of which is immediately preceded by B and also immediately followed by a consonant?
(a) None (b) One
(c) Two (d) Three

35. Which of the following is ninth to the right of the 22nd from the right end of the above arrangement?
(a) A (b) C
(c) B (d) D

Quantitative Aptitude

36. The ratio of monthly salaries of two persons, A and B is 8 : 7. If the salary of A is increased by 20% and that of B by 11%, the new ratio becomes 96:77. What is A's salary?
(a) ₹ 800
(b) ₹ 775
(c) ₹ 750
(d) Cannot be determined

37. Simple interest on a certain sum at 7 p.c.p.a for 4 years is ₹ 3584. What will be the compound interest on the same principal at 4 p.c.p.a. in two years?
(a) ₹ 1054.48 (b) ₹ 1044.48
(c) ₹ 938 (d) ₹ 1064.84

38. The cost of pure milk is ₹ 16 per litre. On adding water, the mixture is sold at ₹ 15 per litre. In this way, the milkman earns 25% profit. What is the ratio of milk and water in the mixture?
(a) 25 : 7 (b) 7 : 25
(c) 15 : 1 (d) 1 : 15

39. Four persons—M, N, O and P—distributed a sum of ₹ 44352 among themselves. M got $\frac{3}{8}$th of total amount. N got $\frac{1}{6}$th part of the remaining amount. Thereafter, the remaining amount was divided between O and P in the ratio 3 : 2. The amount received by P is
(a) ₹ 1988 (b) ₹ 1848
(c) ₹ 1884 (d) ₹ 1684

40. Three persons A, B and C start a business with ₹ 12800, ₹ 16800 and ₹ 9600 respectively. At the end of the year, B received ₹ 13125 as share in total profit. What is the share of Mr C in the profit?
(a) ₹ 7850 (b) ₹ 7550
(c) ₹ 7500 (d) ₹ 8500

41. A shopkeeper has goods of worth ₹ 6000. He sold half of the goods at a gain of 12%. At what profit per cent should he sell the remaining half of the stock so that he gets 18% profit on the whole?
(a) 25% (b) 24%
(c) 18% (d) 8%

42. A 210- metre long train crosses a man running at 9 kmph in opposite direction in 6 seconds. Find the speed of the train.
(a) 58 kmph (b) 97 kmph
(c) 107 kmph (d) 117 kmph

43. Average score of a cricketer in 13 matches is 42 runs. If the average score in the first 5 matches be 54 runs, what is the average score in the last eight matches?
(a) 36.5 (b) 34.5
(c) 35.4 (d) 38

44. The perimeter of a rectangle whose length is 6 metres more than its breadth is 84 metres. What is the area of the triangle whose base is equal to the diagonal of the rectangle and height is equal to the length of the rectangle?
(a) 360 sq metres
(b) 380 sq metres
(c) 360 metres
(d) 400 sq metres

45. Due to decrease of 10% in the price of tea per kg, a consumer buys 250 gm of tea more than before for ₹ 270. What is the original price of tea?
(a) ₹ 130/kg (b) ₹ 120/kg
(c) ₹ 115/kg (d) ₹ 140/kg

Directions (Q. 46-57): What will come in place of the question mark(?) in the following questions?

46. $-676.76 + 1237.87 + 897.34 - ? = 1294.25$
(a) 173 (b) 164.2
(c) 154.2 (d) 164.8

47. $\frac{3}{8}$ of $\{4624 \div (564 - 428)\} = ?$
(a) 11.75 (b) 15.73
(c) 21.75 (d) 12.75

48. $\frac{6 \times 136 \div 8 + 132}{628 \div 16 - 26.25} = ?$
(a) 18 (b) 17
(c) 15 (d) 19

49. $(216)^4 \div (36)^4 \times 6^5 = (6)^?$
(a) 8 (b) 9
(c) 7 (d) 10

50. **$456 \div 24 \times 38 - 958 + 364 = ?$**
(a) 228 (b) 124
(c) 128 (d) 138

51. $3\frac{6}{17} \div 2\frac{7}{34} - 1\frac{9}{25} = (?)^2$
(a) $\frac{2}{5}$ (b) $\frac{3}{5}$
(c) $\frac{5}{2}$ (d) $\frac{5}{3}$

52. **$(43)^2 + 841 = (?)^2 + 1465$**
(a) 15 (b) 65
(c) 45 (d) 35

53. $4\frac{1}{2} + \left(1 \div 2\frac{8}{9}\right) - 3\frac{1}{13} = ?$
(a) $\frac{23}{13}$ (b) $\frac{13}{25}$
(c) $\frac{25}{13}$ (d) $\frac{25}{26}$

54. $\dfrac{\{(441)^{1/2} \times 207 \times (343)^{1/3}\}}{\{(14)^2 \times (529)^{1/2}\}} = ?$
(a) 5.75 (b) 6.75
(c) 7.75 (d) 6.25

55. **(1097.63 + 2197.36 – 2607.24) ÷ 3.5 = ?**
(a) 196.5 (b) 186.5
(c) 196.75 (d) 200.5

56. $\{\sqrt{7744} \times 11^2\} - 2^3 = (?)^3$
(a) 121 (b) 11
(c) 9 (d) 12

57. $3\frac{3}{8} \times 6\frac{5}{12} - 2\frac{3}{16} \times 3\frac{1}{2} = ?$
(a) 16 (b) 12
(c) 14 (d) 18

Directions (Q. 58-62): What will come in place of the question mark (?) in the following number series?

58. **960 839 758 709 ? 675**
(a) 698 (b) 694
(c) 684 (d) 648

59. **3 ? 14 55 274 1643**
(a) 5 (b) 6
(c) 7 (d) 8

60. **36 38.8 42.8 ? 54.4 62**
(a) 46 (b) 48
(c) 45 (d) 48.2

61. **37 ? 103 169 257 367**
(a) 49 (b) 46
(c) 56 (d) 59

62. **46 12 ? 90 315**
(a) 25 (b) 27
(c) 30 (d) 48

Directions (Q. 63-67): In the following table, the number of pages printed by 6 printers in 5 weeks has been given. Read the following table carefully and answer the questions.

Number of pages printed by 6 printers in 5 weeks

Printer / Week	A	B	C	D	E	F
First	664	618	628	552	638	419
Second	569	441	519	438	621	437
Third	440	614	503	527	541	742
Fourth	256	563	347	651	412	321
Fifth	717	429	598	582	519	693

63. **What is the average number of pages printed by all printers in the first week?**
(a) 586.5 (b) 540
(c) 545.4 (d) 546.5

64. **What is the average number of pages printed by printer C taking all the weeks together?**
(a) 529 (b) 519
(c) 591 (d) 592

65. **In which week was the number of printed pages maximum?**
(a) First (b) Second
(c) Third (d) Fifth

66. **The difference between the pages printed by printers A and E in the second week is**
(a) 46 (b) 42
(c) 62 (d) 52

67. **The difference between the total pages printed by printers B and C (all weeks taken together) is**
(a) 65 (b) 70
(c) 73 (d) 77

68. **Pipe A can fill a tank in 8 hours while another pipe B can fill it in 16 hours. A third pipe C can empty the full tank in 32 hours. All three pipes are opened simultaneously. In what time will an empty tank be filled?**
(a) 5.5 hours (b) 6 hours
(c) 6.4 hours (d) 7 hours

69. **A and B are two numbers. Six times square of B is 540 more than square of A. The ratio of A and B is 3 : 2. Find the number B?**
(a) 12 (b) 18
(c) 14 (d) 28

70. **Eight years ago, the age of Vishal was four times that of Shekhar's. After 8 years, Vishal's age will be twice of Shekhar's age. Vishal's present age is**
(a) 24 years (b) 28 years
(c) 30 years (d) 32 years

English Language

Directions (Q. 71-75): In each of these questions, two sentences (I) and (II) are given. Each sentence has a blank in it. Four words (a), (b), (c) and (d) are suggested. Out of these, only one fits at both the places in the context of each sentence. Number of that word is the answer.

71. **I.** Future generations will be left with a _______ of pollution and destruction.
II. They each received a _______ of $ 10000
(a) legacy (b) sum
(c) fortune (d) amount

72. **I.** He was _______ in bringing about an end to the conflict.
II. Mr Hari Prasad Chaurasia is an exponent of _______ music.
(a) instrument (b) instrumental
(c) keen (d) instructor

73. **I.** Many _______ men remarry and have second families.
II. When he was depressed, he felt utterly _______ from reality.
(a) divided (b) separate
(c) disturbed (d) divorced

74. **I.** Most of our employees get _______ stage.
II. The aircraft and its crew were _______ missing.
(a) announced (b) arrested
(c) sent (d) posted

75. **I.** He admired his _______ in the mirror.
II. The article is an accurate

_______ of events that day.

(a) reflection (b) description
(c) imagery (d) photograph

Directions (Q. 76-80): In each question below, four words printed in bold type are given. These are numbered (a), (b), (c) and (d). One of these words printed in bold may either be wrongly spelt or inappropriate in the context of the sentence. Find out the word that is in appropriate or wrongly spelt, if any. The number of that word is your answer.

76. Only the **golkeeper's** (a)/ **reflexes** (b)/ stopped the **ball** (c)/ from **going in.** (d)/

77. He **has** (a)/ **refrain** (b)/ from **criticizing** the **government** (c)/ in the public. (d)

78. To save his own **skull** (a)/ he lied and **blamed** (b)/ the **accident** (c)/ on his **friend.** (d)/

79. He was **badly** (a)/ **shaken** (b)/ by the news (c)/ of her **dead.** (d)/

80. **We lost** (a)/ **our** way (b)/ in the **laybarinth** (c)/ of **streets.** (d)/

Directions (Q. 81-85): Read each sentence to find out whether there is any grammatical error in it. The error if any will be in one part of the sentence, the number of that part will be the answer.

81. Let's wait and see (a)/how the land (b)/ laid before (c)/ we do anything. (d)/

82. In ancient Greece (a)/ a messenger ran from Marathon (b)/ to Athens with the news of (c)/ a victory of the pensians. (d)

83. Grammar information enables (a)/ students to map a (b)/ structure of a foreign (c)/ language onto their own. (d)

84. Their wedding (a)/ turned out to be (b)/ quite (c)/ a occasion. (d)/

85. I may be stated (a)/ the obvious but (b)/ without morernoney the (c)/ project cannot survive. (d)/

Directions (Q. 86-90): Rearrange the following six sentences/group of sentences (A), (B), (C), (D), (E) and (F) in the proper sequence to form a meaningful paragraph, then answer the questions given below them.

(A) The storm-given the name Hercules-closed major roads with snowdrifts.

(B) A fierce winter storm brought dangerous glacial temperature in New York on Friday.

(C) Weather experts said the wind chill temperature would plummet to –25° in New York.

(D) With more than 24 inches of snow falling in the city, a state of emergency was declared.

(E) More than 4000 international and domestic flights were also cancelled.

(F) Indeed storms are disastrous.

86. Which of the following should be the **FIRST** sentence after the rearrangement?

(a) E (b) B
(c) D (d) C

87. Which of the following should be the **FOURTH** sentence after the rearrangement?

(a) D (b) F
(c) B (d) E

88. Which of the following should be the **FIFTH** sentence after the rearrangement?

(a) E (b) D
(c) B (d) C

89. Which of the following should be the **SIXTH (LAST)** sentence after the rearrangement?

(a) A (b) D
(c) F (d) E

90. Which of the following should be the **SECOND** sentence after the rearrangement?

(a) A (b) D
(c) F (d) B

Directions (Q. 91-100): Read the following passage carefully and answer the questions given below it. Certain words have been printed in bold to help you locate them while answering some of the questions.

Internet banking is the term used for new age banking system. Internet banking is also called as online banking and it is an outgrowth of PC banking. Internet banking uses the internet as the delivery channel by which to conduct banking activity, for example, transferring funds, paying bills, viewing checking and savings account balances, paying mortgages and purchasing financial instruments and certificates deposits. Internet banking is a result of explored possibilit; to use internet application in one of the various domains of commerce. It is difficult to infer whether the internet tool has been applied for convenience of bankers or for the customers' convenience. But ultimately it contributes in increasing the efficiency of the banking operation as well providing more convenience to customers. Without even interacting with the bankers, customers **transact** from one corner of the country to another corner.

There are many advantages of online Banking. It is convenient, it isn't bound by operational timings, there are no geographical barriers and the services can be offered at a **minuscule** cost. Electronic banking has experienced explosive growth and has transformed traditional practices in banking.

Private Banks in India were the first to implement internet banking services in the banking industry. Private Banks, due to late entry into the industry, understood that the establishing network in remote corners of the country is a very difficult task. It was clear to them that the only way to stay connected to the customers at any place and at any time is through internet applications. They took the internet applications as a weapon of competitive advantage to corner the great **monoliths** like State bank of India, Indian Bank etc. Private Banks are pioneer in India to explore the versatility of internet applications in delivering services to customers.

Several studies have attempted to assess the relative importance of B2B and B2C business domains. There is wide difference in estimates of volume of business transacted over Internet and its components under B2C and B2B. However, most studies agree that volume of transactions in B2B domain far exceeds that in B2C. This is expected result. There is also a growing opinion that the future of e-business lies in B2B domain, as compared to B2C. This has several reasons, like low penetration of PCs to households, low bandwidth availability etc in a large part of the world. The success of B2C ventures depends; to a large extent on the shopping habits of people in different parts of the world. A survey sponsored jointly by Confederation of Indian Industries and Infrastructure Leasing and Financial Services on e-commerce in India in 2010 the following observations. 62% of PC owners and 75% of PC non-owners but who have access to Internet would not buy through the net, as they were not sure of the product offered. The same study estimated the size of B2B business in Ind ia by the year 2011 to be varying between ₹ 1250 billion to ₹ 1500 billion. In a recent study done by Arthur Anderson, it has been estimated that 84% of total e-business revenue is generated from B2B segment and the growth prospects in this segment are substantial. It has estimated the revenues to be anywhere between US $21 trillion to over US$21 trillion within the next three years (2014).

91. Which bank(s) is/are pioneer in India to explore the versatility of internet banking in serving customers?
(a) State Bank of India
(b) Indian Bank
(c) Public Sector Banks
(d) Private Banks

92. Which of the following is not an advantage of online banking?
(a) It is convenient.
(b) It is bound by operational timings.
(c) The services can be offered at a minimum cost.
(d) There is no geographical barrier.

93. What percentage of PC non-owners but who have access to Internet would not prefer to buy through the net, as they are not sure of the product offered?
(a) 75% (b) 62%
(c) 84% (d) 76%

94. Which type of activities are performed by internet banking?
(a) Paying bills
(b) Transferring funds
(c) Paying mortgages
(d) None of these

95. What estimate was made by confederation of Indian Industries regarding the size of B2B business in India by the year 2014?
(a) Between ₹ 250 billion to ₹ 500 billion
(b) Between ₹ 1250 billion to ₹ 1500 billion
(c) Between ₹ 850 billion to ₹ 1050 billion
(d) Between $8.7 trillion to $21 trillion

Directions (Q. 96-98): Choose the word which is most similar in meaning to the word printed in bold as used in the passage.

96. Versatility
(a) multi-utility
(b) vesicle
(c) dullness
(d) necessity

97. Monoliths
(a) large blocks of stone
(b) large organisations
(c) monopoly
(d) dwarfs

98. Transact
(a) do business (b) tranquillize
(c) transcend (d) exceed

Directions (Q. 99-100): Choose the word which is most opposite in meaning to the word printed in bold as used in the passage.

99. Substantial
(a) meagre (b) considerable
(c) large (d) submissive

100. Minuscule
(a) small (b) minimum
(c) minute (d) large

Answer sheet

1. (b)	**2.** (a)	**3.** (c)	**4.** (b)	**5.** (d)	**6.** (b)	**7.** (d)	**8.** (c)	**9.** (a)	**10.** (d)
11. (c)	**12.** (c)	**13.** (d)	**14.** (c)	**15.** (a)	**16.** (d)	**17.** (d)	**18.** (b)	**19.** (b)	**20.** (c)
21. (a)	**22.** (c)	**23.** (b)	**24.** (d)	**25.** (a)	**26.** (d)	**27.** (a)	**28.** (c)	**29.** (d)	**30.** (b)
31. (b)	**32.** (d)	**33.** (a)	**34.** (d)	**35.** (c)	**36.** (d)	**37.** (b)	**38.** (a)	**39.** (b)	**40.** (c)
41. (b)	**42.** (d)	**43.** (b)	**44.** (a)	**45.** (b)	**46.** (b)	**47.** (d)	**48.** (d)	**49.** (b)	**50.** (c)
51. (a)	**52.** (d)	**53.** (a)	**54.** (b)	**55.** (a)	**56.** (b)	**57.** (c)	**58.** (c)	**59.** (a)	**60.** (b)
61. (d)	**62.** (c)	**63.** (a)	**64.** (b)	**65.** (d)	**66.** (d)	**67.** (b)	**68.** (c)	**69.** (a)	**70.** (a)
71. (a)	**72.** (b)	**73.** (d)	**74.** (d)	**75.** (a)	**76.** (a)	**77.** (b)	**78.** (a)	**79.** (d)	**80.** (c)
81. (c)	**82.** (d)	**83.** (b)	**84.** (d)	**85.** (a)	**86.** (b)	**87.** (d)	**88.** (d)	**89.** (c)	**90.** (b)
91. (d)	**92.** (b)	**93.** (a)	**94.** (d)	**95.** (b)	**96.** (a)	**97.** (b)	**98.** (a)	**99.** (a)	**100.** (d)

Solutions

Hint for (1-5):

Doctor Engineer Teacher Lawyer Reporter Painter Actor

→ • • • • • • • ←

A G E D B F C

1. (b) **2.** (a) **3.** (c) **4.** (b) **5.** (d)

Hint for (6-7):

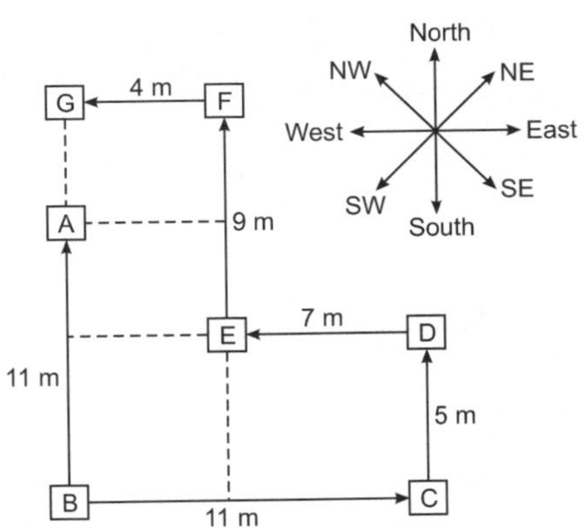

6. (b) It is clear from the diagram that point D is in the South- East direction of point F.

7.(d) Points G, A and B lie in a straight line.

Hint for (8-10):

Floor Number	Person
6	O
5	K
4	L
3	M
2	P
1	N

8. (c) **9.** (a) **10.** (d)

11.(c)**From statement I:**

L and D have only three children.

From statement II:

N, P and S are children of L.

From both the statements:

N, P and S are children of L and D.
so, D is mother of N, P and S.

12.(c)**From statement I:**

The number of students in the class
= 21, 22, 23, 24, 25 or 26

From statement II:

The number of students in the classs = 25 or 30

From both the statements:

There are 25 students in the class.

13.(d) **From statement I:**

N > M > K

From statement II :

□ > J

L > N

From both the statements:

L > N > M > K
(J between N and K)

14.(c) **From statement I:**

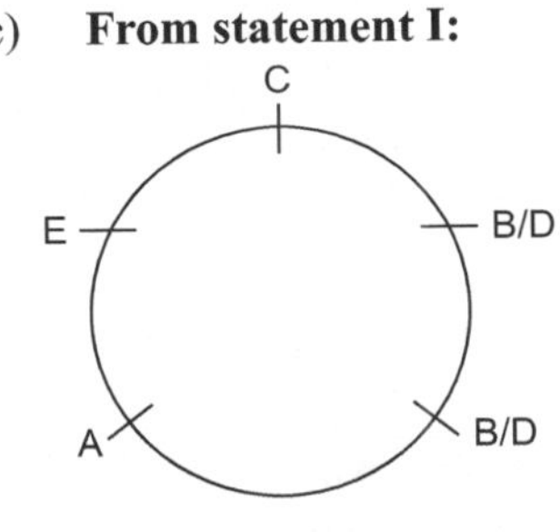

From statement II:

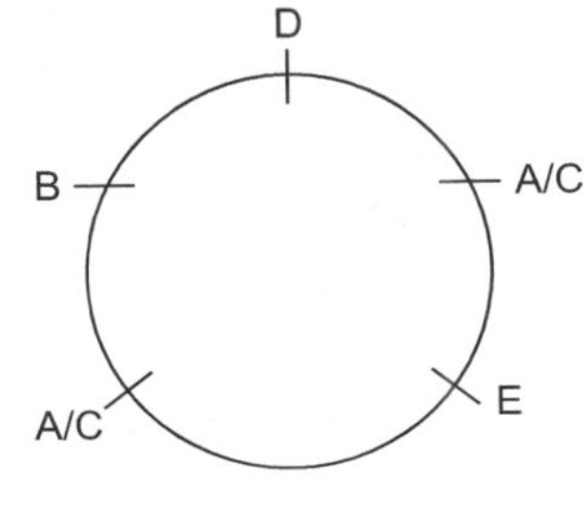

From both the statements:

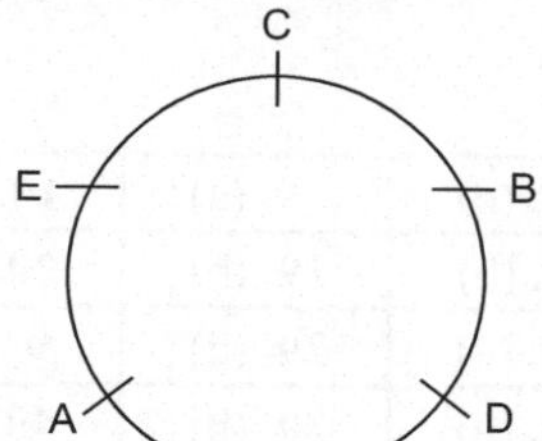

15.(a)**From Statement I:**

tell me the cost ⇒ @ 0 # 9......... (i)

cost was very high ⇒ & 6 # 1............ (ii)

From (i) and (ii),

cost ⇒ #

From statement II:

some cost was discount ⇒ 187#.............. (i)

some people like discount ⇒ 875 %................ (ii)

From (i) and (ii), some discount ⇒ 87

16.(d) O < R < K > I ≥ T ≥ E

Conclusions:

I. R < E: Not True

II. O < T: Not True

17.(d) B > A > S < I > C > L < Y

Conclusions:

I. B > L: Not True

II. A > Y: Not True

18.(b) C < L < O = U = D ≥ S > Y

Conclusions:

I. O > Y: True

II. C < D: True

19.(b)B > R > E > A > K

H > A > S

Conclusions:

I. H > K: True

II. S < B: True

20.(c) J = A

C ≥ K ≥ S ≥ A = J

Conclusions:

I. C > J: Not True

II. C = J: Not True

But, C is either greater than or equal to J.

Hint for (21-25):

21. (a) Some alphabets are letters → conversion → Some letters are alphabets + All alphabets are numbers = I + A = I = Some letters are numbers ⇒ At least some letter are numbers. Therefore, conclusion I follows.

22. (c) Both the Premisses are Particular Affirmative (I-type). No Conclusion follows from the two Particular Premises. Both the Conclusions form Complementary Pair. Therefore, either Conclusion I or II follows.

23. (b) All colleges are buildings + No building is an office (Conversion of the given statement 'No office is a building') = A + E = E = No college is an office. Therefore, conclusion II follows.

24. (d)

25. (a) The pattern is as follows:

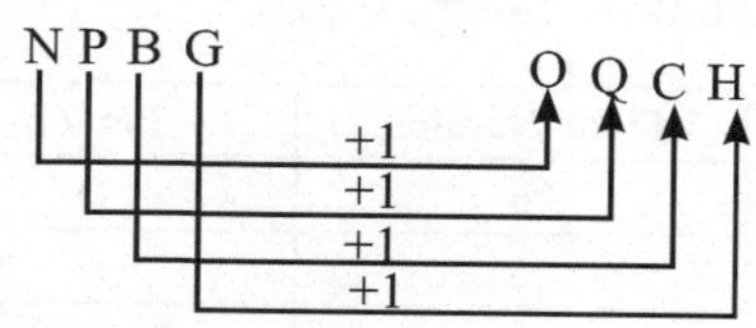

Similarly,

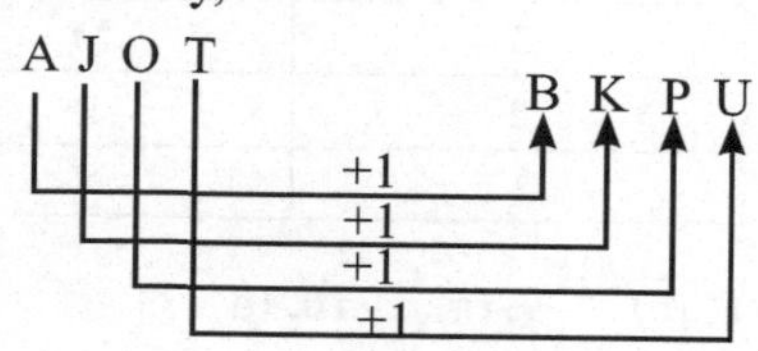

Given letters group is increasing a step a head. therefore, the place of questions mark(?) B K P U letters group will be kept.

Hinds for (26-30)

very large risk associated ⇒ *nu ta ro gi* .... (i)

risk is very low ⇒ *gi se nu mi* .... (ii)

is that also associated ⇒ *ta mi po fu* .... (iii)

inherent risk al so damaging ⇒ *fu nu di yu* .... (iv)

From (i) and (ii'), is ⇒ *mi* .... (v)

From (i), (ii) and (iv), risk ⇒ *nu* .... (vi)

From (i), (ii) and (vi), very ⇒ *gi* .... (vii)

From (ii), (v), (vi) and (vii), low ⇒ *se* .... (viii)

From (iii) and (iv), also ⇒ *fu* .... (ix)

From (i) and (iii"), associated ⇒ *ta* .... (x)

From (v), (ix) and (x), that ⇒ *po* .... (xi)

From (i), (vi), (vii) and (x), large ⇒ *ro* .... (xii)

26. (d) Code for *'damaging'* is either *'di'* or *'yu'*.

30. (b) The code for *'industry'* may be *'hi'*.

31. (b)

32. (d)

33. (a) New arrangement

CEACDCDACEDEOCAADACEDUAND

34. (d)

C E I **BAC** I D B C D A C E D E

D C A B A D A C E D U I B A N I B D

35. (c) 9th to the right of 22nd from the right end means 13th from the right end ie, B.

36. (d) Let, A's salary be ₹ 8x and B's salary be ₹ 7x. After respective increases, we have,

A's salary = ₹$\left(\frac{120 \times 8x}{100}\right)$

B's salary = ₹$\left(\frac{110 \times 7x}{100}\right)$

∴ A : B = 96 : 77

Hence, answer can't be determined.

37. (b) $P = \frac{SI \times 100}{Time \times Rate} = \frac{3584 \times 100}{4 \times 7}$

= ₹12800

$$CI = P\left[\left(1 + \frac{R}{100}\right)^T - 1\right]$$

$$= 12800\left[\left(1 + \frac{4}{100}\right)^2 - 1\right]$$

$$12800\left[\left(\frac{26}{25}\right)^2-1\right]$$

$$=12800\left(\frac{676}{625}-1\right)$$

$$=12800\times\frac{51}{625}=₹1044.48$$

38. (a) SP of 1 litre of mixture = ₹ 15, Gain = 20%

$$\therefore\ CP=\frac{100}{120}\times15=₹\frac{25}{2}$$

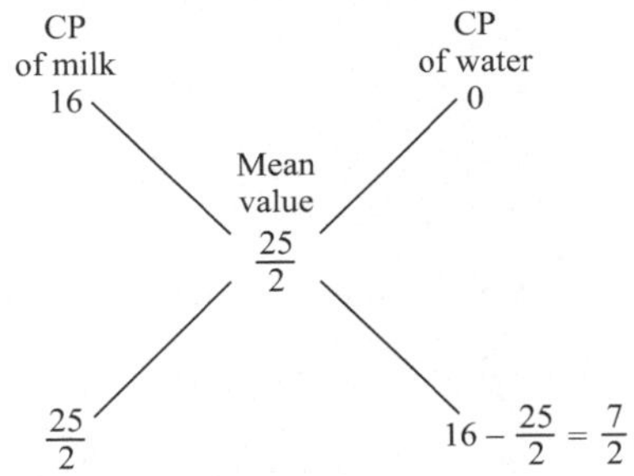

∴ Required ratio = 25 : 7

39. (b) M's share

$$=₹\left(\frac{3}{8}\times44352\right)=₹16632$$

Remaining amount = ₹ (44352 – 16632) = ₹ 27720

N's share =

$$₹\left(\frac{1}{6}\times27720\right)=₹4620$$

∴ P's share

$$=₹\left(\frac{2}{5}\times4620\right)=₹1848$$

40. (c) Ratio of their respective capitals = A : B : C

= 12800: 16800 : 9600

= 16 : 21 : 12

Let the total profit be Rs x.

$$\therefore\ \text{B's share}=₹\frac{21x}{49}$$

$$\therefore\ \frac{21x}{49}=13125$$

$$x=\frac{13125\times49}{21}=₹30625$$

$$\therefore\ \text{C's share}=\frac{12}{49}\times30625=7500$$

41. (b) For 18% gain,

$$\text{Total SP}=\frac{6000\times118}{100}=₹7080$$

SP of goods worth Rs 3000 at 12% profit

$$=\frac{3000\times112}{100}=₹3360$$

Expected SP of remaining goods

= ₹ (7080 – 3360) = ₹ 3720

Let the gain per cent be x%.

Now, according to the question,

$$=\frac{3000\times(100+x)}{100}=3720$$

$$\Rightarrow 100+x=\frac{3720}{300}=124$$

$$\Rightarrow x=124-100=24\%$$

42. (d) Let the speed of train be x kmph.

∴ Relative speed = $(x + 9)$ kmph

$$\because\ \frac{\text{Length of train}}{\text{Relative speed}}=\text{Time}$$

$$\Rightarrow \frac{\frac{210}{1000}}{x+9}=\frac{6}{60\times60}\Rightarrow\frac{21}{(x+9)}=\frac{1}{6}$$

$\Rightarrow x + 9 = 21 \times 6 = 126 \Rightarrow x = 126 - 9 = 117$ kmph

43. (b) Total runs in the last eight matches

= 13 × 42 – 5 × 54 = 546 – 270

= 276

∴ Required average

$$=\frac{276}{8}=34.5$$

44. (a) Let the breadth be x metres.

∴ length = $(x + 6)$ metres

Now, according to the question,

$2(x + 6 + x) = 84$

$\Rightarrow 2x + 6 = 42 \Rightarrow 2x = 36$

$\Rightarrow x = 18$

∴ Length = (18 + 6) = 24 metres = height of triangle

Diagonal of rectangle

$$=\sqrt{18^2+24^2}$$

$$=\sqrt{324+576}=\sqrt{900}=30\text{ metres}$$

= Base of triangle

⇒ Area of triangle

$$=\frac{1}{2}\times\text{base}\times\text{height}$$

$$=\frac{1}{2}\times30\times24=360\text{ sq metres}$$

45. (b) Original rate of tea = Rs x/kg

$$\text{New rate}=₹\,x\times\frac{90}{100}=\frac{9x}{10}/kg$$

New, according to the question,

$$\frac{270}{9x}-\frac{270}{x}=\frac{250}{1000}$$

$$\Rightarrow \frac{300}{x}-\frac{270}{x}=\frac{1}{4}$$

$$\Rightarrow \frac{30}{x}=\frac{1}{4}$$

$\Rightarrow x = 30 \times 4 =$ ₹ 120 per kg

46. (b) $2135.21 - 676.76 - ? = 1294.25$

$\Rightarrow 1458.45 - ? = 1294.25$

$\Rightarrow ? = 1458.45 - 1294.25 = 164.2$

47. (d)

$$?=\frac{3}{8}\times(4624\div136)=\frac{3}{8}\times\frac{4624}{136}$$

= 12.75

48. (d)

$$?=\frac{6\times\frac{136}{8}+132}{\frac{628}{10}-26.25}=\frac{102+132}{39.25-26.25}$$

$$=\frac{234}{13}=18$$

49. (b) $(6^3)^4 \div (6^2)^4 \times 6^5 = (6)^?$

$\Rightarrow 6^{12} \div 6^8 \times 6^5 = (6)^?$

$\Rightarrow (6)^{12-8+5} = (6)^? \Rightarrow 6^9 = 6^?$

$\Rightarrow ? = 9$

50. (c) $? = \frac{456}{24}\times38-958+364$

= 722 – 958 + 364 = 128

51. (a) $(?)^2=\frac{57}{17}\div\frac{75}{34}-\frac{34}{25}$

$= \frac{57}{17} \times \frac{34}{75} - \frac{34}{25}$

$= \frac{114}{75} - \frac{34}{25}$

$= \frac{114-102}{75} = \frac{12}{75} = \frac{4}{25}$

$\Rightarrow ? = \sqrt{\frac{4}{25}} \Rightarrow ? = \frac{2}{5}$

52. (d) $1849 + 841 = (?)^2 + 1465$

$\Rightarrow 2692 = (?)^2 = 2690 - 1465$
$= 1225$

$\therefore ? = \sqrt{1225} = 35$

53. (a) $? = \frac{9}{2} + \left(1 \div \frac{26}{9}\right) - \frac{40}{13}$

$= \frac{9}{2} + \frac{9}{26} - \frac{40}{13}$

$= \frac{117+9-80}{26} = \frac{46}{24} = \frac{23}{13}$

54. (b) $? = (21^2)^{1/2} \times 207 \times (7^3)^{1/3} \div \{196 \times (23^2)^{1/2}\}$

$= \frac{21 \times 207 \times 7}{196 \times 23} = 6.75$

55. (a) $? = (3294.99 - 2607.24) \div 3.5$
$= 687.75 \div 3.5 = 196.5$

56. (b) $\left\{\sqrt{7744} \times 11^2\right\} \div 2^3 = (?)^3$

$\Rightarrow \frac{88 \times 11^2}{8} = (?)^3$

$\Rightarrow (?)^3 = (11)^3 \quad \Rightarrow ? = 11$

57. (c) $? = \frac{27}{8} \times \frac{77}{12} - \frac{35}{16} \times \frac{7}{2}$

$= \frac{693}{32} - \frac{245}{32} \frac{448}{32} = 14$

58. (c) The pattern is
$960 - 839 = 121 = (11)^2$
$839 - 758 = 81 = (9)^2$
$758 - 709 = 49$
$= (7)^2$

$\therefore ? = 709 - 5^2 = 709 - 25 = 684$

59. (a) The pattern is
$3 \times 2 - 1 = 5$
$5 \times 3 - 1 = 14$
$14 \times 4 - 1 = 55$
$55 \times 5 - 1 = 274$
$274 \times 6 - 1 = 1643$

60. (b) The pattern is
$38.8 - 36 = 2.8$
$42.8 - 38.8 = 4 (= 2.8 + 1.2)$
$\therefore ? = 42.8 + (4 + 1.2) = 48$
$\therefore 54.4 - 48$
$= 6.4 (= 4 + 1.2 + 1.2)$

61. (d) The pattern is
$37 + 22 = 59$
$59 + 44 = 103$
$103 + 66 = 169$
$169 + 88 = 257$
$257 + 110 = 367$

62. (c) The pattern is as given below:
$4 \times 1.5 = 6$
$6 \times 2 = 12$
$12 \times 2.5 = 30$
$30 \times 3 = 90$
$90 \times 3.5 = 315$

Hint for (63 –67):

63. (a) Required average

$= \frac{1}{6}(664 + 618 + 628 + 552 + 638 + 419)$

$= \frac{1}{6} \times 3519 = 586.5$

64. (b) Required average

$= \frac{628 + 519 + 503 + 347 + 598}{5}$

$= \frac{2595}{5} = 519$

65. (c) Number of printed pages:
First week $\Rightarrow$ 3519
Second week $\Rightarrow$ 3025
Third week $\Rightarrow$ 3367
Fourth week $\Rightarrow$ 2550
Fifth week $\Rightarrow$ 3538

66. (d) Required difference
$= 621 - 569 = 52$

67. (b) Total pages:
Printer B $\Rightarrow$ 2665
Printer C $\Rightarrow$ 2595
$\therefore$ Difference $= 2665 - 2595 = 70$

68. (c) Part of the tank filled in 1 hour by all three pipes

$= \frac{1}{8} + \frac{1}{16} - \frac{1}{32}$

$= \frac{4+2-1}{32} = \frac{5}{32}$

Hence, the tank will be filled in $\frac{32}{5} = 6.4$ hours.

69. (a) let the number A and D be $3x$ and $2x$ resepectively.
Now, according to the question,
$6 \times B^2 - A^2 = 540$
$\Rightarrow 6 \times 4x^2 - 9x^2 = 540$
$\Rightarrow 15x^2 = 540$
$x^2 = \frac{540}{15} = 36$
$\Rightarrow x = \sqrt{36} = 6$
$\therefore B = 2x = 2 \times 6 = 12$

70. (a) 8 years ago, Let Shekhar's age be x years.
$\Rightarrow$ Vishal's age $= 4x$ years
$\therefore$ Present age of Vishal $= 4x + 8$
After 8 years from the present, we have,
$4x + 8 = 2(x + 8)$
$\Rightarrow 4x + 8 = 2x + 16 \Rightarrow 2x = 8$
$\Rightarrow x = 4$
Hence, present age of Vishal will be $= 4x + 8 = 4 \times 4 + 8 = 24$ year

2 Practice Set

Reasoning

1. **In a certain code 'CAREFUL'is written as 'SBDDMVG'. How is 'SECURED' written in that code?**
(a) DFTVEFS (b) DFTTEFS
(c) BDRTEFS (d) BTCDTQF

2. **How many such pairs of digits are there in the number 935126 each of which has as many digits between them in the number as when the digits are rearranged in descending order within the number?**
(a) Zero (b) One
(c) Two (d) More than Three

3. **Shyam walked 30 metres towards North, took a left turn and walked 20 metres. He again took a left turn and walked 30 metres. How far is he from the starting point?**
(a) 30 metres
(b) 50 metres
(c) 80 metres
(d) None of these

4. **Among P, Q, R, S and T each having a different weight, R is heavier than only T. P is lighter than only S. Who among is the third heaviest?**
(a) Q
(b) R
(c) S
(d) Data not sufficient

5. **Pointing to a boy, Tina said, "He is the only child of my father's only brother". How is the boy related to Tina?**
(a) Brother
(b) Cousin brother
(c) Uncle
(d) Data not sufficient

6. **If '×' means '–', '÷' means '+', '–' means '÷' and '+' means '×', then —**
64 ÷ 32 – 8 × 4 + 6 = ?
(a) 18 (b) 28
(c) 38 (d) 44

7. **How many such pairs of letters are there in the word CHANGES each of which has as many letters between them in the word as in the English alphabet?**
(a) Zero (b) One
(c) Two (d) Three

8. **Each even digit in the number 8795342 is replaced by the next higher digit and each odd digit is replaced by the previous lower digit and the digits so obtained are rearranged in ascending order. Which of the following will be the third from ths left end after the rearrangement?**
(a) 2 (b) 3
(c) 5 (d) 4

9. **If it is possible to make only one meaningful English word with the second, the fourth, the seventh and the ninth letters of the word ADMINISTER using each latter only once in each word, which of the following will be the third letter of that word? If no such word can be made, give 'X' as the answer and if more than one such word can be made, give 'Y' as the answer.**
(a) D (b) 1
(c) E (d) Y

10. **Sharda correctly remembers that her mother's birthday is after fourteenth April but before nineteenth April whereas her brother correctly remembers that their mother's birthday is before sixteenth April but after twelfth April. On which date in April was definitely their mother's birthday?**
(a) Thirteenth
(b) Fifteenth
(c) Sixteenth
(d) Data not sufficient

11. **What should come next in the following number series?**
9 8 7 6 5 4 3 2 1 9 8 7 6 4 3 2 1 9 8 7 6 4 3 2 9 8 7
(a) 6 (b) 4
(c) 3 (d) 1

Directions (Q. 12-15): *Following questions are based on the five three-digit numbers given below:*

826 391 435 678 283

12. **If the positions of the first and the second digits within each number are interchanged, which of the following will be the second digit of the highest number?**
(a) 8 (b) 3
(c) 4 (d) 6

13. **Which of the following is the difference between the second and third digits of the second lowest number?**
(a) 5 (b) 8
(c) 2 (d) 6

14. **Which of the following is the sum of the first and the second digits of the lowest number?**
(a) 10 (b) 11
(c) 12 (d) 13

15. **Which of the following is the third digit of the second highest number?**
(a) 7 (b) 1
(c) 5 (d) 8

16. **In a certain code 'GATE' is written as '9321' and 'TERM' is written as '2148'. How is 'MARE' written in that code?**
(a) 8241 (b) 8431
(c) 8341 (d) 8531

Directions (Q. 17-21): *In each of the questions below are given three statements followed by two conclusions numbered I & II. You have to take the given statements to be true even if they seem to be at variance from commonly known facts. Read all the conclusions and then decide which of the given conclusions logically follows from the given statements disregarding commonly known facts. Give answer*

(a) if only Conclusion I follows.
(b) if only Conclusion II follows.
(c) if either Conclusion I or II follows.
(d) if neither Conclusion I nor II follows.

17. **Statements:** Some pens are buses. Some buses are trucks. All trucks are trains.
Conclusions:
I. Some trucks are pen.
II. No truck is pens.

18. **Statements:** All letters are boxes. Some boxes are irons. All irons are magnets.
Conclusions:
I. Some magnets are letters.
II. Some magnets are boxes.

19. **Statements:** All glasses are pens. No pen is chalk. No chalk is stationary.
Conclusions:
I. No glass is chalk.
II. No glass is stationary.

20. **Statements:** All jungles are roads. All roads are rivers. All rivers are ponds.
Conclusions:
I. Some ponds are roads.
II. Some rivers are jungles.

21. **Statements:** All ropes are sticks. No stick is pen. Some pens are knives.
Conclusions:
I. Some knives are ropes.
II. Some knives are sticks.

22. In the following question, select the related number from the given alternatives.

101 : 10201 : : 107 : ?

(a) 10707 (b) 10749
(c) 11449 (d) 11407

Directions (Q. 23-28): *Study the following arrangement carefully and answer the questions given below :*

R M 4 A @ J H 1 N © # 2 B 9 E V W 5 ★ P U 6 3 I Z 8 8 Q

23. What should come in the place of question mark (?) in the following series based on the above arrangement?

MAJ N#B V5P ?

(a) 3 I Z (b) 6 $ Z
(c) 4 © E (d) 3 $ Z

24. Which of the following is the tenth to the right of the nineteenth from the right end of the above arrangement?

(a) U (b) N
(c) 3 (d) None of these

25. Four of the following five are alike in a certain way based on their positions in the above arrangement and so form a group. Which is the one that does not belong to that group?

(a) 2 # B (b) W V 5
(c) J @ H (d) δ δ Z

26. How many such numbers are there in the above arrangement, each of which is immediately preceded by a consonant and immediately followed by a symbol?

(a) Zero (b) One
(c) Two (d) Three

27. How many such consonants are there in the above arrangement, each of which is immediately preceded by a letter but not immediately followed by a number?

(a) Four (b) One
(c) Two (d) Three

28. If all the symbols in the above arrangement are dropped, which of the following will be the twelfth from the left end?

(a) 6 (b) E
(c) V (d) N

Directions (Q. 29-34): *Study the following information carefully and answer the questions given below:*

A, B, C, D, E, F, G, H and K are sitting around a circle facing the centre. B is fourth to the right of H and second to the left of A. F is fourth to the left of A and third to the right of C. G is third to the right of K. E is second to the left of D.

29. What is second to the left of K?

(a) A (b) D
(c) C (d) H

30. In which of the following pairs is the second person sitting to the immediate left of the first person?

(a) FG (b) EB
(c) HG (d) AK

31. Who is fifth to the right of F?

(a) A (b) K
(c) F
(d) Data not sufficient

32. Who is third to the right of E?

(a) A (b) H
(c) G (d) K

33. Who is second to the right of A?

(a) H (b) G
(c) C (d) B

Directions (Q. 34-35): *In the following questions, the symbols $, @ %, # and © are used with the following meaning as illustrated below:*

'P @ Q' means 'P is not smaller than Q'.
'P % Q' means 'P is not greater than Q'.
'P © Q' means 'P is neither smaller than nor equal to Q',
'P # Q' means 'P is neither greater than nor equal to Q'.
'P$Q' means 'P is neither greater than nor smaller than Q'.

Now in each of the following questions assuming the given statements to be true, find which of the two conclusions I and II given below them is/are definitely true?

Give answer

(a) if only Conclusion I is true.
(b) if only Conclusion II is true.
(c) if either Conclusion I or II is true.

(d) if neither Conclusion I nor II is true.

34. **Statements: K$Z, Z%M, M©N**
Conclusions: I. N#K II. M@K

35. **Statements: I©F, F#B, B@K**
Conclusions: I. K#F II. B©I

Quantitative Aptitude

Directions (Q. 36-47) : *What should come in place of the question mark (?) in the following questions?*

36. **9% of 1800 + $\frac{7}{13}$ of 221= ?**
(a) 441 (b) 381
(c) 271 (d) 281

37. **26% of 350 – 20% of 110 = ? × 23**
(a) 3 (b) 10
(c) 13 (d) 40

38. **182 ÷ 13 × 12 – 32 = ? + 93**
(a) 43 (b) 53
(c) 83 (d) 113

39. **23.141 – 32.417 = ? – 25.132**
(a) 15.866 (b) 17
(c) 15.566 (d) 15.856

40. **$455 \div 13 \times 2 - 37 = (?)^2 + 8$**
(a) 5 (b) $\sqrt{5}$
(c) 17 (d) 33

41. **$9^{3.5} \times 3^{2.2} \div 9^{(?)} = 9^{1.4}$**
(a) 3.1 (b) 6.4
(c) 3.2 (d) 4.6

42. $3\frac{1}{7} \times 1\frac{1}{132} \div 3\frac{1}{6} = ?$
(a) 1 (b) 2
(c) $\frac{2}{3}$ (d) $\frac{3}{7}$

43. **$3 \times 4^2 + 5^2 \times 5 - 7^2 = ? + 3$**
(a) 9^2 (b) 11^2
(c) 12^2 (d) 13^2

44. **75% of 560 – 40% of ? = 35**
(a) 20 (b) 25
(c) 40 (d) 30

45. **2321 + 2332 – 1234 = ? + 1113**
(a) 2316 (b) 2312
(c) 2306 (d) 3304

46. **437 – 382 + 639 = 76 – 354 + 23 + ?**
(a) 929 (b) 969
(c) 1049 (d) None of these

47. **(74 + 25 – 58) + (48 ÷ 12 × 3) = ?**
(a) 53 (b) 54
(c) 63 (d) 78

48. **The average age of father and son at present is 27 years. Also, the difference between their ages is 30 years. What is the respective ratio between the present age of father and the present age of son?**
(a) 8 : 3 (b) 7 : 2
(c) 6 : 7 (d) 3 : 8

49. **What is the value of two-seventh of thirty five per cent of two-third of 660?**
(a) 11 (b) 22
(c) 44 (d) 154

50. **In a test Manjit got 232 marks which were 56 more than that of the Saurabh's marks. Supriya got 40% marks out of the total marks of the test which were 24 marks more than the Saurabh's marks. What percentage of marks did Saurabh get?**
(a) 35
(b) 35.2
(c) 42
(d) Cannot be determined

51. **If a certain sum of money is equally distributed among 73 people, each one gets ₹ 154. What is the total sum of money distributed?**
(a) ₹ 11,222 (b) ₹ 11,422
(c) ₹ 12,242 (d) ₹ 11,242

52. **The total cost of the 12 kg of rice is ₹ 432 and the total cost of the 15 kg of pulse is ₹ 675. What is the ratio between the cost of the 2 kg of pulse and one kg of rice respectively?**
(a) 8 : 7 (b) 7 : 5
(c) 8 : 5 (d) 5 : 2

53. **Out of the fractions $\frac{3}{5}, \frac{2}{7}, \frac{5}{11}, \frac{5}{7}$ and $\frac{9}{13}$ what is the sum of the highest and the lowest fractions together?**
(a) 1 (b) $\frac{31}{35}$
(c) $\frac{59}{77}$ (d) 2

54. **Pranita gave ₹ 900 to her brother which is equal to two-fifth of the simple interest that she got in 6 years at the rate of 15 p.c.p.a. What was the sum of money (principal) that she had deposited?**
(a) ₹ 2,250 (b) ₹ 2,400
(c) ₹ 2,600 (d) ₹ 2,500

55. **Sumit has ₹ 36 more than Arnav. Arnav has 25% of the total amount that Anil has. Anil has a total of ₹ 1,540. What amount does Sumit have?**
(a) ₹ 420 (b) ₹ 385
(c) ₹ 422 (d) None of these

56. **The length of a rectangle is 6 cm more than its breadth. If the area of the rectangle is 112 sq cm. What is the perimeter of the rectangle?**
(a) 22 cm (b) 44 cm
(c) 34 cm (d) 28 cm

57. **Half of Sonit's monthly income is equal to four-seventh of Rohit's monthly income. Ragini's monthly income is ₹ 32000 which is double the monthly income of Sonit. What is Rohit's monthly income?**
(a) ₹ 16000
(b) ₹ 4571
(c) ₹ 14000
(d) Cannot be determined

Directions (Q. 58-59): *In the following number series only one number is wrong. Find out the wrong number.*

58. **2 2 4 12 48 228 1440**
(a) 2 (b) 4
(c) 12 (d) 288

59. **2 7 14 24 34 47 62**
(a) 7 (b) 14
(c) 24 (d) 47

Directions (Q. 60-62): *What approximate value should come in place of the question mark (?) in the following questions? (You are not expected to calculate the exact value.)*

60. **546% of 149 + 38.899 – 211.978 = ?**
(a) 440 (b) 350
(c) 270 (d) 650

61. 54.95% of 154.89 × 7.01 = ?
(a) 510 (b) 600
(c) 650 (d) 700

62. 1236.56 ÷ 48.99 × 9.87 = ?
(a) 250 (b) 150
(c) 300 (d) 325

63. The ratio between the angles of a triangle is 3 : 5 : 2 respectively. If the sum of the largest and the smallest angles of the triangle is equal to the largest angle of a parallelogram. What is the measure of the smallest angle of the parallelogram?
(a) 108° (b) 120°
(c) 80° (d) 54°

64. In how many different ways can the letter of word 'READERS' can be arranged?
(a) 1260 (b) 2520
(c) 5040 (d) 6250

65. A man crossed a stationary train in 5 minutes. Also, the same train crossed a man in 50 seconds. What is the ratio between the speed of the man and the speed of the train respectively?
(a) 1 : 8
(b) 5 : 14
(c) 1 : 9
(d) None of these

Direction (66-70): *Study the table carefully to answer the questions that follow:*

Number of Employees (in Thousands) working in six different companies in six years

Years	Company					
	K	L	M	N	P	R
2004	3.4	2.4	2.8	3.9	4.2	5.6
2005	1.2	3.4	3.0	4.1	1.9	4.5
2006	5.4	4.9	3.7	3.4	2.7	5.7
2007	6.3	4.7	5.5	5.3	5.6	2.9
2008	11.0	5.9	5.7	6.7	4.8	6.7
2009	7.2	7.4	5.9	9.6	6.4	4.8

66. What was the respective ratio between the employees working in company R in year 2005 and employees working in company L in year 2004?
(a) 8 : 15 (b) 15 : 8
(c) 13 : 9 (d) 9 : 13

67. What was the total number of employees working ir company M and P together in year 2008 and employees working in company L and R together in year 2005?
(a) 1,84,000 (b) 18,040
(c) 1,80,400 (d) 18,400

68. In which company was the total number of employees working in year 2007 the second highest?
(a) R (b) N
(c) L (d) P

69. Number of employees working in company K in year 2009 was what percentage of all the employees working in company N in all the years together?
(a) 25 (b) 30
(c) 21 (d) 31

70. What was the average number of employees working in year 2007 in all the companies together?
(a) 5,05,000 (b) 50,050
(c) 50,500 (d) None of these

English Language

Directions (71-85): *Read the following passage carefully and answer the questions given below it. Certain words/phrases have been printed in bold to help you local them while answering some of the questions.*

Once upon a time, there was a royal elephant which usa to reside in the premises of the king's palace. The elephant was very dear to the king, so he was well-fed and well-treated .There was also a Dog who lived near the Elephant's shed. He was very weak and skinny. He was always fascinated by the smell of rich sweet rice being fed to the royal elephant.

One day, the Dog could no longer **resist** the aroma of the rice and somehow managed to sneak into the Elephant's shed. He ate the grains of sweet rice that fell from the Elephant's mouth. He liked the rice so much, that he started going there daily to eat the rice. For days, the huge Elephant didn't notice the small dog as he was busy enjoying the delicious food. Gradually, the Dog grew bigger and stronger eating such rich food. Finally the Elephant noticed, him and allowed him access to the food.

The Elephant enjoyed the company of the Dog and started sharing his food with him. They also started spending time with each other and soon became good friends. They ate together, slept together and played together. While playing, the Elephant would hold the Dog in his trunk and swing him back and forth. Soon neither of them was Happy without the other. They became great friends and didn't want to be **separated** from each other.

Then one day a man saw the Dog and asked the Elephant-keeper, 'I want to buy this Dog. What price do you want for it ?" The Elephant-keeper didn't own the Dog but sold it and **extracted** a sum of money from this deal. The man took the Dog to his home village, which was quite far away. The King's Elephant became very sad after .this incident. He missed his friend a lot and started neglecting everything. He didn't want to do anything without his dear friend, so he stopped eating, drinking and even bathing.

Finally, the Elephant-keeper .reported this to the King; however he didn't mention anything about the Dog. The King had a wise minister, who was known for his **keen** understanding of animals. The King ordered the minister, "Go to the Elephant shed and find out the reason for the Elephant's condition". The intelligent minister went to the Elephant shed and found the Elephant very sad. He examined the Elephant and asked the Elephant-keeper, "There is nothing wrong with this Elephant's body, then why does he look so sad ? I think this Elephant is grief stricken, possibly due to the loss of a dear friend. Do you know if this Elephant shared a close friendship with anyone ?"

The Elephant-keeper said, "There was a Dog who used to eat, sleep and play with the Elephant. He was taken by a stranger three days ago". The minister went back to the King and said, "Your majesty, in my opinion, the royal Elephant is not sick, but he is lonesome without his dear friend, the Dog". The King said, "You're right, friendship is one of the most wonderful things of life. Do you know where that Dog is?"

The Minister replied, "Elephant-keeper has informed me that a stranger took him away and he doesn't know his whereabouts". The King asked, "How can we bring back my Elephant's friend and make him happy again ?" The Minister suggested, "Your Majesty, make a **declaration**, that whoever has the dog that used to live at the royal Elephant's shed will be penalized". The King did the same and the man who had taken the dog, instantly turned him loose when he heard the proclamation.

As soon as he was freed, the Dog ran back as fast as he could to the Elephant's shed. The Elephant was so delighted to see the Dog that he picked his friend up with his trunk and swung him back and forth. The Dog wagged his tail, while the Elephant's eyes sparkled with happiness. The King was content to see the Elephant happy once again and rewarded the minister for his wise judgment.

71. What was the. Minister's diagnosis of the Elephant's condition?
(a) The Elephant hated his keeper
(b) The Elephant was lonely
(c) The Elephant was starving
(d) The Elephant had hurt his leg and was in pain

72. What method did the Minister suggest to the King to get back the Dog?
(a) To declare that whoever had that particular Dog would be punished
(b) To keep a bowl of rice for the Dog in the Elephant's shed so that he could be lured back to the palace
(c) To command the Elephant - keeper to look for the Dog in the village
(d) To persuade the Elephant to call out to the Dog

73. Why had the Elephant become very sad?
(a) He no longer got his daily bowl of rice
(b) He was unhappy with the King for having sold the Dog
(c) He missed his friend the Dog
(d) He was sold to an unknown man by his keeper

74. Which of the following would be the most appropriate title for the passage?
(a) Friends and Enemies
(b) The Playful Dog
(c) The King and the Minister
(d) The Bond of Friendship

75. Which of the following can definitely be said about the King?
(A) He was compassionate.
(B) He was deceitful.
(C) He loved animals.
(a) Only (A)
(b) Only (A) and (C)
(c) Only (A) and (B)
(d) Only (B)

Directions (76-78): *Choose the word/ group of words which is most similar in meaning to the word/group of words printed in bold as used in the passage.*

76. EXTRACTED
(a) pulled (b) inserted
(c) wring (d) received

77. DECLARATION
(a) pact
(b) praise
(c) announcement
(d) writ

78. KEEN
(a) shallow
(b) urgent
(c) concentrated
(d) eager

Directions (79-80): *Choose the word/ group of words which is most opposite in meaning to the word/group of words printed in bold as used in the passage.*

79. RESIST
(a) give in (b) please
(c) struggle (d) try put

80. SEPARATED
(a) stuc (b) united
(c) estranged (d) bound

Directions (Q. 81-85): *Rearrange the following six sentences* (A), (B), (C), (D) (E) *and* (F) *in the proper sequence to form a meaningful paragraph; then answer the questions given below them.*

(A) He immediately acknowledged Mohan's good work and invited him to his home for dinner.
(B) One day a wealthy merchant sent his son's bicycle to the shop for repair.
(C) The next day the merchant came to claim the bicycle and noticed that it was shiny.
(D) After repairing the bicycle, Mohan cleaned it up and made it look new.
(E) Once upon a time, there was a boy named Mohan who worked as an apprentice in a bicycle shop.
(F) Other apprentices in the shop laughed at Mohan for doing unnecessary work.

81. Which of the following should be the SECOND sentence after rearrangement?
(a) A (b) B
(c) C (d) F

82. Which of the following should be the THIRD sentence after rearrangement?
(a) A (b) B
(c) C (d) D

83. Which of the following should be the FIRST sentence after rearrangement?
(a) A (b) B
(c) C (d) E

84. Which of the following should be the LAST (SIXTH) sentence after rearrangement ?
(a) A (b) B
(c) D (d) E

85. Which of the following should be the FOURTH sentence after rearrangement?
(a) B (b) C
(c) D (d) E

Directions (Q. 86-90): *Read each sentence to find out whether there is any grammatical error or idiomatic error in it. The error, if any, will be in one part of the sentence. The number of that part is the answer.*

86. In about five minutes, they would (a) cover the distance from the road to the point (b) where the waves would (c) begin lick their feet (d)

87. The devastating experiences (a) of many wars taught some countries

(b) the necessary of pursuing peace (c) at the expense of nationalist egos (d)

88. The former superstar recently (a) visit an orphanage, (b) fuelling speculation that (c) she is planning to adopt a child (d)

89. Accordance to a new study (a) taking steps to remain healthy and young (b) may help delay (c) the onset of Alzheimer's disease (d)

90. A day after he was diagnosed with (a) swine flu, preventive measures were put in place (b) to ensure that others were not (c) affected with the dreaded virus (d)

Directions (91-100): *In the following passage there are blanks, each of which has been numbered. These numbers are printed below the passage and against each, **four** words are suggested, one of which fits the blank appropriately. Find out the appropriate word in each case.*

Once upon a time there was a prince who wanted to marry a princess; but she would have to be a real princess. He (**91**) all over the world to find one, but nowhere could he get what he wanted. One evening during a terrible storm; there was thunder and lightning, and the rain poured down in torrents. Suddenly a knocking was (**92**) at the palace door, and the old king went to open it. It was a princess standing out there. But, good gracious ! What a sight the rain and the wind had made her look. The water ran down her hair and clothes; into the toes of her shoes and out again at the heels. And yet she insisted that she was a real princess. Well, we'll soon (**93**) out, thought the old queen. But she said nothing, went into the bedroom, took all the bedding off the bedstead, and (**94**) a pea on the bottom; then she took twenty mattresses and laid them on the pea, and then twenty quilts on (**95**) of the mattresses. On this the princess had to lie all night. In the (**96**) she was asked how she had slept. "Oh, very badly!" said she. "I scarcely closed my eyes all night. Heaven only knows what was in the bed, but I was lying on something hard, as a (**97**). I am black and blue all over my body. It's horrible !" Now they knew that she was a real princess because she had (**98**) the pea right through the twenty mattresses and the twenty quilts. Nobody but a real princess could be as (**99**) as that. So the prince took her for his wife, for now he (**100**) that he had a real princess.

91. (a) called (b) tour (c) sent (d) travelled

92. (a) made (b) felt (c) heard (d) seen

93. (a) assure (b) find (c) judge (d) mark

94. (a) drew (b) flung (c) placed (d) cooked

95. (a) top (b) head (c) bottom (d) between

96. (a) morning (b) dinner (c) room (d) fields

97. (a) vengeance (b) price (c) cause (d) result

98. (a) slept (b) felt (c) located (d) carried

99. (a) worried (b) rough (c) irritable (d) sensitive

100. (a) trust (b) assured (c) wanted (d) knew

Answer Sheet

1. (b)	**2.** (d)	**3.** (d)	**4.** (a)	**5.** (b)	**6.** (d)	**7.** (c)	**8.** (d)	**9.** (d)	**10.** (b)
11. (b)	**12.** (b)	**13.** (b)	**14.** (a)	**15.** (d)	**16.** (c)	**17.** (c)	**18.** (d)	**19.** (a)	**20.** (a)
21. (d)	**22.** (c)	**23.** (d)	**24.** (d)	**25.** (d)	**26.** (c)	**27.** (b)	**28.** (b)	**29.** (b)	**30.** (a)
31. (b)	**32.** (a)	**33.** (c)	**34.** (b)	**35.** (d)	**36.** (d)	**37.** (a)	**38.** (a)	**39.** (d)	**40.** (a)
41. (c)	**42.** (a)	**43.** (b)	**44.** (d)	**45.** (c)	**46.** (d)	**47.** (a)	**48.** (b)	**49.** (b)	**50.** (b)
51. (d)	**52.** (d)	**53.** (a)	**54.** (d)	**55.** (d)	**56.** (b)	**57.** (c)	**58.** (d)	**59.** (d)	**60.** (d)
61. (b)	**62.** (c)	**63.** (d)	**64.** (a)	**65.** (d)	**66.** (b)	**67.** (d)	**68.** (d)	**69.** (c)	**70.** (d)
71. (b)	**72.** (a)	**73.** (c)	**74.** (d)	**75.** (b)	**76.** (d)	**77.** (c)	**78.** (d)	**79.** (a)	**80.** (b)
81. (d)	**82.** (b)	**83.** (d)	**84.** (a)	**85.** (c)	**86.** (d)	**87.** (c)	**88.** (b)	**89.** (a)	**90.** (d)
91. (d)	**92.** (c)	**93.** (b)	**94.** (c)	**95.** (a)	**96.** (a)	**97.** (d)	**98.** (b)	**99.** (d)	**100.** (d)

Solutions

1. **(b)** As,

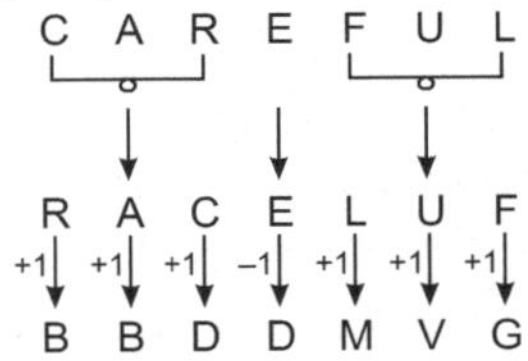

Similarly,

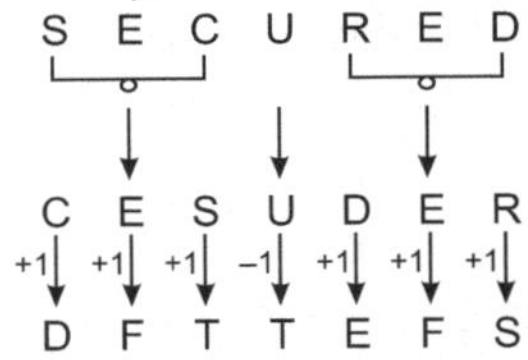

2. **(d)** Given number: 9 3 5 1 2 6

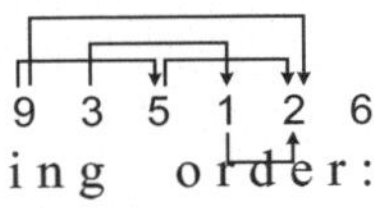

Descending order:

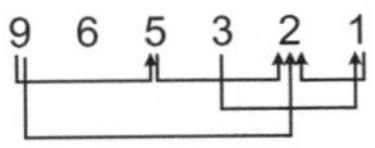

Such pairs are : 9-5, 9-2, 3-1, 5-2 and 1-2

3. **(d)**

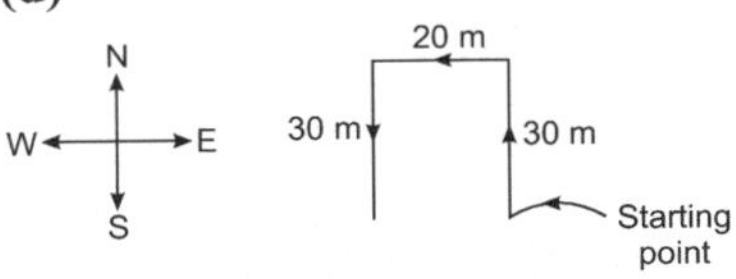

∴ Required distance = 20m

4. **(a)** • > • > • > • > •
S P Q R T
∴ The third heaviest is Q.

5. **(b)** Only child of my fathers only brother
⇒ Only child of my uncle
(∵ fathers only brother is uncle)
⇒ Only child (boy) of my uncle
⇒ my cousin brother.

6. **(d)** After the change the equation
$= 64 + 32 - 8 \times 4 + 6$
$= 64 + 32 \div 8 - 4 \times 6$
$= 64 + 4 - 24 = 44$

7. **(c)**

∴ Required such pairs are C-G and A-C.

8. **(d)** 8 7 9 5 3 4 2
9 6 8 4 2 5 3
Ascending order:
2 3 4 5 6 8 9
Hence, third digit from the left end is '4'.

9. **(d)** Second, fourth, seventh and the ninth letters of the word ADMINISTRATION are D, I, S and E respectively. The words that can be made using them are : SIDE and DIES.

10. **(b)** According to Sharda, her mother's birthday = 15, 16, 17 and 18
According to her brother her mother's birthday = 10, 11, 12, 13, 14 and 15
Clearly, 15th April was definitely their mother's birthday.

11. **(b)** 987654321, 98764321, 9876432, 987 [4]

12. **(b)** 826 391 435 678 283
286 [931] 345 768 823
Clearly, the highest number is 931:
Hence, the second digit of the highest number is 3.

13. **(b)** The second lowest number = 391
Required difference = 9 – 1=8

14. **(a)** The lowest number = 283
Required sum = 2 + 8 = 10

15. **(d)** The second highest number = 678
Its third digit = 8

16. **(c)**

A	E	G	M	R	T
3	1	9	8	4	2

Hence the code for MARE is 8341.

17. **(c)** Some pens are buses (I) + Some buses are trucks (I) = I + I = – ie "No conclusion" Hence conclusion I doesnot follow. Similarly, conclusion 11 doesnot follow. But conclusions I and II form I-E type of complementary pair. Hence eithe I or II follow.

18. **(d)** All letters are boxes (A) + Some boxes are irons (I) + All irons are magnets (A) = A + I + A = (A + I) + A = No conclusion [∴ A + I = No conclusion]. Hence conclusion I does not follow.

19. **(a)** All glasses are pens (A) + No pen is chalk (E) = A + E = E = No glass is chalk. Hence conclusion I follows. Again, All glasses are pens + No pen is chalk + No chalk is stationary = A + E + E = (A + E) + E = E + E = No conclusion. Hence conclusion II does not follow.

20. **(a)** All jungles are roads + All roads are rivers = A+A = All jungles are rivers → conversion → Some rivers are jungles. Hence conclusion II follows. Again, All roads are rivers + All rivers are ponds = A + A = A = All roads are ponds → conversion → Some ponds are roads. Hence conclusion I follows.

21. **(d)**

22. **(c)** Given sequence : 101 : 10201 or 10 (1+1)1^2 or 10201
Similarly, 107; 11449 or 10 (7 + 7) 7^2 11449

23. **(d)** $M \xrightarrow{+7} N \xrightarrow{+7} V \xrightarrow{+7} 3$
$A \xrightarrow{+7} \# \xrightarrow{+7} 5 \xrightarrow{+7} Z$
$J \xrightarrow{+7} B \xrightarrow{+7} P \xrightarrow{+7} \delta$

24. **(d)** Tenth to the right of the nineteenth from the right end means (19 – 10) = 9th from the right end, ie P.

25. **(d)** $2 \xrightarrow{-1} \# \xrightarrow{+2} B$
$W \xrightarrow{-1} V \xrightarrow{+2} 5$
$J \xrightarrow{-1} @ \xrightarrow{+2} H$
$8 \xrightarrow{+1} \delta \xrightarrow{-2} Z$

$6 \xrightarrow{-1} U \xrightarrow{+2} 3$

26. **(c)** Such numbers are W5* and Z8δ

27. **(b)** EVW

28. **(b)** When the symbols in the given arrangment are dropped, it becomes as follows:

R M 4 A J H 1 N 2 B 9 E V W 5 P U 6 3 I Z 8 Q

Hence, Twelfth letter from the left end is E

Hints for (29-34):

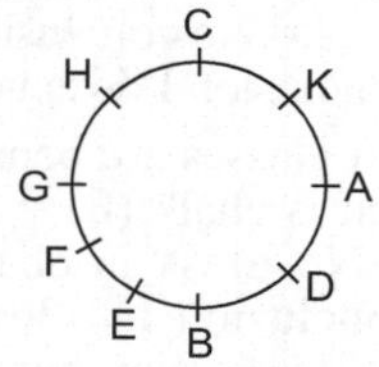

34. **(b)** $K\$Z \Rightarrow K = Z$

$\% M \Rightarrow Z \leq M$

$M©N \Rightarrow M > N$

Therefore, $K = Z \leq M > N$

Conclusions

I. $N\#K \Rightarrow N < K$ (Not True)

II. $M@K \Rightarrow M \geq K$ (True)

35. **(d)** $I © F \Rightarrow I > F$

$F\#B \Rightarrow F < B$

$B@K \Rightarrow B \geq K$

Therefore, $I > F < B \geq K$

Conclusions

I. $K\#F \Rightarrow K < F$ (Not True)

II. $B@I \Rightarrow B > I$ (Not True)

36. **(d)** $1800 \times \frac{9}{100} \times 221 \times \frac{7}{13}$

$= 162 + 119 = 281$

37. **(a)** $? \times 23 = 350 \times \frac{26}{100} - 110 \times \frac{20}{100}$

or, $? \times 23 = 91 - 22 = 69$

$\therefore ? = \frac{69}{23} = 3$

38. **(a)** $? + 93 = 182 \div 13 \times 12 - 32$

$= 14 \times 12 - 32 = 168 - 32 = 136$

$\therefore ? = 136 - 93 = 43$

39. **(d)** $? - 25.132 = 23.141 - 32.417$

or, $? - 25.132 = -9.276$

$\therefore ? = 25.132 - 9.276 = 15.856$

40. **(a)** $(?)^2 + 8 = 455 \div 13 \times 2 - 37$

or, $(?)^2 + 8 = 35 \times 2 - 37 = 70 - 37 = 33$ or, $(?)^2 = 33 - 8 = 25$

$\therefore ? = \sqrt{25} = 5$

41. **(c)** $9^{3.5} \times 3^{2.2} \div (9)^{(?)} = 9^{1.4}$

or, $3^{2\times3.5} \times 3^{2.2} \div 3^{2(?)} = 3^{2\times1.4}$

or, $3^{7+2.2-2(?)} = 3^{2.8}$

Hence, $9.2 - 2(?) = 2.8$

$\therefore -2(?) = 6.4 \quad \therefore ? = 3.2$

42. **(a)**

$3\frac{1}{7} \times 1\frac{1}{132} \div 3\frac{1}{6} = \frac{22}{7} \times \frac{133}{132} \times \frac{6}{19}$

$= \frac{22}{19} \times \frac{19}{22} = 1$

43. **(b)** $\because 3 \times 4^2 + 5^2 \times 5 - 7^2 = ? + 3$

Or, $48 + 125 - 49 = ? + 3$

Or, $124 = ? + 3$

$\therefore ? = 124 - 3 = 121 = (11)^2$

44. **(d)** $\because 560 \times \frac{75}{100} \div ? \times \frac{40}{100} = 35$

Or, $420 \div ? \times \frac{2}{5} = 35$

$\therefore ? = 420 \times \frac{5}{2 \times 35} = 30$

45. **(c)** $\because ? + 1113 = 2321 + 2332 - 1234$

$\therefore ? = -1113 + 2321 + 2332 - 1234 = 2306$

46. **(d)** $\because 437 - 382 + 639 = 76 - 354 + 23 + ?$

Or, $694 = -255 + ?$

$\therefore ? = 694 + 255 = 949$

47. **(a)** $\because (74 + 25 - 58) + (48 \div 12 \times 3) = 41 + 12 = 53$

48. **(b)** Let the present ages of father and son be x and y years respectively.

Then, according to the question,

$\frac{x + y}{2} = 27$

Or, $x + y = 54$ ....(i) and

$x - y = 30$ ....(ii)

On solving equation (i) and (ii), we have $x = 42$ and $y = 12$

$\therefore$ required ratio $= x : y = 42 : 12 = 7 : 2$

49. **(b)** Required value

$= 660 \times \frac{2}{3} \times \frac{35}{100} \times \frac{2}{7}$

$= 66 \times \frac{2}{3} \times \frac{5}{10} \times 2$

$= 22 \times 2 = 44$

50. **(b)** According to the question, Saurabh's marks

$= 232 - 56 = 176$

Supriya's marks $= 176 + 24 = 200$

Let the total marks be x.

Then, 40% of $x = 200$

or, $\frac{40}{100} \times x = 200$

$\therefore x = \frac{200 \times 100}{40} = 500$

Percentage marks obtained by Saurabh $= \frac{176}{500} \times 100 = 35.2$

51. **(d)** Required total sum of money

$= ₹ (154 \times 73) = ₹ 11242$

52. **(d)** Cost of 2kg of pulse

$= \frac{675}{15} \times 2 = ₹ 90$

Cost of 1kg of rice $= \frac{432}{12} = ₹ 36$

$\therefore$ Required ratio $= 90 : 36 = 5 : 2$

53. **(a)** $\frac{3}{5} = 0.6; \frac{2}{7} = 0.285; \frac{5}{11} = 0.454;$

$\frac{5}{7} = 0.714; \frac{9}{13} = 0.692$

Hence, the highest fraction is $\frac{5}{7}$ and the lowest fraction is $\frac{2}{7}$

54. **(d)** Let the sum ₹ P and the simple interst be ₹ x

Now, accroding to the question

$x \times \frac{2}{5} = 900$

Or, $x = \frac{900 \times 5}{2} = ₹ 2250$

$\therefore$ Principal

$= ₹ \left(\frac{2250 \times 100}{15 \times 6}\right) = ₹ 2500$

55. **(d)** Arnav's amount

$= ₹\left(1540\times\frac{25}{100}\right) = ₹\,385$

Sumit's amount = ₹ (385 + 36) = ₹ 421

56. **(b)** Let the bradth of the rectangle be x cm.

So, Length of the reactangle = $(x + 6)$

Then, $(x + 6)\,x = 112$

or, $x^2 + 6x - 112 = 0$

or, $(x + 14)(x - 8) = 0$

or, $x = -14$ or 8

∴ Perimeter of the rectangle = 2(8 + 14) cm = 44 cm

57. **(c)** Sonit's monthly income = $₹\frac{32000}{2} = ₹16000$

Let the Rohit's monthly income be Rs x

Now, according to the question.

$\frac{4}{7}\times x = \frac{16000}{2}$ or, $4x = 800 \times 7$

or, $x = \frac{8000\times 7}{4} = 14000$

∴ Rohit's monthly income = ₹ 14000

58. **(d)** $2_{\times1}\ 2_{\times2}\ 4_{\times3}\ 12_{\times4}\ 48_{\times5}\ \boxed{240}_{\times6}\ 1440$

59. **(d)** $2_{+5}\ 7_{+7}\ 14_{+9}\ \boxed{23}_{+11}\ 34_{+13}\ 47_{+15}\ 62$

60. **(d)** $150\times\frac{550}{100} + 39 - 212$

$\approx 825 + 39 - 112 \approx 652 \approx 650$

61. **(b)** $155\times\frac{55}{100}\times 7 = 596 \approx 600$

62. **(c)** $1240 \div 50 \times 10 = 248 \approx 250$

63. **(d)** Let the angles of a triangle be $3x°$, $5x°$ and $2x°$

Now, according to the question

$3x° + 5x° + 2x° = 180°$

or, $10x° = 180°$

$\therefore x = \frac{180}{10} = 18°$

Sum of the largest and the smallest angles of trianlge

$= 18° \times 5 + 18° \times 2$

$= 90° + 36° = 126°$

Hence, the largest angle of parallelogram = 126°

and Smalllest angle of the paralleogram = 180° – 126° = 54°

64. **(a)** There are 7 letters in the given work READERS.

Hence, It has two R and two E.

∴ Required number of arrangements.

$= \frac{7!}{2!\times 2!} = \frac{7\times6\times5\times4\times3\times2\times1}{2\times1\times2\times1}$

= 1260

65. **(d)** Let the length of the train be a m, speed of the man be x m/sec and speed of the train is y m/sec.

Now, according to the question,

$\frac{a}{x} = 5\times 60$ and $\frac{a}{y} = 50$

Or, $5 \times 60 \times x = 50 \times y$

Or, $\frac{x}{y} = \frac{50}{5\times 60} = \frac{1}{6}$

$\therefore x : y = 1 : 6$

Hints for (66-70):

66. **(b)** Required ratio $= \frac{4.5}{2.4} = 15.8$

67. **(d)** Total number of employees

$= (5.7 + 4.8 + 3.4 + 4.5) \times 1000$

$= 18.4 \times 1000 = 18400$

68. **(d)** ∵ K = 6.3, L = 4.7. M = 5.5. N = 5.3,

$\boxed{P = 5.5}$ R = 2.9

So, Required company = P

69. **(c)** Required per cent

$= \left(\frac{7.2}{3.9+4.1+3.4+5.3+6.7+9.6}\right)\times 100$

$= \frac{7.2\times 100}{33}\%$

$= 21.82\% \approx 21\%$ (Approx.)

70. **(d)** ∵ Required average

$= \frac{6.3+4.7+5.5+5.3+5.6+2.9}{6}\times 1000$

$= \frac{30.3\times 1000}{6} = \frac{30300}{6} = 5050$

3 Practice Set

Reasoning

1. 'Players' are related to 'Team' in the same way as 'Books' are related to

(a) Exams (b) Library
(c) Reading (d) School

2. Shreya started from Point P and walked 2 m towards West. She then took a right turn and walked 3 m before taking a left turn and walking 5 m. She finally took a left turn, walked 3 m and stopped a Point Q. How far is Point Q from Point P?

(a) 5 m (b) 6 m
(c) 7 m (d) 11 m

3. In a certain code 'where have you been' is written as 'been 4 have 3 where 2 you 1' and 'visiting London this summer' is written as 'London 4 summer 3 this 2 visiting 1'. How will 'repair may computer yesterday' be written in the same code?

(a) computer 4 repair 3 may 2 yesterday 1
(b) yesterday 4 repair 3 may 2 computer 1
(c) computer 1 may 2 repair 3 yesterday 4
(d) computer 4 may 3 repair 2 yesterday 1

4. Four of the following five are alike in a certain way based on the English alphabetical series and so form a group. Which is the one that does not belong to that group?

(a) MLJ (b) PJO
(c) OMK (d) JIG

5. Four of the following five are alike in a certain way and so form a group. Which is the one that does not belong to that group?

(a) Diameter
(b) Circumference
(c) Centre
(d) arc

Directions (Q. 6-10): *Read she following information carefully and answer the given questions.*

A, B. C, D, E, F, G and H are sitting around a circular table facing the centre but not necessarily in the same order. G sits third to the right of F. G sits second to the left of H. H is not an immediate neighbour of E and C. F and A are immediate neighbours of each other. Only one person sits between F and B. E and G sit opposite each other.

6. Four of the following five are similar in a certain way based on their position in the seating arrangement. Which of the following does not belong to that group?

(a) EH (b) CF
(c) AG (d) BD

7. Who amongst the following represent immediate neighbours of D?

(a) E, H (b) C, G
(c) F, B (d) H, G

8. What is the position of A with respect to G in the above arrangement ?

(a) Third to the right
(b) Second to the left
(c) Fifth to the right
(d) Immediate right

9. What will come in place of the question mark (?) according to the above seating arrangement?

EF CG HB FA ?

(a) GD (b) CG
(c) GH (d) BH

10. Who sits to the immediate right of A?

(a) E (b) C
(c) B (d) F

Directions (Q. 11-15): *Study the following arrangement carefully and answer the questions given below:*

6 4 2 5 2 8 5 2 6 4 1 3 9 1 8 1 2 5 8 6 3 5 1 4 9 4 7 3 2 7 2 5 9

11. How many 4s are there in the above arrangement, each of which is immediately preceded by a digit which has a numerical value of more than four?

(a) None (b) One
(c) Two (d) Three

12. Which of the following is seventh to the left of the twentieth from the left end of the above arrangement?

(a) 3 (b) 9
(c) 2 (d) 7

13. If all the even digits are deleted from the above arrangement, which of the following will be tenth from the right end of the arrangement?

(a) 9 (b) 5
(c) 1 (d) 3

14. How many such 5s are there in the above arrangement each of which is immediately preceded by an odd digit and immediately followed by an even digit?

(a) None (b) One
(c) Two (d) Three

15. **How many such Is are there in the above arrangement, each of which is immediately preceded by a perfect square?**

(a) None (b) One
(c) Two (d) Three

Directions (Q. 16-20): *Study the following information to answer the given questions:*

In a certain code 'ring a bell' is written as '5 8 2', 'did not ring' is written as '359' and 'not a reason' is written as '729'.

16. **Which of the following represents 'did not'?**

(a) '23' (b) '29'
(c) '35' (d) '93'

17. **What is the code for 'bell'?**

(a) 5 (b) 8
(c) 2 (d) 7

18. **What does '2' stand for?**

(a) ring (b) a
(c) bell (d) reason

19. **What does'7'stand for?**

(a) not (b) a
(c) ring (d) reason

20. **What is the code for 'ring'?**

(a) 8 (b) 2
(c) 5 (d) 3

Directions (Q. 21-25): *Following questions are based on the five three-digit numbers given below:*

219 742 936 587 853

21. **If all the numbers are arranged in descending order from left to right, which of the following will be the product of the first and the second digits of the number which is exactly in the middle of the new arrangement?**

(a) 18 (b) 28
(c) 54 (d) 21

22. **One is subtracted from the first digit and two is subtracted from third the digit of each of the numbers. What will be the difference between the first digit of the highest number and the third digit of the lowest number?**

(a) 3 (b) 4
(c) 5 (d) 1

23. **What will be the resultant if the third digit of the highest number is divided by the first digit of the lowest number?**

(a) 3 (b) 4
(c) 5 (d) 2

24. **If the positions of the first and the third digits of each of the numbers are interchanged, what will be sum of all the digits of the second highest number thus formed ?**

(a) 20 (b) 16
(c) 18 (d) 13

25. **If all the digits in each of the numbers are arranged in descending order within the number, which of the following will form the lowest number in the new arrangement of numbers?**

(a) 219 (b) 742
(c) 936 (d) 587

Directions (Q. 26-30): *Read the following information carefully and answer the given questions.*

P, Q, R, S, T, V and W are sitting in a straight line facing North but not necessarily in the same order.

(a) Q sits third to the right of T. W sits second to the right of Q.
(b) V and R are immediate neighbours of each other. V is not an immediate neighbour of T.
(c) Only one person sits between S and P.
(d) S is not an immediate neighbour of Q.

26. **Four of the following five are alike in a certain way based on their seating positions in the above arrangement and so form a group. Which is the one that does not belong to that group?**

(a) QW (b) TV
(c) RQ (d) VW

27. **How many persons sit between R and P ?**

(a) None (b) One
(c) Two (d) Three

28. **Which of the following pairs sits at the extreme corners of the line ?**

(a) R,W (b) S,T
(c) W,Q (d) T, R

29. **What is the position of T with respect to V?**

(a) Second to the left
(b) Third to the right
(c) Immediate right
(d) Fourth to the left

30. **If all the persons are made to sit in alphabetical order from right to left, the positions of how many will remain unchanged as compared to the original seating positions?**

(a) None (b) One
(c) Two (d) Three

Directions (Q. 31-33): *In each question below are two statements followed by two conclusions numbered I and II. You have to take the two given statements to be true even if they seem to be at variance with commonly known facts and then decide which of the given conclusions logically follows from the given statements, disregarding commonly known facts. Given answer*

(a) if only conclusion I follows.
(b) if only conclusion II follows.
(c) if either conclusion I or conclusion II follows.
(d) if neither conclusion I nor conclusion II follows.

31. **Statements:** No house is an apartment.
Some apartments are bungalows.
Conclusions:
I. No house is a bungalow.
II. All bungalows being houses is a possibility.

32. Statements: All pens are ink.
No ink is an eraser.
Conclusions:
I. No pen is an eraser.
II. Some erasers are pens.

33. Statements: Some trains are buses.
All trains are ships.
Conclusions:
I. All ships are buses.
II. All those trains if these are buses are also ships.

34. In the following question, select the missing number from the given series.
2, 5, 12, 27, ?
(a) 53 (b) 56
(c) 57 (d) 58

35. If 'P 3 Q' means 'P is daughter of Q', 'P 5 Q' means 'P is father of Q', 'P 7 Q' means 'P is mother of Q' and 'P 9 Q' means 'P is sister of Q', then how is J related to K in J 3 L 9 N 3 O 5 K?
(a) Mother (b) Wife
(c) Niece (d) Daughter

Quantitative Aptitude

Directions (Q. 36-50): *What will come in place of the question mark (?) in the following equations?*

36. $\frac{8}{15}+\frac{2}{5}-\frac{1}{3}=?$
(a) $\frac{3}{7}$ (b) $\frac{2}{5}$
(c) $\frac{3}{8}$ (d) $\frac{3}{5}$

37. 4500 ÷ 18 – 122 = ? × 4
(a) 32 (b) 26
(c) 28 (d) 34

38. $\sqrt[3]{32768}=?$
(a) 38 (b) 34
(c) 36 (d) 32

39. $(19)^2 + (28)^2 - (16)^2 = ?$
(a) 889 (b) 888
(c) 883 (d) 885

40. $63 \times 14 + 334 = ? + (12)^2$
(a) 1078 (b) 1072
(c) 1077 (d) 7074

41. [(452 ÷ 4) + 62] ÷ 5 = ?
(a) 48 (b) 37
(c) 45 (d) 35

42. (14 × 24) + (27 × 12) = ?
(a) 650 (b) 665
(c) 660 (d) 655

43. (4.7 × 12 × 8) + (6 .8 × 16 × 10) = ?
(a) 1533.9 (b) 1539.2
(c) 1532.9 (d) 1536.9

44. $\frac{1}{5}$th of $\frac{3}{4}$ the of $\frac{3}{5}$ of 6000 = ?
(a) 360 (b) 330
(c) 370 (d) 350

45. $4^{10} \times 64 \div 256 = 4^{?} \times 16$
(a) 6 (b) 5
(c) 8 (d) None of these

46. (5994 ÷ 18) × (468 ÷ 18) = ?
(a) 8658 (b) 8656
(c) 8655 (d) 8654

47. 451.34 + 322.69 – 242.88 = ?
(a) 533.33 (b) 551.15
(c) 531.15 (d) 539.34

48. $321 \times 16 \div 8 + 34 = (?)^2$
(a) $\sqrt{26}$ (b) $(26)^2$
(c) $(676)^2$ (d) None of these

49. 4334 – 1515 + 4242 – 2222 = ?
(a) 4834 (b) 4838
(c) 4839 (d) 4836

50. $\frac{3}{4}$**th of 24% of 400 – 32 = ?**
(a) 50 (b) 45
(c) 40 (d) 55

51. The sum of five consecutive even numbers is 400. What is the half of the sum of the smallest number and the largest number of the set?
(a) 80 (b) 81
(c) 79 (d) 82

52. The ratio of Binoy's and Alisha's present ages is 5 : 6. Three years hence the ratio of their ages will be 6 : 7 respectively. What was Alisha's age eight years ago?
(a) 7 years (b) 10 years
(c) 26 years (d) 18 years

53. In how many different ways can the letters of the word 'QUOTED'be arranged?
(a) 720 (b) 360
(c) 1440 (d) 320

54. Sohail scored 33 marks in English, 37 marks in Science, 28 marks in Mathematics, 26 marks in Hindi and 32 marks in Social Studies. The maximum marks a student can score in each subject is 60. How much percentage did Sohail get in this exam ?
(a) 52 (b) 54
(c) 48 (d) 53

55. 37% of a number is 114.7. What is 130% of that number?
(a) 406 (b) 405
(c) 403 (d) 407

56. What will be the average of the following set of scores?
69, 89, 34, 76, 54, 68, 28, 46
(a) 53 (b) 55
(c) 57 (d) None of these

57. What will be the resultant if the square of 109 is subtracted from the square of 210?
(a) 32220 (b) 32209
(c) 32291 (d) None of these

58. What will be the compound interest accrued on a principal amount of ₹32,500 at the rate of 5 pcpa after a period of 2 years?
(a) ₹ 3332.78 (b) ₹ 3335.35
(c) ₹ 3333.27 (d) ₹ 3331.25

59. The average of five numbers is 50.8. The average of the first and the second number is 29. The average of the fourth and the fifth number is 66.5. What is the third number?
(a) 65 (b) 73
(c) 61 (d) None of these

60. A train covers 430 km in 5 hours. The speed of a bike is half the speed of the train. How much time will the bike take to cover a

distance of 301 km?

(a) 6 hours (b) 7 hours

(c) 8 hours (d) 9 hours

61. If the following fractions are arranged in ascending order (from left to right), which of them will be second from the right end?

$\frac{2}{9}, \frac{4}{7}, \frac{12}{17}, \frac{7}{13}, \frac{5}{11}$

(a) $\frac{4}{7}$ (b) $\frac{12}{17}$

(c) $\frac{2}{9}$ (d) $\frac{5}{11}$

62. Last year the total number of students in a school was 4500.48% of the total students were females. This year 60 males left the school. What is the present ratio of the number of males to the number of females in the school?

(a) 19 : 17 (b) 18 : 17

(c) 23 : 18 (d) None of these

63. What is the least number that can be added to 2020 to make it a perfect square ?

(a) 4 (b) 6

(c) 5 (d) 3

Directions (Q. 64-65): *What approximate value should come in place of question mark(?) in the following questions? (Note: You are not expected to calculate the exact value.)*

64. $\sqrt{62627} = ?$

(a) 280 (b) 220

(c) 250 (d) 330

65. 44.979 × 20.011 ÷ 9.968 = ?

(a) 30 (b) 60

(c) 150 (d) 90

Directions (Q. 66-70): *What should come in place of the question mark (?) in the following number series?*

66. 600 564 539 523 514 ?

(a) 500 (b) 520

(c) 510 (d) 540

67. 55000 11000 2200 440 88 ?

(a) 16.4 (b) 18.3

(c) 17.6 (d) 14.5

68. 2 12 60 240 720 ?

(a) 1445 (b) 1440

(c) 1420 (d) 1444

69. 80 48 64 56 60 ?

(a) 57 (b) 68

(c) 54 (d) 58

70. 32 38 50 68 92 ?

(a) 118 (b) 128

(c) 124 (d) 122

English Language

Directions (Q. 71-85): *Read the following passage carefully and answer the questions given below it. Certain words are printed in bold to help you locate them while answering some of the questions.*

Once upon a time, there was a shrewd shopkeeper called Makarand. He had a friend called Mihir, who had saved a lot of money. Mihir was **keen** on going on a pilgrimage, but he did not know where to leave his precious savings. So he came to Makarand's shop and said, 'My friend. I trust you more than anyone. Could you please look after my life's savings till I return from my pilgrimage?' Makarand pretended to be deep in thought, and then said, 'I would rather not. Money spoils relationships. What if something happens to your money while you are away? You will no longer be my friend.'

As Mihir stood there by his shop thinking about what his friend had just said, an old woman entered the shop and bought some things. One of the boys helping Makarand gave her less change than he should have. Makarand saw this and pretended to scold the boy. He then ordered him to return the remaining money to the woman. Mihir, not knowing that this was an act put up by Makarand to make him believe that he was honest, was convinced about his decision and said to Makarand, 'I have decided I will leave the money only with you.' Makarand smiled. 'Then, let us do something. Let us take the bag of coins and bury it in a place that only you and I will know of. That way, even if something happens to me while you are away, you will know where your money is.'

Mihir, simple that he was, thought this was a good idea and the two went and hid the bag in a secret place. Mihir left the next day on his pilgrimage, happy that his savings were in safe hands. Six months later, Mihir returned. He dumped his luggage at home and went to dig out his bag of savings.

But, even though he searched and searched for his valuables, there was no sign of the bag anywhere. In panic, he ran to Makarand, who was busy in his shop. When Mihir asked him about the bag, Makarand pretended to be surprised, 'But I did not go that way in all these months. Why don't you search for it again?' he said, putting on his most innocent look. Mihir had no **choice** but to believe him. Sadly, he went home.

On the way, as luck would have it, he met the old woman he had seen in Makarand's shop. Seeing him sad, she asked him what the matter was. Mihir told her the **whole** story. Then, she smiled and whispered a plan to him. Not long after, the woman came to Makarand's shop, carrying a big box. 'Brother, I heard you are a good and honest man. My son went on a pilgrimage many months ago and has still not returned. I am worried and have decided to go and look for him. Will you look after my box of two hundred gold coins while I am away?'

Makarand could not believe his luck. He was about to launch into his idea about hiding the box when an angry Mihir entered the shop, 'Where is ...' But before he could **complete** his sentence, Makarand, afraid of being accused in front of the old woman, said quickly, **'I forgot.** I had seen some pigs digging around there and had removed the bag just to keep it safe. Here it is.' And he handed Mihir the bag he had stolen many months ago.

Now, the old woman pretended she was seeing Mihir for the first time, 'Son, did you also go on a pilgrimage? Could you tell me if you met my son anywhere? His name is Jahangir.' Mihir, **clutching** onto his precious bag, said, 'Yes auntie, I met him on the road a few villages away. He was on his way home. He should be here in a week.'

The old woman leaned over and took her box away from Makarand. 'Thank you brother. You have saved me an unnecessary trip. Now, I will need some money to prepare for my son's welcome,' she added and the two left the shop. Makarand could only stare at them open-mouthed.

71. What incident in the passage convinced Mihir that Makarand was indeed an honest man?
(A) The incident where he scolded his helper boy for returning less change to the old woman who was a customer in his shop.
(B) The fact that Makarand refused to keep Mihir's money in the event that it might destroy their friendship
(C) The incident where Makarand told Mihir that he had kept his bag with him as he saw pigs digging at the very spot where the treasure was buried
(a) Only (A) (b) Only (B)
(c) Only (C) (d) Only (B) and (C)

72. What was Makarand's real intention for wanting to bury Mihir's bag of valuables?
(a) He wanted Mihir to know where the money would be in case something happened to him while Mihir was away.
(b) He did not feel safe keeping Mihir's bag of valuables with him.
(c) He wanted to steal the money while Mihir was away.
(d) He wanted the pigs to dig out the bag so he could steal it.

73. Where did Makarand and Mihir bury the bag of coins?
(a) In a secret place in Mihir's garden
(b) In the ground under Makarand's shop
(c) In the old woman's backyard
(d) Not indicated in the passage

74. Which of the following is true with regard to Mihir?
(a) He accused Makarand of stealing his valuables.
(b) He helped the old woman find her son.
(c) He left his life's savings with the old woman.
(d) He trusted Makarand with his valuables.

75. Why did Mihir want to keep his life's savings with Makarand?
(A) Makarand had a locker in his shop.
(B) He trusted his friend Makarand more than anyone else.
(C) He was scared that if he buried his savings, the pigs would dig it out.
(a) Only (A)
(b) Only (B)
(c) Only (C)
(d) Either (B) or (C)

76. Which of the following statements is false according to the passage?
(a) The old woman's son went on the same pilgrimage as Mihir.
(b) The old woman helped Mihir recover his savings from Makarand.
(c) Makarand was a very shrewd shopkeeper.
(d) Mihir had gone away on a pilgrimage.

77. Why was Mihir sad after returning from the pilgrimage?
(A) He lost all his valuables while returning from the pilgrimage.
(B) The valuables that he had buried safely had all disappeared.
(C) He had spent far too much of his savings on the pilgrimage.
(a) Only (A)
(b) Only (B)
(c) Only (C)
(d) Only (A) and (C)

78. In the end, why did Makarand return Mihir's money?
(A) He realised that he had done the wrong thing b; pretending to be unaware of Mihir's misfortune.
(B) The old woman offered to give him two hundred gold coins if he returned Mihir's money back.
(C) He did not want to be accused of having stolei Mihir's money in front of the old woman.
(a) Only (A)
(b) Only (B)
(c) Only (C)
(d) Only (A) and (C)

Directions (Q.79-82): *Choose the word which is mos neaHy the SAME in meaning as the word printed in bold a used in the passage.*

79. Clutching
(a) Releasing (b) Fixing
(c) Holding (d) Sticking

80. Keen
(a) Eager (b) Hurried
(c) Planning (d) Fortunate

81. Choice
(a) Understanding (b) Regard
(c) Value (d) Option

82. Whole
(a) Partial (b) Some
(c) Entire (d) Total

Directions (Q. 83-85): *Choose the word which is mos OPPOSITE in meaning of the word printed in bold as usei in the passage.*

83. Complete
(a) Partial (b) Start
(c) Incomplete (d) End

84. Sadly
(a) Quietly (b) Dejectedly
(c) Happily (d) Disturbingly

85. Forgot
(a) Found (b) Memorised
(c) Lost (d) Remembered

Directions (Q. 86-90): *Read each sentence to fim out whether there is any grammatical error in it. The error if any, will be in one part of the sentence. The number of the part is the answer.*

86. The more enlightened (a) factory owners (b) build homes to their (c) workers in Britain in the 19th century. (d)

87. Most criminals (a) realises that they may be caught, (b) but nevertheless, (c) they are prepared to take the risk. (d)

88. Strictly speaking, (a) spiders are not insects, (b) although most people (c) think them are (d)

89. The actress is also (a) widely respected in (b) the music world (c) and deserving so.(d)

90. The story was (a) inspired by (b) a chance meeting (c) with an old Russian duke. (d)

Directions (Q. 91-95): *Which of the phrases* (a), (b), (c) *and* (d) *given below each sentence should replace the phrase printed in bold in the sentence to make it grammatically correct?*

91. He is held regard as the Chief's right-hand man.
(a) regards as
(b) to regard as
(c) regarded as
(d) being regarded for

92. The inquiry has to bring to light some startling facts.
(a) bring light to
(b) brought to the lights
(c) brings to light
(d) brought to light

93. My friend went his way out to oblige me.
(a) out on his way
(b) out of his way
(c) so out of the way
(d) little way Out

94. They are determined to stand up for their rights.
(a) be standing up
(b) for standing up
(c) stand up to
(d) No correction required

95. Recently, my expenses have gone run up considerably.
(a) run up (b) to rise up
(c) had to run up (d) got upwards

Directions (Q. 96-100): *Each question below has two blanks. Each blank indicates that something has been omitted. Choose the set of words which best fits the meaning of the sentence as a whole.*

96. Rachana saw me ____ for a bus; she stopped and ____ me a lift.
(a) standing, took
(b) stopped, gave
(c) walking, sat
(d) waiting, offered

97. During winter, we can wearing ____ clothes.
(a) protect, warm
(b) establish, light
(c) save, good
(d) stop, thick

98. The school refused to ____ acts of ____ behaviour.
(a) overcome, spoilt
(b) tolerate, violent
(c) overlook, sudden
(d) appreciate, bravery

99. The actor was not ___ by public criticism and paid no ____ even to the poor reviews in the media.
(a) affected, attention
(b) troubled, mind
(c) effected, regard
(d) bothered, justification

100. The ___ words of the teacher comforted the ___ student.
(a) harsh, sorrowful
(b) encouraging, anxious
(c) reality, nervous
(d) wise, happy

Answer sheet

1. (b)	**2.** (c)	**3.** (d)	**4.** (c)	**5.** (c)	**6.** (c)	**7.** (d)	**8.** (b)	**9.** (a)	**10.** (b)
11. (d)	**12.** (b)	**13.** (b)	**14.** (a)	**15.** (c)	**16.** (d)	**17.** (b)	**18.** (b)	**19.** (d)	**20.** (c)
21. (b)	**22.** (d)	**23.** (a)	**24.** (a)	**25.** (b)	**26.** (d)	**27.** (c)	**28.** (b)	**29.** (a)	**30.** (a)
31. (d)	**32.** (a)	**33.** (b)	**34.** (d)	**35.** (c)	**36.** (d)	**37.** (a)	**38.** (d)	**39.** (a)	**40.** (b)
41. (d)	**42.** (c)	**43.** (b)	**44.** (a)	**45.** (d)	**46.** (a)	**47.** (c)	**48.** (d)	**49.** (c)	**50.** (c)
51. (a)	**52.** (b)	**53.** (a)	**54.** (a)	**55.** (c)	**56.** (d)	**57.** (d)	**58.** (d)	**59.** (d)	**60.** (b)
61. (a)	**62.** (d)	**63.** (c)	**64.** (c)	**65.** (d)	**66.** (c)	**67.** (c)	**68.** (b)	**69.** (d)	**70.** (d)
71. (a)	**72.** (c)	**73.** (d)	**74.** (d)	**75.** (b)	**76.** (a)	**77.** (b)	**78.** (c)	**79.** (c)	**80.** (a)
81. (d)	**82.** (c)	**83.** (b)	**84.** (c)	**85.** (d)	**86.** (c)	**87.** (b)	**88.** (d)	**89.** (d)	**90.** (d)
91. (c)	**92.** (d)	**93.** (b)	**94.** (d)	**95.** (a)	**96.** (d)	**97.** (a)	**98.** (b)	**99.** (a)	**100.** (b)

Solutions

1. (b)

2. (c)

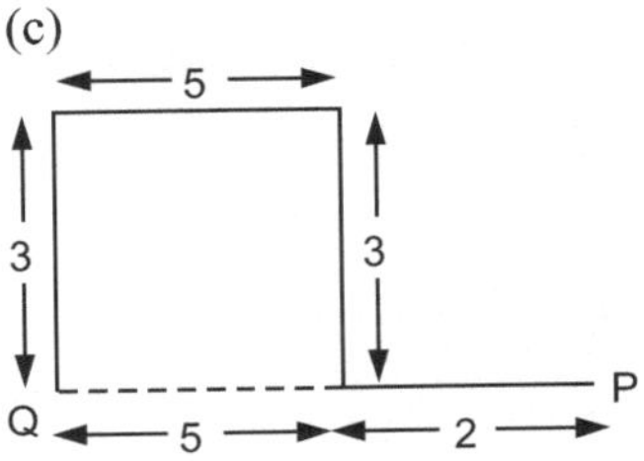

3. (d) The words are arranged in alphabetical order with numbers 4, 3, 2, 1 coming alternately.

4. (c) In all others, 1st letter – 1 = 2nd letter; and 2nd letter – 2 = 3rd letter.

5. (c) All others consist some sort of line whether it be round or straight.

Hints for (6-10):

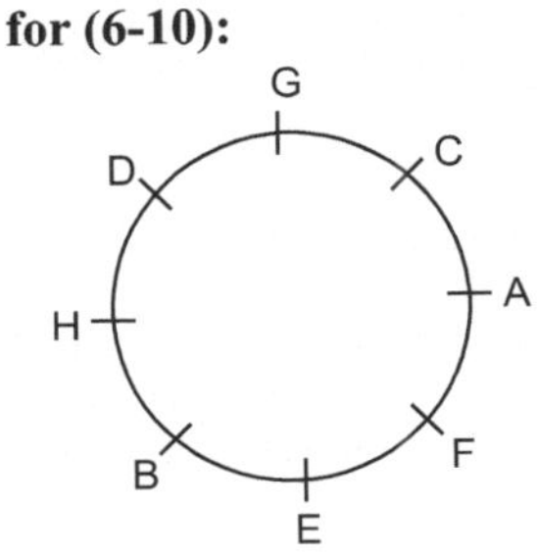

11. (d) 6 4 2 5 2 8 5 2 6 4 1 3 9 1 8 1 2 5 8 6 3 5 1 4 9 4 7 3 2 7 2 5 9

12. (b) 7th to the left of 20th from left = (20 – 7) = 13th from left.

13. (b) Arrangement after deleting all the even digits:
5 5 1 3 9 1 1 5 3 5 1 9 7 3 7 5 9

14. (a) 6 4 2 5 2 8 2 6 4 1 3 9 1 8 1 2 5 8 6 3 5 1 4 9 4 7 3 2 7 2 5 9
None of the 5s in the arrangement satisfy the given condition.

15. (c) 6 4 2 5 2 8 5 2 6 4 1 3 9 1 8 1 2 5 8 6 3 5 1 4 9 4 7 3 2 7 2 5 9

(16-20):

ring a bell → 5 8 2 ... (i)
did not ring → 3 5 9 ... (ii)
not a reason → 7 2 9 ... (iii)
Using (i) and (ii),
ring → 5
Using (ii) and (iii),
not → 9
∴ did → 3
Using (i) and (iii);
a → 2
Then, bell → 8
reason → 7

21. (b) New arrangement:
936 853 742 587 219
The number exactly in the middle of the new arrangement = 742
Required product = 7 × 4 = 28

22. (d) After subtracting 1 from the first digit and 2 from the third digit of each number, we get
117 640 834 485 751
Highest number → 834
Lowest number → 117
Required answer = 8 – 7 = 1

23. (a) Highest number → 936
Lowest number → 219
Required answer = $\frac{6}{2} = 3$

24. (a) After changing positions of first and third digits, the numbers are
912 247 639 785 358
Second highest number → 785
Sum of digits = 7 + 8 + 5 = 20

25. (b) When all the digits in each number are arranged in descending order, the numbers become
921 742 963 875 853
Lowest number = 742, formed by 742.

Hints for (26-30):

Required sequence: T R V Q P W S

26 (d) **27.** (c) **28.** (b) **29.** (a)

30. (a) Original arrangement: T R V Q P W S
New arrangement: W V T S R Q P

31. (d)

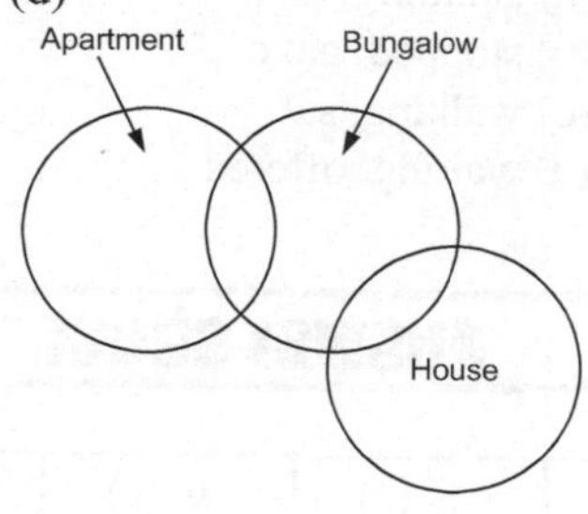

Figure 1
OR

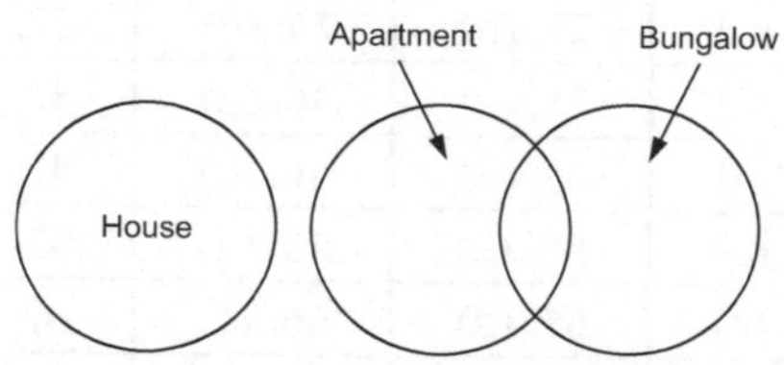

Figure 2

I does not follow as both the cases are possible, ie some houses can be bungalows (figure 1) and no house can be bungalow (figure 2).
II does not follow as is evident from both the Venn diagrams.

32. (a)

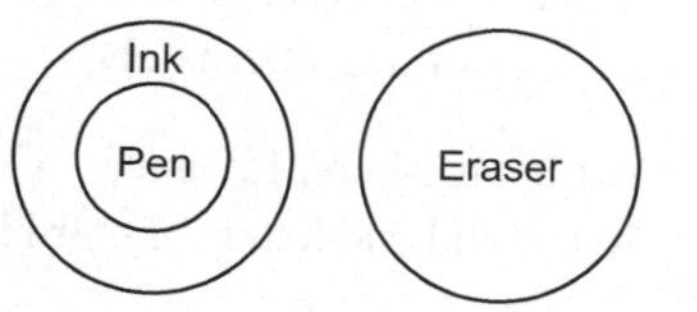

I follows. As no Ink can be eraser, pens also can never be erasers.
II. does not follow as is evident from the Venn diagram.

33. (b)

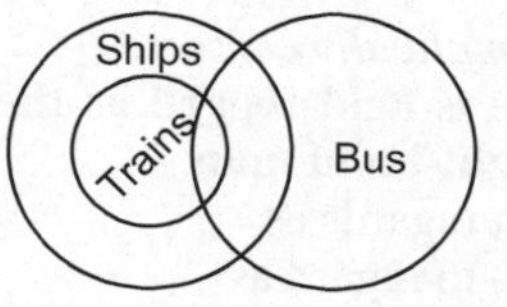

I does not follow as is evident by the Venn diagram.
II follows as all the trains are ships. So, the trains which are buses are also ships.

34. (d) 2, 5, 12, 27, ?
2 × 2 + 1 = 5
5 × 2 + 2 = 12
12 × 2 + 3 = 27
27 × 2 + 4 = 58
therefore, missing number = 58

35. (c) P, 3, Q, means–P, Q's daughter
P, 5, Q, means–P, Q's Father
P, 7, Q, means–P, Q's Mother
P, 9, Q, means–P, Q's sister
then, J 3 L 9 N 3 O 5 K—
J, 3, L, means–J, L's daughter
L, 9, N, means–L, N's is sister
N, 3, O, means–N, O's daughter
O, 5, K, means–O, K's father
therefore, J 3 L 9 N 3 O 5 K—
J, daughter of, L
L, sister of, N
N, daughter of, O
O, Father of, K
or

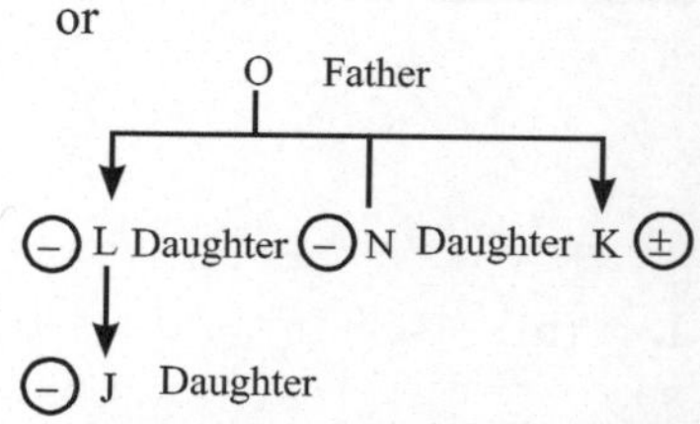

therefore, J is K Niece of k.

36. (d) $? = \frac{8}{15} + \frac{2}{5} - \frac{1}{3} = \frac{8+6-5}{15} = \frac{3}{5}$

37. (a) $\frac{4500}{18} - 122 = ? \times 4$

or, $\frac{250-122}{4}=?$

$\therefore ? = 32$

38. (d) $? = \sqrt[3]{32768}$

$= \sqrt[3]{(32)^3} = 32$

39. (a) 361 + 784 – 256 = ?

or, ? = 889

40. (b) 882 + 334 = ? + 144

? = 1216 – 144 = 1072

41. (d) $\left[\frac{452+62}{5}\right] \div 5 = ? \div 5$

$= \frac{113+62}{5} = \frac{175}{5} = 35$

42. (c) 336 + 324 = ?

or = 660

43. (b) 451.2 + 1088 = 1539.2

44. (a) $\frac{1}{5}\times\frac{3}{4}\times\frac{2}{5}\times 6000$

= 360

45. (d) $4^{10} \times (4)^3 \div (4)^4 = 4^? \times 4^2$

or $4^? = 4^{10+3-4-2}$

$\therefore ? = 7$

46. (a)

$\left(\frac{5994}{18}\right)\times\left(\frac{468}{18}\right) = 33\times 26 = 8658$

47. (c)

48. (d) $321\times\frac{16}{8}+34=(?)^2$

or $(?)^2 = 642 + 34 = 676$

$\therefore ? = 26$

49. (c)

50. (c) $\frac{3}{4}\times\frac{24}{100}\times 400 - 32 = ?$

or 72 – 32 = ?

$\therefore ? = 40$

51. (a) Average of the five numbers is equal to the middle number.

So, middle number $= \frac{400}{5} = 80$

$\therefore$ Smallest number = 80 – 4 = 76

$\therefore$ Largest number = 80 + 4 = 84

$\therefore$ Required answer $= \frac{76+84}{2} = 80$

52. (b) Let the present age of Binoy be b and that age of Alisha be a.

$\frac{b}{a} = \frac{5}{6}$ ....(i)

Three years hence,

$\frac{b+3}{a+3} = \frac{6}{7}$ ...(ii)

Solving the equations (i) and (ii), we get

$b = 15$ and $a = 18$

Alisha's age 8 years ago

= 18 – 8 = 10

53. (a) Letters of the word 'QUOTED' are all different hence, these can be written in 6! ways = 720 ways,

54. (a) Required percent $= \frac{(33+37+28+26+32)}{60\times 5}\times 100$

$= \frac{156}{300}\times 100 = 52\%$

55. (c) Required value

$= \frac{114.7}{37}\times 130 = 403$

56. (d) Required average

$= \frac{69+89+34+76+5.4+6.8+28+46}{8}$

$= \frac{464}{8} = 58$

57. (d) Required resultant $= 210^2 - 109^2$

= (210 + 109) (210 – 109)

= 319 × 101 = 32219

58. (d) $\left(32500\times\frac{105}{100}\times\frac{105}{100}\right) - 32500$

= 3331.25

59. (d) Sum of all 5 numbers = 50.8 × 5 = 254

Sum of 1st and 2nd number = 29 × 2 = 58

Sum of 4th and 5th number = 66.5 × 2 = 133

$\therefore$ 3rd number = 254 – 58 – 133 = 63

60. (b) Speed of train $= \frac{430}{5} = 86$ km/ hr

Speed of the bike $= \frac{86}{2} = 43$ km/hr

Time taken by Bike to cover 301 km

$= \frac{301}{43} = 7$ hrs

61. (a) $\frac{2}{9} < \frac{5}{11} < \frac{7}{13} < \frac{4}{7} < \frac{12}{17}$

62. (d) No. of females in school last year

$= \frac{48}{100}\times 4500 = 2160$

No. of males in school last year

= 4500 – 2160 = 2340

Required ratio

$= \frac{(2340-60)}{2160} = \frac{2280}{2160} = \frac{19}{18}$

63. (c) Root of 2020 lies between 44 and 45

By adding 5, it becomes a perfect square.

64. (c) Square of 250 is 62500 and 62627 is slightly higher than 62500

65. (d) 45 × 20 ÷ 10 = 45 × 2 = 90

66. (c)

600 564 539 523 514 510

$-(6)^2$ $-(5)^2$ $-(4)^2$ $-(3)^2$ $-(2)^2$

67. (c)

55000 11000 2200 440 88 17.6

÷5 ÷5 ÷5 ÷5 ÷5

68. (b)

2 12 60 240 720 1440

×6 ×5 ×4 ×3 ×2

69. (d)

80 48 64 56 60 58

–32 $+\frac{32}{2}$ $-\frac{32}{4}$ $+\frac{32}{8}$ $-\frac{32}{16}$

70. (d)

32 38 50 68 92 122

+(6×1) +(6×2) +(6×3) +(6×4) +(6×5)

4 Practice Set

Reasoning

1. **Four of the following five are alike in a certain way and hence form a group. Which of the following does not belong to that group?**
(a) 196 (b) 16
(c) 144 (d) 25

2. **In a certain code language, 'PLUS' is coded as 'SULQ', similarly 'MASK' is coded as 'KSAN'. How will 'FLIP' be coded in the same code language?**
(a) PILG (b) PILE
(c) CLIP (d) ELDP

3. **If each alternate letter in the word 'MENTION' starting with M is changed to the next letter in the English alphabetical series and each of the remaining letter is changed to the previous letter in the English alphabetical series then how many letters will appear more than once in the new arrangement?**
(a) Five (b) One
(c) Two (d) Three

4. **Four of following five are alike in a certain way and hence form a group. Which of the following does not belong to that group?**
(a) Tyre (b) Speed
(c) Clutch (d) Brake

5. **How many such pairs of letters are there in the word 'LABOUR', each of which has as many letters between them in the word (in both forward and backward directions) as they have between them in the English alphabetical series?**
(a) Four (b) One
(c) Two (d) Three

6. **In a class of 20 students, Mrinal's rank is 12th from the top and Reena's rank is 17th from the bottom. If Mohan's rank is exactly between Mrinal and Reena's rank, what is Mohan's rank from the top?**
(a) Ninth (b) Eighth
(c) Tenth (d) Seventh

7. **Pointing to a boy, Neelu said, "He is the only son of my grandfather's only child." How is the boy related to Neelu?**
(a) Cousin (b) Uncle
(c) Sister (d) Brother

8. **How many meaningful English works can be formed with the letters 'EWF' using all the letters only once in each work?**
(a) Four (b) One
(c) Two (d) Three

9. **What should come next in the letter series given below?**
Z Z Y Z Y X Z Y X W Z Y X W V Z Y X W V U Z Y X W V U T Z Y X W V U T
(a) U (b) Z
(c) R (d) None of these

10. **'Skating' is related to 'Rink' in the same way as 'Badminton' is related to '_______'.**
(a) Court (b) Field.
(c) Stadium (d) Pitch

Directions (Q. 11-15): *Study the following information to answer the given questions:*

Eight friends L, M, N, O, P, Q, R and S are sitting around a circle facing the centre. There are equal number of males and females in the group. No two females are immediate neighbours of each other. N is a male and N sits third to the right of R. O is a female and O is not an immediate neighbour of N. P sits second to the left of O. S sits fourth to the right of L and S is not an immediate neighbour of R. Q is a female.

11. **What is Q's position with respect to O?**
(a) Immediate right
(b) Third to the right
(c) Third to the left
(d) Fourth to the left

12. **Four of the following five are alike' in a certain way based on their seating positions in the above arrangement and so form a group. Which is the one that does not belong to the group?**
(a) LO (b) NL
(c) OP (d) PQ

13. **If all the eight friends are made to sit alphabetically in the clockwise direction starting from L, positions of how many will remain unchanged (excluding L)?**
(a) None (b) One
(c) Two (d) Three

14. **Which of the following is true about M ?**
(a) M sits third to the right of Q.
(b) M sits second to the right of L.
(c) M is a male.
(d) M sits on the immediate left of O.

15. **Which of the following groups represents the females in the group?**
(a) O, P, Q, S (b) Q, R, P, O
(c) Q, L, M, O (d) O, M, Q, R

Directions (Q. 16-20): *In each of the questions below, two statements are given followed by two conclusions numbered I and II. You have to take the two statements to be true even if they seem to be at variance with the* *commonly known facts and then decide which of the given conclusions logically follows from the given statements disregarding commonly known facts.*

Give answer

(a) if only conclusion I follows.

(b) if only conclusion II follows.

(c) if either conclusion I or conclusion II follows.

(d) if neither conclusion I nor conclusion II follows.

16. Statements: All purses are strings.

No string is a bucket.

Conclusions:

I. No purse is a bucket.

II. At least some purses are buckets.

17. Statements: Some glasses are tablets.

All machines are instruments.

Conclusions:

I. All instruments being machines is a possibility.

II. All machines being glasses is a possibility.

18. Statements: Some weathers are rains.

Some winters are weathers.

Conclusions:

I. At least some winters are rains.

II. At least some weathers are winters.

19. Statements: All watches are shoes.

Some watches are clocks.

Conclusions:

I. Some clocks are shoes.

II. All clocks are shoes.

20. Statements: All tents are cabins.

All cabins are crews.

Conclusions:

I. All tents are crews.

II. All crews are tents.

Directions (Q. 21-22): *Study the following information to answer the given questions:*

Seven friends, A, B, C, D, E, F and G, are sitting in a straight line facing north, not necessarily in the same order. E sits fourth to the left of G. Neither E nor G sits at the extreme ends. A sits third to the right of D. C sits fourth to the left of F. C does not sit at one of the extreme ends.

21. Four of the following five are alike in a certain way based on their seating positions in the above arrangement and so form a group. Which is the one that does not belong to that group?

(a) AC (b) GB

(c) FG (d) DE

22. What is B's position with respect to E?

(a) Second to the right

(b) Third to the left

(c) Second to the left

(d) Third to the right

Directions (Q. 23-27): *In each question below is given a group of numbers/symbols followed by four combinations of letter codes numbered* (a), (b), (c) and (d). *You have to find out which of the combinations correctly represents the group of numbers/symbols based on the following coding system and the conditions and mark the number of that combination as your answer.*

Number/

Symbol: 7 3 & 6 % 2 # 8 4 @ 1 + 5 $

Letter

Code: S H P W L D K J X Z Q T N F

Conditions:

I. If the first element is a symbol and the last element is a number, the codes for both are to be interchanged.

II. If both the first and' last elements are symbols, the last element is to be coded as the code for the first element.

III. If the group of elements contains only one symbol, that symbol is to be coded as A.

23. 45631 #

(a) ANWHQX (b) XNWHQK

(c) XNWHQA (d) XNHWQA

24. 2 @ 7$4&

(a) D ASFXP (b) PZS AXD

(c) DZSFXP (d) PZSFXP

25. 3 + 5641

(a) HTNWXQ (b) QANWXH

(c) MANX WQ (d) HANWXQ

26. % 82 & 47

(a) LDJPXS (b) SJDPXL

(c) SJDXPL (d) LJDPXS

27. @ 4153 +

(a) TXQNHT (b) ZQXNHZ

(c) TQXNHT (d) ZXQNHZ

Directions (Q. 28-32): *In these questions, relationships between different elements is shown in the statements. These statements are followed by two conclusions.*

Give answer

(a) if only conclusion I follows.

(b) if only conclusion II follows.

(c) if both conclusions I and II follow.

(d) if neither conclusion I nor conclusion II follows.

28. Statement: $A > L = T < R \leq H > K$

Conclusions: I. $H > L$

II. $K > T$

29. Statement: $P \geq N > D \geq G < B \leq J$

Conclusions: I. $G < P$

II. $G < J$

30. Statement: $Q \leq E < I > N = R \geq S$

Conclusions: I. $E \geq S$

II. $S \leq N$

31. Statement: $R = S \geq Y \geq M < W > O$

Conclusions: I. $Y < M$

II. $O > S$

32. Statement: $F \leq C \leq V = Z < X = U$

Conclusions: I. $V < U$

II. $Z < F$

Directions (Q. 33-35): *Study the following arrangement carefully and answer the questions given below:*

M I & R S 2 K 3 # T 6 L E % A F G U $ H ★ 5 9 J 4 D W 7 @ Q ! © N B

33. If all the symbols are dropped from the arrangement, which of the following will be twelfth from the left end?

(a) F (b) G

(c) E (d) None of these

34. **Which of the following is eighth to the right of the nineteenth from the right end of the above arrangement?**
(a) 4 (b) 3
(c) J (d) 9

35. **How many such consonants are there in the above arrangement, each of which is immediately preceded by a consonant and immediately followed by a number?**
(a) Five (b) One
(c) Two (d) Three

Quantitative Aptitude

Directions (Q. 36-49): *What will come in place of question mark(?) in the following questions ?*

36. **892.33 + 212.87 + 456.99 = ?**
(a) 156823 (b) 1566.99
(c) 1564.73 (d) None of these

37. **3434 + 7979 – 2323 = ?**
(a) 9191 (b) 9190
(c) 9091 (d) None of these

38. **45 × 253 – 782 = ?**
(a) 10205 (b) 10605
(c) 10607 (d) 10603

39. $\frac{1}{2}$ of $\frac{1}{5}$th of $\frac{1}{4}$th of 4500 = ?
(a) 118.3 (b) 117.5
(c) 110.3 (d) None of these

40. **24% of 40% of $\frac{3}{4}$th of 12000 = ?**
(a) 868 (b) 864
(c) 866 (d) 862

41. **0.2 × 222 ÷ 20 × 12 = ?**
(a) 26.64 (b) 28
(c) 24.88 (d) 22.62

42. **23578 + 33872 + 17193 – 52559 = ?**
(a) 22088 (b) 22086
(c) 22082 (d) 22084

43. **4096 × $(16)^3$ ÷ 16 = (4)? × 64**
(a) 8 (b) 12
(c) 7 (d) 10

44. **32.97 + 45.33 + 17.24 = ?**
(a) 95.54 (b) 98
(c) 91.62 (d) 93.84

45. **42% of ? + 18% of 400 = 219**
(a) 370 (b) 360
(c) 350 (d) 340

46. **$\frac{3}{4}$th of 46% of 400 – 12 = ?**
(a) 126 (b) 125
(c) 124 (d) 122

47. **$(15)^2 + (12)^2 - (18)^2$ = ?**
(a) 42 (b) 43
(c) 48 (d) None of these

48. **3.44 + 5.22 + 7.23 + 5.24 = ?**
(a) 23.34 (b) 21.13
(c) 25.57 (d) 20.05

49. **45698 – 23367 + 43237 = ?**
(a) 65568 (b) 65586
(c) 65569 (d) 65589

50. **The side of a square is twice the radius of a circle. The area of that square is 9604 sq cm. What is the area of the circle?**
(a) 7545 sq cm (b) 7543 sq cm
(c) 7548 sq cm (d) None of these

51. **In how many different ways can the letters of the word 'BOUNTY'be arranged?**
(a) 720 (b) 725
(c) 732 (d) 740

52. **Four years ago the ratio of the age of Ramesh to that of Lina was 5:3. The ratio of their present ages is 11 : 7. What will be Lina's age 3 years hence?**
(a) 18 years (b) 29 years
(c) 33 years (d) 31 years

53. **If the following fractions are arranged in a descending order (from left to right), which of them will be second from the left end?**
$\frac{4}{7}, \frac{7}{9}, \frac{1}{5}, \frac{8}{11}, \frac{2}{9}$
(a) $\frac{2}{9}$ (b) $\frac{4}{7}$
(c) $\frac{7}{9}$ (d) $\frac{8}{11}$

54. **Manish spent 12% of his income on bills, 22% on rent and 28% on shopping. $\frac{1}{4}$ of the remaining amount is ₹ 3,610. How much did he spend on bills?**
(a) ₹ 4,580 (b) ₹ 4,530
(c) ₹ 4320 (d) ₹ 4,560

55. **Find the average of the following sets of scores:**
556, 224, 778, 442, 336, 112
(a) 405 (b) 408
(c) 402 (d) 406

56. **The average of five numbers is 40.8. The average of the first and the second number is 46. The average of the fourth and the fifth number is 37. What is the third number?**
(a) 28 (b) 34
(c) 38 (d) 42

57. **Bina scored 110 marks in English, 13 5 marks in Science, 140 marks in Mathematics, 120 marks in Hindi and 115 marks in Social studies. The maximum marks a student can score in each subject is 150. How much approximate percentage did Bina get in this exam?**
(a) 83 (b) 89
(c) 93 (d) 95

58. **A truck covers 448 km in eight hours. The average speed of a bicycle is one-fourth the average speed of the truck. How much distance will the bicycle cover in 7 hours ?**
(a) 101 km (b) 98 km
(c) 95 km (d) 96 km

59. **What will be the compound interest accrued on a principal amount of ₹ 12000 at the rate of 4 pcpa after a period of two years ?**
(a) ₹ 971.5 (b) ₹ 973.4
(c) ₹ 979.2 (d) ₹ 975.9

Directions (Q. 60-62): *The following questions are based on the given information:*

A publisher published 3400 copies of a book. 28% of the total copies were sold in City A. 32% of the total copies were sold in City B. 22% of the total copies were sold in City C. The remaining copies are yet to be sold.

60. How many copies were sold in City B and City C together?

(a) 1833 (b) 1838
(c) 1836 (d) 1832

61. What is the difference between the number of copies sold in City A and that in City C?

(a) 178 (b) 184
(c) 200 (d) None of these

62. How many copies are yet to be sold ?

(a) 588 (b) 612
(c) 616 (d) 618

Directions (Q. 63-65): *What approximate value should come in place of question mark(?) in the following questions? (**Note**: You are not expected to calculate the exact value.)*

63. 4005.33 ÷ 19.89 × 1.9 = ?

(a) 275 (b) 300
(c) 400 (d) 370

64. 0.501 × 10.011 × 52.83 = ?

(a) 205 (b) 225
(c) 245 (d) 265

65. 16.002 × 14.897 × 20.334 = ?

(a) 4100 (b) 4300
(c) 4500 (d) 4800

Directions (Q. 66-70): *What should come in place of question mark (?) in the following number series?*

66. 13 14 17 22 29 ?

(a) 33 (b) 35
(c) 36 (d) 38

67. 6 8 4 12 –4 ?

(a) 28 (b) 26
(c) 24 (d) 22

68. 53 318 1590 6360 19080 ?

(a) 38165 (b) 38170
(c) 38160 (d) 38175

69. 17 18 22 31 47 ?

(a) 72 (b) 77
(c) 83 (d) 68

70. 222 198 178 162 150 ?

(a) 140 (b) 142
(c) 144 (d) 145

English Language

Directions (Q. 71-77): *Read the following passage carefully and answer the questions given below it. Certain words are printed in bold to help you locate them while answering some of the questions.*

Once upon a time, there were three brothers. They were very clever and one day decided to make a fortune by using their powers of reasoning and logic. As they walked to the nearest city to look for work, they saw some footprints on the mud road. As they stood looking at the marks, a merchant came rushing towards them. 'Did you see anyone go by this road ?' he asked in **panic.** The first brother looked closely at the prints and said, 'Yes, a large camel'. The second said, 'The camel could see with only one eye'. The third, who had been looking further down the road, said, 'The camel was carrying a woman and a child on its back'.

Now the merchant was furious and shouted, 'You have kidnapped my wife and child. Come with me to the king.' The brothers could not get him to reason out and the four men ended up in the king's court. 'Hmm,' the king said, after he had heard the entire story. 'If you three claim to be so clever, let me set a task for you. I will place before you a wooden box which will be locked. You will have to tell me what it contains without looking inside.'

The three brothers agreed, and soon the king's men placed before them a stout wooden box, **firmly** shut, The first brother said immediately,' It has something round inside.' The second said, 'It is a pomegranate.' 'An unripe pomegranate,' added the third. The box was opened and indeed, inside there was an unripe pomegranate.

The king now asked them for an explanation. The first man said, 'When your servant was bringing the box, I heard something rolling inside. That meant there was a round object in it. The second man said, 'I saw your servant coming from the pomegranate orchard, so I knew he had placed a pomegranate in the box.' 'And this is not the season for pomegranates, so it had to be an unripe one, commented the last brother.

The king had now witnessed the brother's powers of observation and was curious to know how they had discovered about the merchant's wife and child being on the camel's back. 'The footprints we saw were large ones, so I **deduced** it was a big camel that had passed that way,' said the first brother.' The camel had grazed on only one side of the road," said the second, 'so I knew it was one-eyed.'

'And I saw the footprints of a woman and a child where the camel had sat down to rest,' said the third, 'which meant they were on the camel's back.' The king, now convinced of their cleverness, appointed the three brothers as ministers in his court.

71. Why did' the merchant take the three brothers to the king's court?

(a) They confessed to having kidnapped his wife and child.
(b) He found them acting very strange.
(c) He thought they were responsible for his missing wife and child.
(d) He found their observations hilarious and wanted them to narrate them to the king.

72. How did the second brother arrive at the conclusion that the camel could see with only one eye?

(A) He saw the camel passing by.
(B) He took a guess.
(C) The grass on only one side of the road was eaten.

(a) Only (A)
(b) Only (B)
(c) Only (C)
(d) Only (B) and (C)

73. Which of the following word is most opposite of the word 'panic' printed in bold in the above story?

(a) Calm (b) Frightened
(c) Hesitation (d) Anxious

74. Which of the following sentences are true in the context of the three brothers?

(A) They were fortune tellers.

(B) They were responsible for kidnapping the merchant's wife and child.

(C) They used logic in order to determine the contents of the wooden box.

(a) Only (A)
(b) Only (B) and (C)
(c) Only (B)
(d) Only (C)

75. What task did the king give to the three brothers on their arrival to the court ?

(A) He asked them to reveal the contents of a wooden box that he placed before them.

(B) The task of handling the day-to-day affairs of the state

(C) He asked them to explain the secret of their reasoning abilities.

(a) Only (A)
(b) Only (B)
(c) Only (C)
(d) Only (A) and (B)

75. Which of the following statements is false according to the passage?

(a) One of the brothers saw the king's servant coming out from the pomegranate orchard.

(b) One of the brothers saw the camel carrying a lady along with a child on its back.

(c) The three brothers were appointed as ministers in the king's court.

(d) The king was convinced with the brothers' story after listening to their logic.

Directions (Q. 76-77): *Choose the word which is most nearly the SAME in meaning as the word printed in bold as used in the passage.*

76. Closely

(a) Openly (b) Watchfully
(c) Personally (d) Slyly

77. Firmly

(a) Unevenly (b) Drastically
(c) Tightly (d) Steadily

Directions (Q. 78-82): *Read each sentence to find out whether there is any grammatical error in it. The error, if any, will be in one part of the sentence. The number of that part is the answer.*

78. I requested my friend (a) to come (b) and shopping (c) with me. (d)

79. The passage is (a) more difficult (b) that I am unable (c) to comprehend it. (d)

80. Janet is determined (a) to be success (b) in whatever field (c) she chooses. (d)

81. My friend lives (a) at a beautiful house (b) not more than (c) five minutes from the beach.(d)

82. If you breaks the law (a) you must be prepared (b) to suffer (c) the consequences.

Direction (Q. 83-87): *In each question below, four words printed in bold are given. These are numbered* (a), (b), (c) *and* (d). *One of these words printed in bold may either be wrongly spelt or inappropriate in the context of the sentence. Find out the word that is inappropriate or wrongly spelt, if any. The number of that word is your answer.*

83. My **friend (a) deserved** of **(b) succeed** for **(c)** he **worked** hard (d).

84. My **parents (a)** were poor **though (b)** they were of **nobel (c) birth. (d)**

85. The doctor **advised (a)** me to **switch (b)** over to a **healthier (c) diet (d)**

86. Over the (a) **succeeding (b) weak (c)** things went from bad to **worse** (d)

87. Abdul, **quiet (a) pale (b)** with **fright (c)** rushed into the **room (d)**

Directions (Q. 88-90): *Rearrange the following four sentences* (A), (B), (C) and (D) *in the proper sequence to form a meaningful paragraph; then answer the questions given below them.*

(A) The victor flew up to the roof of the barn and began to crow, "I have won, I have won!"

(B) Finally one of them was beaten and he went and hid himself in the corner of the hen-house.

(C) The rooster that had been defeated suddenly found himself to be the unchallenged master of the farmyard.

(D) Just then an eagle swooped down and carried him away.

88. Which of the following should be the SECOND sentence after rearrangement?

(a) A (b) B
(c) C (d) D

89. Which of the following should be the THIRD sentence after rearrangement?

(a) A (b) B
(c) C (d) D

90. Which of the following should be the FIRST sentence after rearrangement ?

(a) A (b) D
(c) C (d) B

Directions (91-92): *In the following question, out of the four alternatives, select the alternative which is the best substitute of the phrase.*

91. That which cannot be corrected.

(a) Impregnable
(b) Immolation
(c) Incorrigible
(d) Ineligible

92. A person who is blamed for the wrong doings of others.

(a) Bursar (b) Captor
(c) Phlegmatic (d) Scapegoat

Directions (Q. 93-100): *In the following passage there are blanks, each of which has been numbered. These numbers are printed below the passage and against each, four words are suggested, one of which fits the blank appropriately. Find out the appropriate word in each case.*

Birbal was in Persia at the invitation of the king of that country. During his stay parties were given in his honour. On the eve of his (**93**) for home, a nobleman (**94**) him how he would compare the king of Persia to his own king. "Your King is a full moon," said Birbal. "Whereas mine could be (**95**) of as the quarter moon." The Persians were very happy. But when Birbal went home he found that Emperor Akbar was furious with him. "How (**96**) you belittle your own king?" demanded Akbar. "You are a traitor!".

"No, Your Majesty," said Birbal. "I did not belittle you. The full moon (**97**) and disappears whereas the quarter moon grows with strength. What I, in fact, (**98**) to the world is that your power is (**99**) from day to day whereas that of the king of Persia is about to go into decline." Akbar smiled in satisfaction and welcomed Birbal back (**100**) a warm embrace.

93. (a) arrival (b) depart (c) leave (d) departure

94. (a) asked (b) comented (c) said (d) made

95. (a) pass (b) celebrated (c) imagined (d) thought

96. (a) must (b) could (c) should (d) will

97. (a) appear (b) decrease (c) diminishes (d) reduce

98. (a) proclaimed (b) show (c) restored (d) promised

99. (a) sure (b) fixed (c) growing (d) new

100. (a) with (b) giving (c) granting (d) shaving

Answer sheet

1. (d)	**2.** (a)	**3.** (c)	**4.** (b)	**5.** (c)	**6.** (b)	**7.** (d)	**8.** (b)	**9.** (d)	**10.** (a)
11. (d)	**12.** (a)	**13.** (b)	**14.** (c)	**15.** (b)	**16.** (a)	**17.** (a)	**18.** (b)	**19.** (a)	**20.** (a)
21. (d)	**22.** (d)	**23.** (c)	**24.** (c)	**25.** (d)	**26.** (b)	**27.** (d)	**28.** (a)	**29.** (c)	**30.** (b)
31. (d)	**32.** (a)	**33.** (d)	**34.** (c)	**35.** (c)	**36.** (d)	**37.** (d)	**38.** (d)	**39.** (d)	**40.** (b)
41. (a)	**42.** (d)	**43.** (c)	**44.** (a)	**45.** (c)	**46.** (a)	**47.** (d)	**48.** (b)	**49.** (a)	**50.** (d)
51. (a)	**52.** (d)	**53.** (d)	**54.** (d)	**55.** (b)	**56.** (c)	**57.** (a)	**58.** (b)	**59.** (c)	**60.** (c)
61. (d)	**62.** (b)	**63.** (c)	**64.** (d)	**65.** (d)	**66.** (d)	**67.** (a)	**68.** (c)	**69.** (a)	**70.** (b)
71. (c)	**72.** (c)	**73.** (a)	**74.** (d)	**75.** (b)	**76.** (b)	**77.** (c)	**78.** (c)	**79.** (b)	**80.** (b)
81. (b)	**82.** (a)	**83.** (b)	**84.** (c)	**85.** (d)	**86.** (c)	**87.** (a)	**88.** (b)	**89.** (a)	**90.** (b)
91. (c)	**92.** (d)	**93.** (d)	**94.** (a)	**95.** (d)	**96.** (b)	**97.** (c)	**98.** (a)	**99.** (c)	**100.** (b)

Solutions

1. (d) 25 is the square of a prime number whereas rest of the numbers are the squares of even numbers.
2. (a) As,

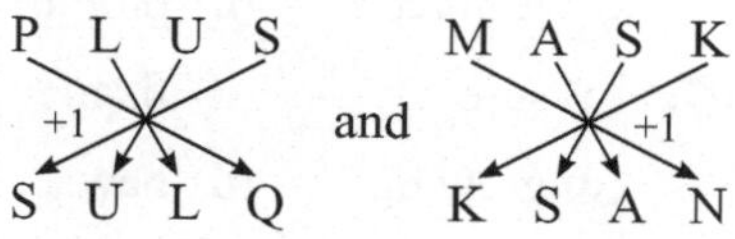

Similarly,

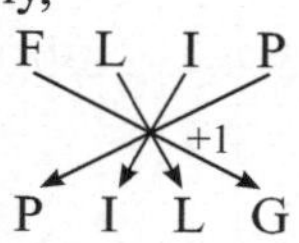

3. (c) M E N T I O N
N D O S J N O
N and O appear more than once in the new arrangement.
4. (b) All the other four options are components of a vehicle.
5. (c) L A B O U R
LO and AB are such pairs.
6. (b) Reena's rank is 17th from the bottom means Reena's rank is 4th from the top. Mohan's rank is exactly between 4th and 12th, ie 8th.
7. (d)

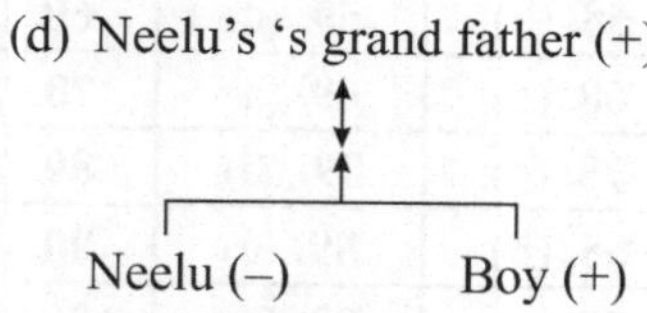

The boy is Neelu's brother.
8. (b) 'FEW' is the only word possible.
9. (d) Z, ZY, ZYX, ZYXW, ZYXWV, ZYXWVU, ZYXWVUT, ZYXWVUTIS

(11-15):

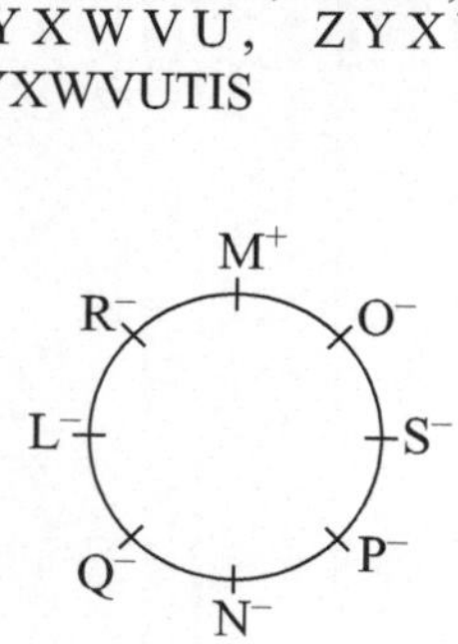

16. (a) All purses are strings + No string is a basket = A + E = E = No purse is a basket. Hence, conclusion I follows. Consequently conclusion II doesnot follow.
17. (a) Some glasses are tablets + Some tablets are machines (conversion of the statement "All machines are tablets") = I + I = No conclusion. Hence conclusion II doesnot follow. Again, draw all the possibilities for the given statement "All machines are tablets" as given below:

Possibility I:

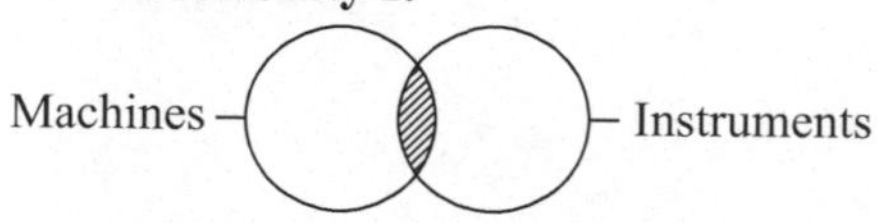

(Some machines are tablets)

Possibility II:

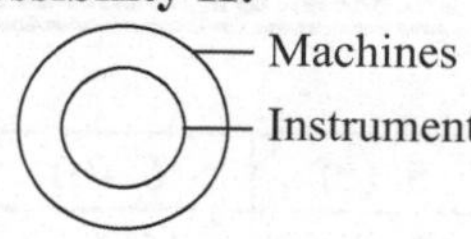

Therefore, "All instruments being machines is a possibility" exists. Hence, option (a) is the correct answer.
18. (b) Both the given statements are particular positive propositions. These propositions cannot be combined. Hence conclusion I does not follow. Again, Some winters are weathers (I) → conversion → Some weathers are winters (I) ⇒ At least some weathers are winters . Therefore, conclusion II follows.
19. (a) Some watches are clocks (I) → conversion → Some clocks are watches + All watches are shoes = I + A = I = Some clocks are shoes. Hence conclusion I follows. Consequently, conclusion II doesnot follow.
20. (a) All tents are cabins + All cabins are crews = A + A = A = All tents are crews. Hence, conclusion 1 follows.

Hints for (21-22): D E C A B G F

23. (c) It follows condition III.
24. (c) It does not follow any of the given conditions.
25. (d) It follows condition III.
26. (b) It follows condition I.
27. (d) It follows conditon II.
33. (d) When all the symbols are dropped from the arrangement, the new arrangement becomes as follows:
M I R S 2 K 3 T 6 L E A F G U H 5 9 J 4 D W 7 Q N B
Twelfth element from the left end is A.
34. (c) Eighth to the right of the nineteenth from the right end means (19 – 8) = 11th from the right end ie J.
35. (c) Only two consonants, S and W, follow the given condition
36. (d) 1562.19
37. (d) 9090
38. (d) 11385 – 782 = 10603
39. (d) $\frac{1}{2}\times\frac{1}{5}\times\frac{1}{4}\times 4500 = 112.5$
40. (b) $\frac{24}{100}\times\frac{40}{100}\times\frac{3}{4}\times 12000 = 864$
41. (a) $0.2\times\frac{222}{20}\times 12 = 26.64$
42. (d) 22084
43. (c) $(4)^? = \frac{4096\times(16)^2}{64\times 16} = \frac{(4)^6\times(4)^{2\times 3}}{(4)^3\times(4)^2}$
$= 4^{6+6-3-2} = 4^7 \quad \therefore ? = 7$
44. (a) 95.54
45. (c) 42% of $? = 219 - \frac{18}{100}\times 400$
$26, \frac{42}{100}\times ? = 219 - 72 = 147$
$\therefore ? = \frac{147\times 100}{42} = 350$
46. (a) $\frac{3}{4}\times\frac{46}{100}\times 400 - 12 = 138 - 12$
$= 126$

47. (d) $? = (15)^2 + (12)^2 - (18)^2$
$= 225 + 144 - 324 = 45$

48. (b) 21.13 **49.** (a) 65568

50. (d) Side of the square
$= \sqrt{9604} = 98$ cm

Radius of the circle $= \frac{98}{2} = 49$ cm

Area of the circle

$= \frac{22}{7} \times 49 \times 49 = 7546 \text{ cm}^2$

51. (a) Required number of ways $= {}^6P_6$
$= 6!$ ways $= 720$

52. (d) Let the present age of Ramesh be S and that of Lina be D.

Then, $\frac{S}{D} = \frac{11}{7} \Rightarrow 7S - 11D = 0$ ...(a)

Four year ago

$\frac{S-4}{D-4} = \frac{5}{3}$

or, $3S - 12 = 5D - 20$

or, $3S - 5D = -8$ ...(b)

Lina's age after 3 years will be 31 years.

53. (d) Descending order of fractions is $\frac{7}{8} > \frac{8}{11} > \frac{4}{7} > \frac{2}{9} > \frac{1}{5}$

54. (d) One-fourth of the remaining amount = 3610

Remaining amount = 100 – (12 + 22 + 28) $\Rightarrow 38\% = 3610 \times 4$

Money spent on bills

$= \frac{12}{100} \times \frac{3610 \times 4}{38} \times 100 = ₹\,4560$

55. (b) Average =
$\frac{556 + 224 + 778 + 442 + 336 + 112}{6}$

$= \frac{2448}{6} = 408$

56. (c) Sum of the five number = 40.8 × 5 = 204

Sum of first and second number = 46 × 2 = 92

Sum of fourth and fifth number = 37 × 2 = 74

Thrid number = 204 – 92 – 74 = 38

57. (a) Maximum marks that Bina can score = 150 × 5 = 750

Bina's score = 110 + 135 + 140 + 120 + 115 = 620

∴ % marks

$= \frac{620}{750} \times 100 = 82.66 \approx 83\%$

58. (b) Speed of the truck

$= \frac{448}{8} = 56$ km/hr

Speed of bicycle $= \frac{56}{4} = 14$ km/hr

Distance covered by bicycle in 7 hours = 14 × 7 = 98 km

59. (c) Amount after 2 years = 12000 × 1.04 × 1.04 = 12979.2

Compound Interest = 12979.2 – 12000 = ₹ 979.2

60. (c) Copies sold in City B and C together

$= \frac{(32 + 22)}{100} \times 3400 = 1836$

61. (d) Required difference

$= \frac{(28 - 22)}{100} \times 3400 = 204$

62. (b) No. of copies yet to be sold

$= \frac{(100 - 28 - 32 - 22)}{100} \times 3400 = 612$

63. (c) 4005 ÷ 20 × 2

$\approx \frac{4005}{20} \times 2 \approx 400.5 \approx 400$

66. (d)

13 14 17 22 29 38
+1 +3 +5 +7 +9

67. (a)

6 8 4 12 –4 28
+2 –4 +8 –16 –32

68. (c)

53 318 1590 6360 19080 38160
×6 ×5 ×4 ×3 ×2

69. (a)

17 18 22 31 47 72
$+(1)^2$ $+(2)^2$ $+(3)^2$ $+(4)^2$ $+(5)^2$

70. (b)

222 198 178 162 150 142
–24 –20 –16 –12 –8

5 Practice Set

Reasoning

1. **Ravi cycles 3 km towards the east and takes the first right turn and cycles for another 5 km to point A. From point A, he takes a left turn and cycles 7 km to point B, after covering another 4 km he rests for a little time. How much distance has Ravi covered from point A till the time he stops?**

   (a) 6 km (b) 11 km
   (c) 19 km (d) 14 km

2. **The position of how many digits will remain the same if the digits in the number 2567394 are rearranged in ascending order from left to right?**

   (a) Four (b) One
   (c) Two (d) Three

3. **How many meaningful English words can be made from the letters IRA, using each letter only once in each word?**

   (a) None (b) One
   (c) Two (d) Three

4. **How many such pairs of letters are there in the word INTRUDE each of which has as many letters between them in the word (in both forward and backward directions) as they have between them in the English alphabetical order?**

   (a) None (b) One
   (c) Two (d) Three

5. **If A means '+', B means '×', C means '–'and D means '÷', then 12 B 8C 6 D 2 A 4 = ?**

   (a) 87 (b) 94
   (c) 86 (d) 97

6. **If each of the vowels in the word HONESTLY is changed to the next letter in the English alphabetical series and each consonant is changed to the previous letter in the English alphabetical series, and then the alphabets so formed are arranged in alphabetical order from left to right, the positions of how many of the following alphabets will remain unchanged ? (from that of before arranging in alphabetical order)**

   (a) None (b) One
   (c) Three (d) Two

7. **'AB' is related to 'EF' in the same way as 'IJ' is related to_____**

   (a) MN (b) KL
   (c) OP (d) LM

8. **A, B, C and D live in a building having 14 floors, A lives two floors above B. C lives on the 14th floor immediately above A. D neither lives immediately above nor immediately below B. The first 7 floors of the building are vacant. On which of the following floor does D live?**

   (a) 8th
   (b) 10th
   (c) 12th
   (d) Cannot be determined

9. **If it is possible to make only one meaningful word with the second, third, eighth and ninth letters of the word 'ABDUCTION', which one of the following would be the second letter of that word from the left end? If no such word can be made, give 'A' as your answer and if more than one such word can be formed, give your answer as 'Z'.**

   (a) A (b) O
   (c) N (d) B

10. **In a certain code 'AEROBIC' is written as 'BFQNAJD'.**

    How is ADVERTS written in that code?

    (a) BEQUDUT (b) BUEDQUT
    (c) BEUDQUT (d) BEUQDUT

Directions (Q. 11-15): *Study the following information carefully and answer the given questions.*

Eight friends A, B, C, D, E, F, G and H are sitting around a circular table facing the centre and are equidistant, from each other. D sits exactly between E and H. A is third to the left of G, and G sits opposite F. E is third to the left of C.

11. **How many people sit between E and B when counted in an anti-clockwise direction from B?**

    (a) One (b) Two
    (c) Three (d) Four

12. **Who sits second to the left of C?**

    (a) F (b) E
    (c) D (d) H

13. **In which of the following pairs, is the first person sitting to the immediate left of the second person?**

    (a) BC (b) CA
    (c) GB (d) HD

14. **If B : D then C : ?**

    (a) E (b) F
    (c) G (d) H

15. What is the position of F with respect to B in the above arrangement?

(a) Fourth to the left
(b) Second to the right
(c) Third to the left
(d) Fourth to the right

Directions (Q. 16-20): *The following questions are based on the five three-digit numbers given below:*

356 497 812 739 264

16. If all the numbers are arranged in ascending order from left to right, which one of the following will be the sum of all the three-digits of the number which is second from the left of the new arrangement thus formed?

(a) 14 (b) 20
(c) 19 (d) 11

17. What will be the resultant if the third digit of the second lowest number is divided by the third digit of the highest number?

(a) 2 (b) 3
(c) 4 (d) 5

18. If '2' is subtracted from the last digit of every odd number and ' 1' is added to the last digit of every even number, what will be the difference between the highest and the lowest numbers thus formed?

(a) 380 (b) 456
(c) 318 (d) 548

19. If all the digits in each of the numbers are arranged in descending order within the number, which one of the following will form the second highest number in the new arrangement of numbers?

(a) 356 (b) 497
(c) 812 (d) 739

20. If the positions of the first and the second digits of each of the numbers are interchanged, in how many numbers thus formed will the first digit be a perfect square ? ('1' is also a perfect square)

(a) One (b) Two
(c) Three (d) Four

Directions (Q. 21-25): *In each of the questions below are given three statements followed by two conclusions numbered I and II. You have to take the given statements to be true even if they seem to be at variance from commonly known facts and then decide which of the given conclusions logically follows from the statements disregarding commonly known facts. Give answer*

(a) if only conclusion I follows.
(b) if only conclusion II follows.
(c) if either conclusion I or conclusion II follows.
(d) if neither conclusion I nor conclusion II follows.

21. Statements: Some drawings are pictures.
All drawings are sketches.
Some sketches are interesting.
Conclusions:
I. All pictures are sketches.
II. Some interesting are drawings.

22. Statements: All pebbles are stones.
No stone is a coral.
Some precious are corals.
Conclusions:
I. Some pebbles are cotals.
II. Some stones are precious.

23. Statements: All journeys are distances.
Some distances are not journeys.
Some journeys are vacations.
Conclusions:
I. Some distances are vacations.
II. Some vacations are not journeys.

24. Statements: All Printers are machines.
All machines are expensive.
All expensive are scanners.
Conclusions:
I. At least some scanners are machines.
II. Some Printers are not expensive.

25. Statements: All colleges are institutions.
Some institutions are buildings.
Some buildings are colleges.
Conclusions:
I. Some institutions are both colleges and buildings.
II. No college is a building.

Directions (Q. 26-30): *In each question below is given a number/symbol followed by four combinations of letter codes numbered* (a), (b), (c) and (d). *You have to find out which of the combinations correctly represents the number/ symbol based on the following coding system and the conditions and mark the number of that combination as your answer.*

Number/ Symbol	β 5 4 # 3 8 @ 7 2 1 $ 6 π W 9 Ω
Letter Code	P V R T S C K M B G E N X D A

Conditions:

(i) If the first element is an even digit and the last a symbol, the even digit is to be coded as the code for the last symbol.
(ii) If the group of elements contains only one symbol, that symbol is to be coded as the code for the element following it.
(iii) If both the second and the fifth elements are numbers, the fifth number is to be coded as the code for the second number.

26. #95π2@
(a) TDVXDK (b) TDXVDK
(c) TDVXBK (d) TBVXBK

27. 76#3@β
(a) PNTSKP (b) MNKTSP
(c) MNSTKP (d) MNTSKP

28. 5#9487
(a) VDDMCR (b) VRDDCM
(c) VDDCRM (d) VDDRCM

29. 4#513Ω
(a) RTSGVR (b) ATVGSA
(c) RTVGSR (d) ATGVSA

30. π36Ω5$
(a) XVSNAE (b) XSANSE
(b) XSNAVE (d) XSNASE

Directions (Q. 31-35): *In the following questions, the symbols ✶, @, #, & and % are used with the following meaning as illustrated below:*

'A @ B' means 'A is greater than B'.

'A % B'means'A is equal to B'.

'A # B' means 'A is either equal to or smaller than B'.

'A & B' means 'A is either equal to or greater than B'.

'A ✶ B'means'A is smaller than B'.

Now in each of the following questions assuming the given statements to be true, find which of the two conclusions I and II given below them is/are **definitely true?** Give answer

(a) if only Conclusion I is true.
(b) if only Conclusion II is true.
(c) if either Conclusion I or II is true.
(d) if neither Conclusion I nor II is true.

31. **Statements:** S%A, A&D, D★J
Conclusions: I. D#S
II. A ★ J

32. **Statements:** Q @ F, F % C, N★C
Conclusions: I. Q@C
II. F★N

33. **Statements:** R& P, P★K, K★F
Conclusions: I. R@F
II P★F

34. **Statements:** M & F, F★C, C % K
Conclusions: I. M@C
II. F★K

35. **Statements:** P&T, T★R, R#B
Conclusions: I. P@T
II. B&T

Quantitative Aptitude

Directions (36-63): What should come in place of the question mark (?) in the following questions?

36. $\sqrt{1521} \div 3 \times 12 = ?$
(a) 155 (b) 166
(c) 162 (d) 156

37. **672 ÷ 24 × 18 + 153 – 345 = ?**
(a) 318
(b) 324
(c) 314
(d) None of the above

38. $\frac{3}{4}$ **of 26% of 850 = ?**
(a) 165.75 (b) 160.35
(c) 163.75 (d) 167.75

39. **144 ÷ 8 ÷ ? = 9**
(a) 1 (b) 2
(c) 3 (d) 5

40. **?% of 590 – 11.8 = 236**
(a) 46 (b) 44
(c) 42 (d) 42

41. **$(8)^2$ % of ? = 723 + 45**
(a) 1200 (b) 1400
(c) 1100 (d) 10020

42. **5554 – 333 + 45 = 7 + 2525**
(a) 2174 (b) 2417
(c) 2714 (d) 2741

43. $3\frac{1}{4} + 2\frac{1}{2} + 6\frac{1}{6} = ?$
(a) $13\frac{11}{12}$ (b) $11\frac{11}{12}$
(c) $12\frac{11}{12}$ (d) $15\frac{11}{12}$

44. **$(450 \div 30)^2 - (12)^2 = (?)^2$**
(a) 9^2 (b) -9^2
(c) $\sqrt{9}$ (d) None of these

45. **56.73 + 32.88 + 45.23 = ?**
(a) 130.84 (b) 134.84
(c) 140.84 (d) 144.84

46. **$5^2 \times 25^3 \times 625 = (e)^?$**
(a) 14 (b) 11
(c) 15 (d) 12

47. **$5^2 \times 255 \div 5 - 1116 = ?$**
(a) 148 (b) 144
(c) 159 (d) 156

48. $(\sqrt{5}-1)^2 = ? - 2\sqrt{5}$
(a) 6 (b) $6+2\sqrt{5}$
(c) $6\sqrt{5}$ (d) $6-2\sqrt{5}$

49. $? \times \frac{7}{12} \times \frac{5}{7} \times \frac{1}{2} = 2500$
(a) 14000 (b) 13000
(c) 12000 (d) 11000

50. **556 – 441 + 223 – 112 = ?**
(a) 261 (b) 221
(c) 226 (d) 272

51. **168 ÷ 14 + 3 = ?**
(a) 2 (b) 4
(c) 3 (d) 7

52. **9999 – 3434 –2525 + 1313 = ?**
(a) 3535 (b) 5353
(c) 5335 (d) 3553

53. $3\frac{2}{3} \times 4\frac{1}{3} \times 1\frac{4}{7} \div \frac{11}{12} = ?$
(a) $27\frac{4}{21}$ (b) $26\frac{5}{21}$
(c) $27\frac{5}{21}$ (d) $26\frac{4}{21}$

54. $\sqrt{5^2 \times 7^2 + 12^2} = ?$
(a) 37 (b) 35
(c) 36 (d) 34

55. $35\% \text{ of } 180 - \sqrt{49} = ?$
(a) 62 (b) 55
(c) 58 (d) None of these

56. **19.673 – 12.235 + 15.224 + 10.111 = ?**
(a) 32.773 (b) 37.223
(c) 33.772 (d) 34.773

57. **(343 – 103) ÷ (216 + 36) = ?**
(a) 30 (b) 40
(c) 32 (d) 42

58. **$(0.027)^2 \times (0.09)^2 \div (0.3)^6 = (0.3)^?$**
(a) 3 (b) 2
(c) 5 (d) None of these

59. $\sqrt{961} + \sqrt{784} + \sqrt{49} = ?$
(a) 65 (b) 67
(c) 63 (d) 66

60. **35% of 740 – 35% of 520 = ?**
(a) 78 (b) 71
(c) 75 (d) 77

61. **Sushil runs four kilometres every day. On Saturday and Sunday he runs one kilometre extra (on each day). How many kilometres does he run in 2 weeks?**
(a) 40 km (b) 60 km
(c) 50 km (d) 70 km

62. **The angles in a triangle are in a ratio of 19 : 10:7. What is the sum of twice the smallest angle and the largest angle?**
(a) 165° (b) 185°
(c) 155° (d) 175°

63. **In how many different ways can the letters of the word 'TABLE' be arranged?**
(a) 360 (b) 720
(c) 60 (d) None of these

Directions (Q. 64-70): *What will come in place of the question mark(?) in the following series?*

64. 3 4 13 38 87 ?

(a) 178 (b) 188
(c) 158 (d) None of these

65. 150 148 144 136 120 ?

(a) 98 (b) 68
(c) 88 (d) 83

66. 11 16 26 41 61 ?

(a) 68 (b) 72
(c) 78 (d) 86

67. Yesterday, a man covered a distance of 360 k min 8 hours by a car. Today he travelled at a speed 3 times less than yesterday's speed for 10 hours. How much distance did he cover?

(a) 150 km (b) 160 km
(c) 140 km (d) 130 km

68. One of the angles of a parallelogram is 35°. What will be the sum of the largest angle and twice the smallest angle of the parallelogram?

(a) 219° (b) 205°
(c) 215° (d) None of these

69. Out of the following fractions which one is the second lowest?

$\frac{3}{5}$ $\frac{6}{11}$ $\frac{7}{18}$ $\frac{5}{16}$ $\frac{8}{11}$

(a) $\frac{6}{11}$ (b) $\frac{7}{18}$
(c) $\frac{3}{5}$ (d) $\frac{8}{11}$

70. Satish bought an article and sold it for ₹ 4,550 which is 30% more than the original price. What is the original price of that article?

(a) ₹ 3,500 (b) ₹ 3,800
(c) ₹ 3,600 (d) ₹ 3,400

English Language

Directions (Q. 71-80): *Read the following passage carefully and answer the questions given below it, Certain words are printed in bold to help you to locate them while answering some of the questions.*

A fisherman, enfeebled with age, could no longer go out to sea so he began fishing in the river. Every morning he would go down to the river and sit there fishing the whole day long. In the evening, he would sell whatever he had caught, buy food for himself and go home. It was a hard life for an old man. One hot afternoon while he was trying to keep awake and bemoaning his fate, a large bird with silvery feathers **alighted** on a rock near him. It was Kaha, the heavenly bird. "Have you no one to care for you, grandpa?" asked the bird. "Not a soul". "You should not be done such work at your age," said the bird. "From now on I will bring you a big fish every evening. You can sell it and live in comfort:" True to her word, the bird began to drop a large fish at his doorstep every evening. All that the fisherman had to carry it to the market and sell it. As big fish were in great demand, he was soon **rolling in money.** He bought a cottage near the sea, with a garden around it and engaged a servant to cook for him. His wife had died some years earlier. He had decided to marry again and began to look for a suitable woman.

One day he heard the royal courtier make an announcement. "Our king has news of a great bird called Kaha," said the courtier. "Whoever can give information about this bird and help catch it, will be rewarded with half the gold in the royal treasury and half the kingdom!". The fisherman was acutely tempted by the reward. Half the kingdom would make him a prince!

"Why does the king want the bird?" he asked. "He has lost his sight," explained the courtier. "A wise man has advised him to bathe his eyes with the blood of Kaha. Do you know where she can be found?" "No,..l mean...no, no...." **Torn** between greed and his sense of gratitude to the bird, the fisherman could not give a consolidated reply. The courtier, sensing that he knew something about the bird, informed the king. The king brought him to the palace.

"If you have information about the bird, tell me," urged the king. "I will reward you handsomely and if you help catch her, I will personally crown you king of half my domain". "I will get the bird for you," cried the fisherman, suddenly making up his mind. "But Kaha is strong. I will need help." The king sent a dozen soldiers with him. That evening when the bird came with the fish, the fisherman called out to her to wait. "You drop the fish and go and I never get a chance to thank you for all that you've done for me," he said. "Today I have laid out a feast for you inside. Please alight and come in." Kaha was reluctant to accept the invitation but the fisherman pleaded so earnestly that she finally gave in, and alighted. The moment she was on the ground, the fisherman **grabbed** one of her legs and shouted to the soldiers hiding in his house to come out. They rushed to his aid but their combined effort could not keep Kaha down.

She rose into the air with the fisherman still clinging onto her leg. By the time he realised, he was being carried away, the fisherman was too high in the air to let go. He hung on grimly, and neither he nor Kaha were ever seen again.

71. Why was the king desperately looking for Kaha the bird?

(a) The king wanted a pet bird.
(b) A wise man advised the king to capture the bird for good luck,
(c) Kaha was the only heavenly bird with silvery feathers.
(d) The king was blind and required Kaha's blood for his eyes.

72. Why did the bird volunteer to bring fish for the old man?

(a) The old man was inexperienced at fishing.
(b) The bird took pity on the old man and wanted to help him.
(c) The bird had caught more fish than required.
(d) The bird wanted to make the old man rich.

73. What led the courtier to sense that the fisherman might know something about Kaha?

(a) The courtier had observed Kaha alight at the fisherman's house every evening.

(b) The courtier had seen the fisherman talk to Kaha.

(c) The fisherman fumbled when asked about Kaha.

(d) Word went around that the fisherman was in contact with Kaha.

74. Which of the following cannot be said about the royal courtier?

(A) He was a very observant man.

(B) He was jealous of the old fisherman.

(C) He had informed the king about the fisherman.

(a) Only (A)

(b) Only (B)

(c) Only (C)

(d) Only (A) andc(C)

75. What could be an appropriate title for the story?

(a) A Fish a Day.

(b) The Lonely fisherman.

(c) Kaha the Silvery feathered bird.

(d) The Ungrateful old fisherman.

76. Which of the following is not true about Kaha?

(a) Kaha was a very considerate bird.

(b) The blood of Kaha was precious.

(c) Kaha was a strong bird.

(d) Kaha saved the fisherman from the King's wrath.

77. Why did the fisherman stammer when asked if he knew about the bird?

(a) The fisherman thought he was going to be punished for living off the bird.

(b) He was thrilled he would be able to help the king.

(c) He already knew about the reward that was being offered.

(d) He was conflicted between the king's reward and his gratitude towards the bird.

78. How did the fisherman get Kaha to come down?

(A) The fisherman told Kaha that the King was impressed by her kindness and wanted to meet her.

(B) The fisherman invited Kaha to live in his house as he was a lonely man and wanted company.

(C) The fisherman invited Kaha to his house for a feast in order to thank her for everything.

(a) Only (A) (b) Only (B)

(c) Only (C) (d) Only (B) and (C)

79. What does the phrase 'rolling in money' as highlighted in the passage refer to?

(a) To have a large amount of money.

(b) To have just enough of money.

(c) To live a life that is not affordable.

(d) To live off someone else.

80. Why was the fisherman doubtful about revealing information about Kaha to the courtier?

(a) He did not want to lose Kaha.

(b) Kaha was his source of income.

(c) He was worried about his supply offish.

(d) He had heard that kaha was going to be killed for her blood.

Directions (Q. 81-83): *Choose the word which is most nearly the SAME in meaning as the word printed in bold as used in the passage.*

81. Aid

(a) Health (b) Help

(c) Support (d) Freedom

82. Acutely

(a) Happily (b) Painfully

(c) Gainfully (d) Greatly

83. Torn

(a) Conflicted (b) Alarmed

(c) Frightened (d) Strained

Directions (Q. 84-85): *Choose the word which is most OPPOSITE in meaning of the word/s printed in bold as used in the passage.*

84. Alight

(a) Settle (b) take off

(c) Come by (d) Rest

85. Grabbed

(a) Caught (b) Released

(c) Secured (d) Loosened

Directions (Q. 86-90): *Which of the phrases* (a) (b), (c) and (d) *given below each sentence should replace it phrase printed in the sentence to make grammatically correct ? If the sentence is correct as it given and no correction is required, mark* (d) *as the answer.*

86. So successful her business to be, that Marie was able to retire at the age of 50.

(a) So successful her business was

(b) So successful being her business

(c) Her business was so successful

(d) No correction required

87. The ship was in mercy of the waves.

(a) to be in mercy of

(b) at the mercy of

(c) having mercy on

(d) No correction required

88. He not to have resigned, we would have been forced to dismiss him.

(a) Had he not

(b) Had not he

(c) He had not

(d) No correction required

89. A wealthy coin collector was eager to pay the huge sum for the coin because it was one kind.

(a) of one kinds

(b) one of kinds

(c) one of a kind

(d) No correction required

90. The thief carried the knife carefully to not cut himself.

(a) so as not to

(b) so not to

(c) not to

(d) No correction required

Directions (Q. 91-95): *In each question below, four words printed in bold type are given. These are numbered (a), (b), (c) and (d). One of these words printed in bold may either be wrongly spelt or inappropriate in the context of the sentence. Find out the word that is inappropriate or wrongly spelt, if any. The number of that word is your answer.*

91. **The economist (a)** was **hesistant (b)** to **comment (c)** on the government **policy (d).**

92. The king **knew (a)** that he had **definitely (b)** been wrong about his **choice (c)** of **courtiers (d).**

93. **Statistics (a)** are now **compulsory (b)** for all students taking a **cource (c)** in **engineering (d)** All Correct (e)

94. The **caretaker(a)** is **responsible(b)** for the **maintainance (c)** of the school **buildings (d)**

95. The more **scarce (a)** any **collectable (b)** item is, the **higher (c)** the **price** tends to be **(d)**

Directions (Q. 96-100): *Rearrange the following six sentences/ group of sentences (A), (B), (C), (D), (E) and (F) in the proper sequence to form a meaningful paragraph; then answer the questions given below them.*

(A) Seeing the dogs and his master running after the fox, the rooster screamed "No! Don' tcomenearme!"

(B) A fox sneaked into a farm and grabbed a prize rooster. The farmer saw him and raised an alarm.

(C) "My master was very cruel to me," explained the rooster to the fox. "Tell him to stay away from me."

(D) The rooster flew up into a tree and stayed there till he was rescued by his master.

(E) The fox was delighted. In the process of shouting to the farmer he released his hold over the rooster.

(F) Soon the farmer and his dogs started chasing the fox. The fox, was holding the rooster in his mouth, and was running very fast.

96. Which of the following should be the SIXTH (LAST) sentence after the rearrangement?

(a) E (b) B

(c) C (d) D

97. Which of the following should be the FIFTH sentence after the rearrangement?

(a) C (b) D

(c) F (d) E

98. Which of the following should be the FIRST sentence after the rearrangement?

(a) A (b) D

(c) F (d) B

99. Which of the following should be the FOURTH sentence after the rearrangement?

(a) D (b) C

(c) B (d) A

100. Which of the following should be the SECOND sentence after the rearrangement?

(a) B (b) C

(c) F (d) D

Answer sheet

1.(b)	2.(b)	3.(b)	4.(c)	5.(d)	6.(b)	7.(a)	8.(d)	9.(b)	10.(c)
11.(c)	12.(a)	13.(d)	14.(d)	15.(c)	16.(a)	17.(b)	18.(d)	19.(d)	20.(b)
21.(d)	22.(d)	23.(d)	24.(a)	25.(a)	26.(a)	27.(d)	28.(d)	29.(b)	30.(d)
31.(a)	32.(a)	33.(b)	34.(b)	35.(d)	36.(d)	37.(d)	38.(a)	39.(b)	40.(c)
41.(a)	42.(d)	43.(b)	44.(d)	45.(b)	46.(d)	47.(c)	48.(a)	49.(c)	50.(c)
51.(b)	52.(b)	53.(c)	54.(a)	55.(d)	56.(a)	57.(b)	58.(d)	59.(d)	60.(d)
61.(b)	62.(a)	63.(d)	64.(d)	65.(c)	66.(d)	67.(a)	68.(c)	69.(b)	70.(a)
71.(d)	72.(b)	73.(c)	74.(b)	75.(d)	76.(d)	77.(d)	78.(c)	79.(a)	80.(c)
81.(b)	82.(d)	83.(a)	84.(b)	85.(b)	86.(c)	87.(b)	88.(a)	89.(c)	90.(a)
91.(b)	92.(b)	93.(c)	94.(c)	95.(b)	96.(d)	97.(d)	98.(d)	99.(b)	100.(c)

Solutions

1. (b)

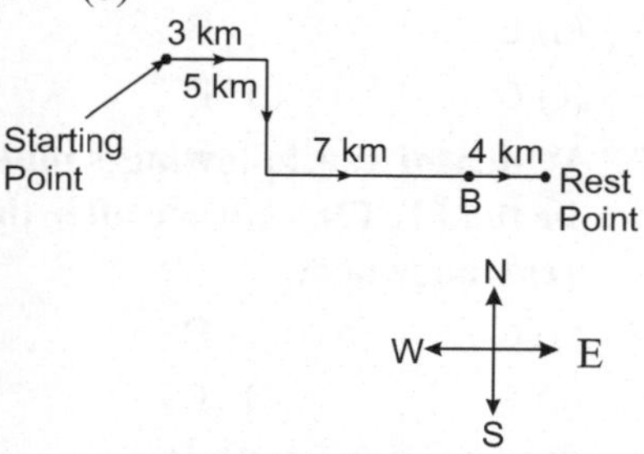

$\therefore$ Required distance= (7+4)=11 km.

2. (b)

Given Number : [2] 5 6 7 3 9 4
Ascending Order : [2] 3 4 5 6 7 9

3. (b) Meaningful word is AIR.

4. (c) I N T R U D E

$\therefore$ Required pair are DE and DI.

5. (d) 12 B 8 C 6 D 2 A 4

$\Rightarrow$ $12 \times 8 - 6 \div 2 + 4 = 96 - 3 + 4 = 97$

6. (b) H O N E S T L Y

↓ ↓ ↓ ↓ ↓ ↓ ↓ ↓

G P M F R S K X

Alphabetical Order:

F G K M P R S X

7. (a)

As, A $\xrightarrow{+4}$ E, B $\xrightarrow{+4}$ F
Similarly, I $\xrightarrow{+4}$ M, J $\xrightarrow{+4}$ N

8. (d) According to the question,

14th	C	8th	
13th	A	7th	Vacant
12th	–	:	
11th	B	Ist	
10th	–		
9th			

D is either on the 9th or 8th floor, therefore, it is not clear. Hence correct position of D cannot be found.

9. (b) The specified letters of the given word ABDUCTION are B, D, O and N. From these letters only one word BOND can be made. Hence, its second letter from the left is O.

10. (c) As, A E R O B I C

+1 +1 –1 –1 –1 +1 +1

B F Q N A J D

Similarly, A D V E R T S

+1 +1 –1 –1 –1 +1 +1

B E U D Q U T

(11-15) :

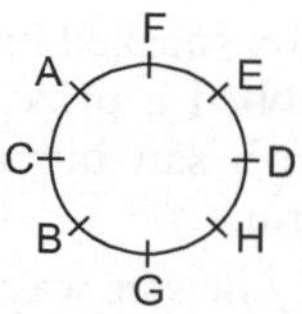

11. (c) Three people G, H and D sit between E and B.

12. (a) F sits second to the left of C.

13. (d) **14.** (d) **15.** (c)

(16-20) :

16. (a) 356 497 812 739 264

264 [356] 497 739 812

$\therefore$ Required sum = 3 + 5 + 6 = 14

17. (b) The second lowest number = 356

Its third digit = 6

The highest number = 812

Its third digit = 2

$\therefore$ Required result = $6 \div 2 = 3$

18. (d) 356 497 812 739 264

357 495 813 737 265

$\therefore$ Required difference = 813 – 265 = 548

19. (d) 356 497 812 739 264

653 974 821 [973] 642

20. (b) 356 497 812 739 264

536 [9]47 [1]82 379 624

(21-25):

21. (d) Some drawings are pictures (I) → conversion → Some pictures are drawings (I) + All drawings are skecthes (A) = I + A = I = Some pictures are sketches (I). Hence conclusion (I) does not follow. Again, All drawings are sketches are drawings (A) → conversion → Some sketches are drawings (I) + Some sketches are intersting (I) = I + I = (–) ie No conlusion. Hence conclusion II does not follow.

22. (d) All pebbles are stones + No stone is a coral A + E = E = No pebble is a coral. Hence conclusion I does not follow. Again, No stone is a coral (E) + Some coral are precious (conversion of "Some precious are coral") = E + I = O* = Some precious are not stones. Hence conclusion II does not follow.

23. (d)

24. (a) All machines are expensive + All expensive are scanners = A + A = A = All machines are scanners → conversion → some scanners are machines (I). It also means "At least some scanners are machines". Hence, conclusion I follows.

25. (a)

26. (a) Condition (iii) is applied

27. (d) MNTSKP

28. (d) Condition (ii) is applied

29. (b) Condition (i) is applied

30. (d) XSNASE

(31-35):

A @ B $\Rightarrow$ A > B
A % B $\Rightarrow$ A = B
A # B $\Rightarrow$ A ≤ B
A & B $\Rightarrow$ A ≥ B
A★B $\Rightarrow$ A < B

31. (a) S % A $\Rightarrow$ S = A
A & D $\Rightarrow$ A ≥ D
D★3 $\Rightarrow$ D < J
Therefore, S = A ≥ D < J
Conclusions
I. D # D $\Rightarrow$ D ≤ S (True)
II. A★J $\Rightarrow$ A < J (Not True)

32. (a) Q @ F $\Rightarrow$ Q > F
F % C $\Rightarrow$ F = C
N ★ C $\Rightarrow$ N<C
Therefore, Q > F = C > N
Conclusions
I. Q @ C $\Rightarrow$ Q > C (True)
II. F★N $\Rightarrow$ F < N (Not True)

33. (b) R & P $\Rightarrow$ R ≥ P
P ★K $\Rightarrow$ P < K
K★F $\Rightarrow$ K < F
Therefore, R ≥ P < K < F
Conclusions
I. R @ F $\Rightarrow$ R > F (Not True)
II. P★F $\Rightarrow$ P < F (True)

34. (b) M & F $\Rightarrow$ M ≥ F
F★C $\Rightarrow$ F < C
C % K $\Rightarrow$ C = K
Therefore, M ≥ F < C = K
Conclusions
I. M @ C $\Rightarrow$ M > C (Not True)
II. F★K $\Rightarrow$ F < K (True)

35. (d) P & T $\Rightarrow$ P $\geq$ T
T★R $\Rightarrow$ T < R
R # B $\Rightarrow$ R $\leq$ B
Therefore, P $\geq$ T < R $\leq$ B
Conclusions
I. P @ T $\Rightarrow$ P > T (Not True)
II. B & T $\Rightarrow$ B $\geq$ T (Not True)

36. (d) ? = $\sqrt{1521} \div 3 \times 12 = \frac{39}{3} \times 12 = 156$

37. (d) ? = 672 ÷ 24 × 18 + 153 – 345
= 28 × 18 + 153 – 345 = 312

38. (a) $? = 850 \times \frac{26}{100} \times \frac{3}{4} = 165.75$

39. (b) $\because$ 144 ÷ 8 ÷ ? = 9
$\Rightarrow \frac{144}{8 \times ?} = 9$
$\therefore ? = \frac{144}{8 \times 9} = 2$

40. (c) $\because 590 \times \frac{?}{100} - 11.8 = 236$
$\Rightarrow$ 5.9 × ? = 236 + 11.8
$\therefore ? = \frac{247.8}{5.9} = 42$

41. (a) $\because ? \times \frac{(8)^2}{100} = 723 + 45$
$\Rightarrow$ 0.64 × ? = 768
$\therefore ? = \frac{768}{0.64} = 1200$

42. (d) ? + 2525 = 5554 – 333 + 45
$\therefore$? = 5266 – 2525 = 2741

43. (b) $? = 3\frac{1}{4} + 2\frac{1}{2} + 6\frac{1}{6}$
$= (3+2+6) + \left(\frac{1}{4} + \frac{1}{2} + \frac{1}{6}\right)$
$= 11 + \left(\frac{3+6+2}{12}\right) = 11\frac{11}{12}$

44. (d) $\because (?)^2 = (450 \div 30)^2 - (12)^2$
$= (15)^2 - (12)^2 = 225 - 144 = 81$
$= (9)^2$
$\therefore ? = 9$

45. (b) ? = 56.73 + 32.88 + 45.23 = 134.84

46. (d) $\because = 5^2 \times 25^3 \times 625 = 5^2 \times 5^6 \times 5^4 = 5^{2+6+4}$
$\therefore ? = 2 + 6 + 4 = 12$

47. (c) $? = 5^2 \times 255 \div 5 - 1116$
$= 25 \times \frac{225}{5} - 1116$
= 1275 – 1116 = 159

48. (a)
$\because ? - 2\sqrt{5} = (\sqrt{5} - 1)^2 = 5 + 1 - 2\sqrt{5}$
$\therefore ? = 6$

49. (c) $\because ? \times \frac{7}{12} \times \frac{5}{7} \times \frac{1}{2} = 2500$
$\therefore ? = \frac{2500 \times 12 \times 7 \times 2}{7 \times 5} = 12000$

50. (c) ? = 556 – 441 + 223 – 112 = 226

51. (b) $? = 168 \div 14 \div 3 = \frac{168}{14 \times 3} = 4$

52. (b) ? = 9999 – 3434 – 2525 + 1313 = 5353

53. (c) $? = 3\frac{2}{3} \times 4\frac{1}{3} \times 1\frac{4}{7} \div \frac{11}{12}$
$= \frac{11}{3} \times \frac{13}{3} \times \frac{11}{7} \times \frac{12}{11} = \frac{572}{21} = 27\frac{5}{21}$

54. (a)
$=? \sqrt{5^2 \times 7^2 + 12^2} = \sqrt{25 \times 49 + 144}$
$= \sqrt{1369} = 37$

55. (d) $? = 180 \times \frac{35}{100} - \sqrt{49}$
= 63 – 7 = 56

56. (a) ? = 19.673 – 12.235 + 15.224 + 10.111 = 32.773

57. (b) ? = (343 – 103) ÷ (216 ÷ 36) = 240 ÷ 6 = 40

58. (d)
$\because (0.3)^? = (0.027)^2 \times (0.09)^2 \div (0.3)^6$
$= (0.3)^6 \times (0.3)^4 \div (0.3)^6$
$= (0.3)^{6+4-6}$
$\therefore ? = 6 + 4 - 6 = 4$

59. (d) $? = \sqrt{961} + \sqrt{784} + \sqrt{49}$
= 31 + 28 + 7 = 66

60. (d) $? = 740 \times \frac{35}{100} - 520 \times \frac{35}{100}$
= 259 – 182 = 77

61. (b) Required distance
= 2(4 × 5 + 5 × 2) km
= 2(20 + 10) = 60 km

62. (a) The smallest angle
$= \frac{7 \times 180}{(19+10+7)} = 35°$
The largest angle
$= \frac{19 \times 180}{(19+10+7)} = 95°$
$\therefore$ Required sum
= 2 × 35° + 95° = 165°

63. (d) Required number of ways
$= 5P_5 = 5! = 120$

64. (d)
$3 \underset{+(1)^2}{} 4 \underset{+(3)^2}{} 13 \underset{+(5)^2}{} 38 \underset{+(7)^2}{} 87 \underset{+(9)^2}{} ?$
$\therefore$? = 87 + 81 = 168

65. (c) $150 \underset{-2}{} 148 \underset{-4}{} 144 \underset{-8}{} 136 \underset{-16}{} 120 \underset{-32}{} ?$
$\therefore$? = 120 – 32 = 88

66. (d) $11 \underset{+5}{} 16 \underset{+10}{} 26 \underset{+15}{} 41 \underset{+20}{} 61 \underset{+25}{} ?$
? = 61 + 25 = 86

67. (a) Yesterday's speed of the car
$= \frac{360}{8} = 45$ km/hr
Today's speed of the car
$= \frac{45}{3} = 15$ km/hr
$\therefore$ Required covered distance
= (15 × 10) = 150 km

68. (c) The largest angle of the parallelogram
= 180° – 35° = 145°
$\therefore$ Required sum = 145° + 2 × 35°
= 145° + 70° = 215°

69. (b) $\frac{3}{5} = 0.60; \frac{6}{11} = 0.54; \frac{7}{18} = 0.38;$
$\frac{5}{16} = 0.31$ and $\frac{8}{11} = 0.72$
$\therefore \frac{7}{18}$ is the second lowest fraction.

70. (a) Original price of the article
$= \frac{4550 \times 100}{130} =$ ₹ 3500

6 Practice Set

Reasoning

1. **How many meaningful English words can be formed with the letters PCYO using all the letters, but each letter only once in each word?**
   (a) One (b) Two
   (c) Three (d) Four

2. **The positions of the first and fifth letters of the word SUITABLE are interchanged. Similarly, the positions of second and sixth letters, third and seventh letters, and fourth and eighth letters are interchanged. In the new arrangement, how many letters are there in the English alphabetical series between the alphabet which is third from the left end and the alphabet which is second from the right end?**
   (a) None (b) One
   (c) Two (d) Four

3. **Arrange the given words in the sequence in which they occur in the dictionary.**
   1. Ropped **2. Roster**
   3. Roasted **4. Road**
   5. Roller
   (a) 35412 (b) 45312
   (c) 34512 (d) 43512

4. **A series is given with one term missing. Select the correct alternative from the given ones that will complete the series.**
   BCF, CDG, DEH, ?
   (a) EFI (b) EFI
   (c) DFI (d) EGI

Directions (Q. 5 - 7): The following questions are based on the alphabetical series given below.

M J L I T Q S R K U F H C B D E A V P O G N

5. **What will come in place of question (?) mark in the following series based on the above alphabetical series? N PO BDE ?**
   (a) UKR (b) SRKU
   (c) RKUF (d) QSRK

6. **If in a certain code, 'BIND' is coded as 'CLGB' and 'HELD' is coded as 'FDJB' based on the series given above. How will 'FORK' be coded in the same code language?**
   (a) HGKU (b) UPKR
   (c) KPSR (d) UPSR

7. **'HC' is related to 'KQ' in a certain way. Similarly, 'OG' is related to 'AB' in the same way. To which of the following is 'RK' related, following the same pattern?**
   (a) TJ (b) SI
   (c) T1 (d) HD

8. **Each vowel of the word SAVOURY is changed to the next letter in the English alphabetical series and each consonant is changed to the previous letter in the English alphabetical series. If the new alphabets thus formed are arranged in alphabetical order (from left to right), which of the following will be fifth from the right?**
   (a) U (b) R
   (c) Q (d) P

9. **How many such pairs of letters are there in the word PACKETS, each of which has as many letters between them in the word (in both forward and backward directions) as they have between them in the English alphabetical series?**
   (a) One (b) Two
   (c) Three (d) Four

10. **Point P is 10m to the West of Point A. Point B is 2m to the South of Point P. Point Q is 6m to the East of Point B. Point C is 2m to the North of Point Q. Which of the following three points fall in a straight line?**
    (a) A, C, P (b) B, C, P
    (c) Q, C, A (d) A, B, Q

Directions (Q. 11 - 15): In these questions, relationship between different elements is shown in the statements. The statements are followed by two conclusions. Give answer

(a) if only conclusion I is true.
(b) if only conclusion II is true.
(c) if both conclusions I and II are true.
(d) if neither conclusion I nor II is true.

11. **Statements:** $H \geq I = J > K \leq L$
    Conclusions: I. $K < H$
    II. $L \geq I$

12. **Statements:** $S > C \geq O; P < C$
    Conclusions: I. $O < P$
    II. $S < P$

13. **Statements:** $A = B \leq C; A > R$
    Conclusions: I. $B > R$
    II. $R < C$

14. **Statements:** $D > E \leq F; J < F$
    Conclusions: I. $D > J$
    II. $E < J$

15. **Statements:** $P < Q > T; R \geq Q$
    Conclusions: I. $R > P$
    II. $T < R$

Directions (Q. 16-20): Study the following information to answer the given questions.

Eight people are sitting in two parallel rows containing four people each in such a way that there is an equal distance between adjacent persons. In row I, A, B, C and D are sitting (but not necessarily in the same order) and all of them are facing North. In row II, P, Q, R and S are sitting (but not necessarily in the same order) and all of them are facing South. Therefore, in the given seating arrangement, each member sitting in a row faces another member of the other row.

S sits second to left of Q. A faces the immediate neighbour of S. Only one person sits between A and C. P does not face A. B is not an immediate neighbour of A.

16. Which of the following is true regarding D?
(a) D sits at one of the extreme ends of the line.
(b) A sits on the immediate left of D.
(c) Q faces D.
(d) C is an immediate neighbour of D.

17. Who among the following faces C?
(a) P (b) Q
(c) R (d) S

18. Who among the following sits on the immediate right of the person who faces C?
(a) P (b) Q
(c) R (d) S

19. Four of the following five are alike in a certain way based on the given seating arrangement and thus form a group. Which is the one that does not belong to that group?
(a) A (b) Q
(c) R (d) S

20. Who among the following faces R?
(a) A (b) B
(c) C (d) D

Directions (Q. 21-26): Study the following information to answer the given questions:
In a certain code, 'time and money' is written as *'ma jo ki'*, 'manage time well' is written as *'pa rujo'*, 'earn more money' is written as *'zi ha ma'* and 'earn well enough' is written as *'siruha'*.

21. What is the code for 'earn'?
(a) si (b) ru
(c) ha (d) ma

22. Which of the following represents 'more time'?
(a) pa jo (b) zi ki
(c) ma ki (d) jo zi

23. What is the code for 'manage'?
(a) ru (b) pa
(c) jo (d) ha

24. Which of the following may represent' 'money matters'?
(a) ki to (b) ma pa
(c) fi ma (d) ha ma

25. What does 'ru' stand for ?
(a) well (b) manage
(c) time (d) enough

26. Which of the following may represent 'good enough'?
(a) ru si (b) da ha
(c) si pa (d) si da

Directions (Q. 27-33): Study the following information carefully and answer the given questions.

Eight friends - A, B, C, D, E, F, G and H - are sitting around a circle facing the centre, but not necessarily in the same order. D sits third to left of A. A is an immediate neighbour of both F and H. Only one person sits between C and F. B is not an immediate neighbour of D. Only one person sits between B and G.

27. A is related to G in a certain way. Similarly, C is related to H, according to the given seating arrangement. Who among the following is related to F, following the same pattern?
(a) A (b) B
(c) C (d) D

28. Who among the following sits second to the right of C?
(a) F (b) A
(c) D (d) G

29. What is the position of C with respect to the position of E?
(a) Third to the left
(b) Second to the left
(c) Immediate right
(d) Third to the right

30. Which of the following is true with respect to the given seating arrangement?
(a) A sits on the immediate left of H.
(b) B sits exactly between C and G.
(c) F sits second to the right of C.
(d) None is true

31. Which of the following pairs represents the immediate neighbours of G?
(a) A, C (b) C, D
(c) D, H (d) D, E

32. Who among the following sits exactly between C and F?
(a) A (b) D
(c) G (d) B

33. Starting from A, if all the friends are made to sit in alphabetical order in clockwise direction, the positions of how many (excluding A) will remain unchanged?
(a) None (b) One
(c) Two (d) Four

Directions (Q. 34-35): In each question below are two statements followed by two conclusions numbered I and II. You have to take the two given statements to be true even if they seem to be at variance with commonly known facts and then decide which of the given conclusions logically follows from the given statements, disregarding commonly known facts. Give answer
(a) if only conclusion I follows.
(b) if only conclusion II follows.
(c) if either conclusion I or II follows.
(d) if neither conclusion I nor II follows.

34. Statements: All exams are tests.
No test is a question.
Conclusions: I. At least some exams are questions.
II. No exam is a question.

35. **Statements:** No bangle is an earring.
Some earrings are rings.
Conclusions: I. No ring is a bangle.
II. Some rings are definitely not earrings.

Quantitative Aptitude

Directions (Q. 36 - 50): What should come in place of question mark (?) in the following questions?

36. **? ÷ 0.5 × 24 = 5652**
(a) 171.75 (b) 117.25
(c) 171.25 (d) 117.75

37. **5 × ? = 4808 ÷ 8**
(a) 122.2 (b) 112.2
(c) 120.2 (d) 102.2

38. **65% of 654 – ?% of 860 = 210.1**
(a) 25 (b) 15
(c) 20 (d) 30

39. **35154 – 20465 – 5201 = ?**
(a) 9488 (b) 9844
(c) 9484 (d) 9848

40. $\frac{8}{13} \div \frac{192}{559} = ?$
(a) $1\frac{19}{24}$ (b) $4\frac{19}{28}$
(c) $2\frac{17}{28}$ (d) $3\frac{17}{2}$

41. **243 × 124 – 25340 = ?**
(a) 4729 (b) 4792
(c) 4972 (d) 4927

42. **92 ÷ 8 ÷ 2 = ?**
(a) 4.75 (b) 5.75
(c) 425 (d) 5.25

43. $(121)^3 \times 11 \div (1331)^2 = (11)^?$
(a) 3 (b) 2
(c) 1 (d) None of these

44. **283.56 + 142.04 + 661.78 = ?**
(a) 1084.28 (b) 1087.28
(c) 1080.38 (d) 1082.48

45. **7028 ÷ 25 = ?**
(a) 218.12 (b) 281.21
(c) 218.21 (d) None of these

46. $390.5 \times \sqrt{?} = 284 \times 22$
(a) $(256)^2$ (b) 16
(c) $\sqrt{16}$ (d) 256

47. **12.5 × 8.4 × 7.6 = ?**
(a) 787 (b) 788
(c) 799 (d) None of these

48. **4477 ÷ (44 × 5.5) = ?**
(a) 24.5 (b) 21.5
(c) 16.5 (d) 18.5

49. **33.5% of 250 = ?**
(a) 76.25 (b) 82.25
(c) 78.75 (d) 83.75

50. $\frac{1}{2}$ **of** $\frac{3}{5}$ **of** $\frac{4}{9}$ **of 5820 = ?**
(a) 766 (b) 777
(c) 776 (d) 767

51. **12 men alone can complete a piece of work in six days, whereas 10 men and 21 women take three days to complete the same piece of work. In how many days can 12 women alone complete the same piece of work?**
(a) 10 (b) 9
(c) 11 (d) 8

52. **The owner of an electronic store charges his customer 11% more than the cost price. If a customer paid ₹ 1,33,200 for an LED TV, what was the original price of the TV?**
(a) ₹ 1,20,000 (b) ₹ 1,14,500
(c) ₹ 1,22,500 (d) ₹ 1,18,000

53. **The average age of a woman and her daughter is 19 years. The ratio of their ages is 16:3. What is the age of the daughter? .**
(a) 9 years (b) 3 years
(c) 12 years (d) 6 years

54. **If the fractions** $\frac{3}{5}, \frac{1}{4}, \frac{5}{6}, \frac{7}{9}$ **and** $\frac{8}{11}$ **arranged in ascending order of their values, which of the following will come at the third position?**
(a) $\frac{5}{6}$ (b) $\frac{3}{5}$
(c) $\frac{7}{9}$ (d) $\frac{8}{11}$

55. **A car covers a certain distance in three hours at the speed of 124 km/hr. What is the average speed of a truck which travels a distance of 120 km less than the car in the same time?**
(a) 88 km/hr (b) 84 km/hr
(c) 78 km/hr (d) 73 km/hr

56. **The cost of four calculators and two stencils is ₹ 6,200. What is the cost of ten calculators and five stencils?**
(a) ₹ 15,500
(b) ₹ 14,875
(c) ₹ 16,200
(d) Cannot be determined

57. **Find the average of the following set of scores:**
214, 351, 109, 333, 752, 614, 456, 547
(a) 482 (b) 428
(c) 444 (d) None of these

58. **The average of four consecutive odd numbers A, B, C and D is 54. What is the product of A and C?**
(a) 2907 (b) 2805
(c) 2703 (d) 2915

59. **The sum of 55% of a number and 40% of the same number is 180.5. What is 80% of that number?**
(a) 134 (b) 152
(c) 148 (d) 166

60. **There are 950 employees in an organisation, out of which 28% got promoted. Find the number of employees who got promoted.**
(a) 226 (b) 256
(c) 266 (d) 216

61. **What is the least number to be added to 3000 to make it a perfect square?**
(a) 191 (b) 136
(c) 25 (d) 84

62. **What would be the compound interest obtained on an amount of ₹ 7,640 at the rate of 15 pcpa after two years?**
(a) ₹ 2,634.9 (b) ₹ 2,643.9
(c) ₹ 2,364.9 (d) ₹ 2,463.9

63. In an examination it is required to get 65% of the aggregate marks to pass. A student gets 847 marks and is declared failed by 10% marks. What is the maximum aggregate marks a student can get?

(a) 1450 (b) 1640
(c) 1500 (d) None of these

64. A juice centre requires 35 dozen guavas for 28 days. How many dozen guavas will it require for 36 days?

(a) 50 (b) 52
(c) 40 (d) 45

65. Mohan sold an item for Rs 4,510 and incurred a loss of 45%. At what price should he have sold the item to have earned a profit of 45%?

(a) ₹ 10,900 (b) ₹ 12,620
(c) ₹ 11,890 (d) None of these

66. What will come in place of both the question marks (?) in the following question?

$$\frac{(?)^{1.5}}{288} = \frac{6}{(?)^{1.5}}$$

(a) 6 (b) 12
(c) 7 (d) 14

67. What would be the circumference of a circle whose area is 745.36 sq cm?

(a) 94.4 cm (b) 88.8 cm
(c) 96.3 cm (d) None of these

Directions (Q. 68 - 70): What will come in place of question mark (?) in the following number series?

68. 5 15 35 75 155 (?)

(a) 295 (b) 315
(c) 275 (d) 305

69. 3 6 18 72 360 (?)

(a) 2160 (b) 1800
(c) 2520 (d) 1440

70. 688 472 347 283 256 (?)

(a) 236 (b) 229
(c) 255 (d) 248

English Language

Directions (Q. 71-75): Pick out the most effective word from the given words to fill in the blank to make the sentence meaningfully complete.

71. The government is planning to set _____ family welfare centres for slums in cities.

(a) another (b) with
(c) for (d) up

72. Economic independence and education have ______ women more assertive.

(a) prepared (b) made
(c) marked (d) resulted

73. In the modern world, the ______ of change and scientific innovation is unusually rapid.

(a) supplies (b) context
(c) pace (d) fantasy

74. The unprecedented economic growth of China has worldwide attention.

(a) Preceived (b) proposed
(c) neither (d) attracted

75. Each business activity _____ employment to people who would otherwise be unemployed.

(a) taking (b) finds
(c) creates (d) provides

Directions (Q. 76-85): Read the following passage carefully and answer the questions given below it. Certain words have been printed in bold to help you locate them while answering some of the questions.

The importance of communication skills cannot be underestimated, especially so, in the teaching learning process. Teaching is generally considered as only fifty per cent knowledge and fifty per cent interpersonal or communication skills. For a teacher, it is not just important to give a lecture rich in content that provides **abundant** information about the subject or topic in question, but a successful teacher develops an **affinity** with, an understanding of, and a harmonious interrelationship with her pupils. Building rapport becomes her primary task in the classroom. But what exactly is rapport? Rapport is a sympathetic relationship or understanding that allows you to look at the world from someone else's perspective. Making other people feel that you understand them creates a strong bond. Building rapport is the first step to better communication the primary goal of all true educators. Communication skills for teachers are thus as important as their in-depth knowledge of the particular subject which they teach. To a surprising **degree,** how one communicates determines one's effectiveness as a teacher. A study on communication styles suggests that 7% of communication takes place through words, 38% through voice intonation and 55% through body language.

Much of teaching is about sending and receiving messages. The process of communication is composed of three elements : the source (sender, speaker, transmitter or instructor), the symbols used in composing and transmitting of the message (words or signs), and the receiver (listener, reader or student). The three elements are dynamically interrelated since each element is dependent on the others for effective communication to take place. Effective communication is all about conveying your message to the other people clearly and unambiguously. It's also about receiving information the others are sending to you, with as little distortion as possible. Doing this involves effort from both the sender and the receiver. And it's a process that can be fraught with error, with messages **muddled** by the sender, or misinterpreted by the recipient. When this isn't detected it can cause tremendous confusion, wasted effort and missed opportunity.

Good communication skills are a prerequisite for those in the teaching profession. Carefully planned and skilfully delivered messages can issue invitations to students that school is a place to share ideas, investigate and collaborate with others. Effective communication is essential for a well-run classroom. A teacher who is able to communicate well with students can inspire them to learn and participate in class and encourage them to come forth with their views, thus creating a proper rapport. Although this sounds simple and obvious, it requires much more than a teacher saying something out loud to a student. They must also realise that all students have different levels of strengths and weaknesses.

Directions (Q. 76-77): Choose the word which is most OPPOSITE in meaning of the word printed in bold as used in the passage.

76. Abundant

(a) Small (b) Little
(c) False (d) Sufficient

77. Muddled

(a) Skilfully organised
(b) Strongly controlled
(c) Clearly conveyed
(d) Isolated

Directions (Q. 78-85): Choose the word which is most SIMILAR in meaning to the word printed in bold as used in the passage.

78. Sounds

(a) Seems (b) Corrects
(c) Noises (d) Takes

79. Affinity

(a) Partnership (b) Partiality
(c) Weakness (d) Compatibility

80. Degree

(a) Extent (b) Goal
(c) Affect (d) Situation

81. Which of the following is/are essential for effective communication?

(A) Conveying the message clearly
(B) Not to waste effort and opportunity
(C) Receiving the information with as little distortion as possible

(a) Only (A) and (C)
(b) Only (B)
(c) Only (A)
(d) Only (C)

82. Which of the following is true about 'rapport' as per the passage?

(A) It is a sympathetic relationship.
(B) It is based on understanding of other people's frame of reference.
(C) It helps in creating a strong bond.
(D) It is important for teachers to build rapport with students.

(a) Only (A) and (B)
(b) Only (B) and (D)
(c) Only (A), (B) and (D)
(d) All are true

83. Which of the following must the teachers keep in mind to facilitate learning in student as per the passage?

(a) To control the students such that they do not share ideas with others within the lecture hours
(b) To maintain rapport with students and compromise on the course content
(c) To realise that all students have different levels of strengths and weaknesses
(d) Only to keep the lecture rich in course content

84. Which of the following are the three elements of communication as per the passage?

(a) Source, Signs and Students
(b) Source, Sender and Speaker
(c) Signs, Words and Students
(d) Instructor, Listener and Reader

85. Which of the following is the finding of the study on communication styles?

(a) The body language and gestures account for 38% of communication and outweighs the voice intonation.
(b) Only 9% communication is about content whereas the rest is about our tone and body language.
(c) The tone of our voice accounts for 55% of what we communicate and outweighs the body language.
(d) More than 90% of our communication is not about content but about our tone and body language.

Directions (Q. 86-95): Read each sentence to find out whether there is any grammatical error in it. The error if any, will be in one part of the sentence. The number of that part is the answer.

86. The economic disparity (a)/ has grown rapid in (b)/ the era of globalisation (c)/ and free market forces. (d)

87. Research shows that people (a)/ is more sensitive to perceiving (b)/ messages that are consistent (c)/ with their opinions and attitudes. (d)

88. Many poverty alleviation schemes (a)/ are not applicable of (b)/ slum dwellers in metro cities (c)/ as they are above the poverty line. (d)/

89. Rather than considering its (a)/ human capital as a drain on (b)/ resources, India needs to (c)/ resource develop its into a huge opportunity. (d)

90. The European nations have (a)/ become one of the (b)/ favourite destinations of the Indian students (c)/ seek specialised knowledge and training. (d)

91. If a credit card bill (a)/ is paid in full and (b)/ on time, none finance (c)/ charges are levied. (d)

92. Training have a (a)/ positive effect at (b)/ development of various (c)/ skills and abilities. (d)

93. Lack of ability to (a)/ read or write is just one of (b)/ the all barriers that keep (c)/ the poor people under developed. (d)

94. Science and technology were (a)/ become dominant actors (b)/ affecting our economic, cultural (c)/ and spiritual development. (d)

95. A social business sells products (a)/ at prices that make it self-sustaining, pays (b)/ no dividends and reinvestment (c)/ the profits in the business. (d)

Directions (Q. 96-100): In the following passage, there are blanks, each of which has been numbered. These numbers are printed below the passage and against each five words are suggested, one of which fits the blank appropriately. Find out the appropriate word in each case.

The latest technology **(96)** put to use or about to arrive in market must be **(97)** to all entrepreneurs. The reason is that it may have an **(98)** effect on business. Valve radios gave way to transistor radios and with micro chips, technology is giving way to digital equipment. Business has **(99)** the same but the technology has kept changing. A notable feature is that the size of the receivers decreased **(100)** so did the use of its material and consequently its price.

96. (a) to (b) needed (c) decided (d) being

97. (a) hoped (b) welcome (c) released (d) known

98. (a) approximate (b) huge (c) uniform (d) enormous

99. (a) maintained (b) remained (c) often (d) mentioned

100. (a) mainly (b) and (c) how (d) also

Answer sheet

1.(a)	2.(c)	3.(d)	4.(a)	5.(b)	6.(d)	7.(a)	8.(c)	9.(b)	10.(a)
11.(a)	12.(b)	13.(c)	14.(d)	15.(c)	16.(d)	17.(a)	18.(b)	19.(d)	20.(a)
21.(c)	22.(d)	23.(b)	24.(c)	25.(a)	26.(d)	27.(d)	28.(c)	29.(a)	30.(d)
31.(b)	32.(d)	33.(d)	34.(b)	35.(d)	36.(d)	37.(c)	38.(a)	39.(a)	40.(a)
41.(b)	42.(b)	43.(c)	44.(a)	45.(d)	46.(d)	47.(d)	48.(d)	49.(d)	50.(c)
51.(b)	52.(a)	53.(d)	54.(d)	55.(b)	56.(a)	57.(d)	58.(b)	59.(b)	60.(c)
61.(c)	62.(d)	63.(d)	64.(d)	65.(c)	66.(b)	67.(d)	68.(b)	69.(a)	70.(d)
71.(d)	72.(b)	73.(c)	74.(d)	75.(d)	76.(b)	77.(c)	78.(a)	79.(d)	80.(a)
81.(a)	82.(d)	83.(c)	84.(a)	85.(d)	86.(b)	87.(b)	88.(b)	89.(d)	90.(d)
91.(c)	92.(b)	93.(c)	94.(a)	95.(c)	96.(d)	97.(d)	98.(d)	99.(b)	100.(b)

Solutions

1. (a) Only one word, COPY, can be formed.

2. (c) After rearranging the word, it becomes

A B [L] E S U [I] T

Now, 3rd from the left is L.
2nd from the right is I.
There are two letters between I and L in English alphabetical series, ie J and K.

3. (d) According to dictionary word sequence :
4. Road 3. Roasted 5. Roller
1. Ropped 2. Roster.

4. (a) Given pattern :

1+ 3+   1+ 3+   1+ 3+   1+ 3+
B C F, C D G, D E H, E F I

the given sequence of group letters follows the pattern +1 for IInd letters, and +3 for IIIrd letters repectively.

5. (b) There is a gap of 1, 2, 3 ... letters between each group. Each sucessive group consists of 1,2, 3,4... letters. And the letters are written from left to right.

6. (d) As,

B I N D and H E A D
−1↓ −1↓ −1↓ −1↓   −1↓ −1↓ −1↓ −1↓
C L G B   F D J B

Similarly,

F O R K
−1↓ −1↓ −1↓ −1↓
U P S R

7. (a) First letter goes (−3) and second (−7).

8. (c)

S A V O U R Y
↓ ↓ ↓ ↓ ↓ ↓ ↓
R B U P V Q X

Now, after arranging in alphabetical order, fifth from the right is Q.

B P [Q] R U V X

9. (b) P A C K E T S

There are two pairs of letters ie, CE and ST.

10. (a)

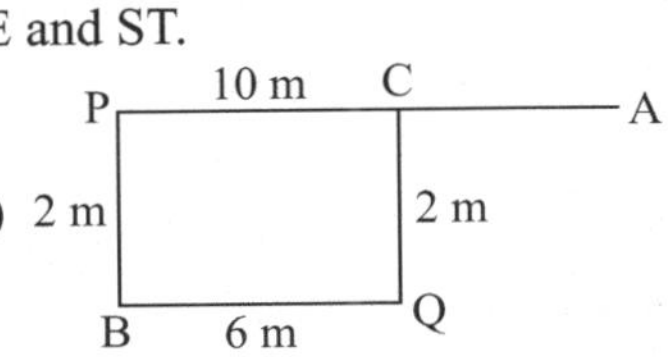

11. (a) H ≥ I = J > K ≤ L

I: H ≥ I = J > K ≤ L

Combining

H ≥ I > K

Thus, I is true.

II. H ≥ I = J > K ≤ L

I > K ≤ L

No definite relation can be found. Thus, II is not true.

Hence, only I is true.

12. (b) S > C > O and C > P

Thus O and P can't be compared. Hence 1 is not true.

Again,

S > C > P or S > P

Hence II is true.

13. (c) R < A = B < C

I. R < A = B < C

Thus, I is true.

II. R < C

Thus, II is also true.

14. (d) D > E < F > J

I. D > E ≤ F > J

Combining

D and J can't be combined. Thus, I is not true.

II. D > E ≤ F > J

Combining

E and J can't be combined. Thus, II is also hot true.

Hence, neither I nor II is true.

15. (c) P < Q > T

Q ≤ R

I. P < Q ≤ R

Combining

Thus, I is true.

II. R ≥ Q > T

Combining

Thus, II is also true.

Hence, both I and II are true.

Hints for (16-20):

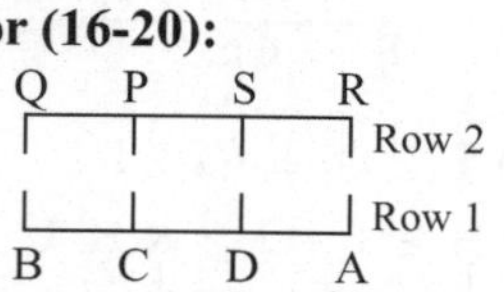

16. (d) **17.** (a) **18.** (b) **19.** (d) **20.** (a)

Hints for (21-26):

time and money → ma jo ki ...(i)

manage time well → pa ru jo ...(ii)

earn more money → zi ha ma ...(iii)

earn well enough → si ru ha ...(iv)

From (i) and (ii), time → jo

From (i) and (iii), money → ma

From (i), and → ki

From (ii) and (iv), well → ru

From (ii), manage → pa

From (iii) and (iv), earn → ha

From (iii), more → zi

From (iv), enough → si

21. (c) **22.** (d) **23.** (b)

24. (c) Since 'matters' is a new word. So, new code is introduced for 'matters' ie, 'fi'. Code for 'money' is 'ma'.

25. (a)

26. (d) Code for 'enough' is 'si' and since 'good' is a new work, so a new code for 'good' ie 'da' is introduced.

Hints for (27-33)

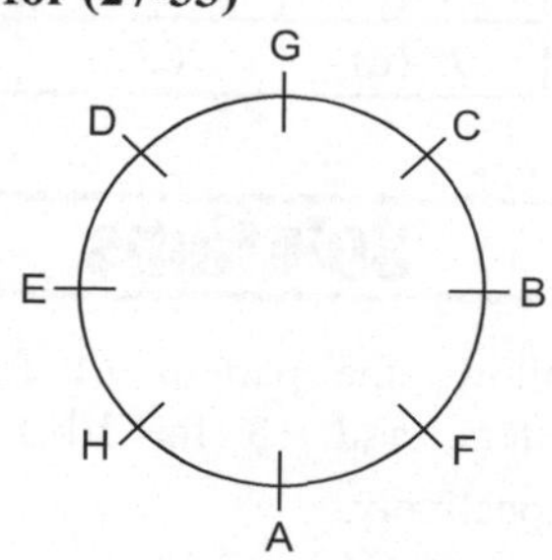

27. (d) **28.** (c) **29.** (a) **30.** (d) **31.** (b)

32. (d) **33.** (d)

34. (b) All exams are tests (A) + No test is a question (E) = A + E → E = No exam is a question.
Hence, only conclusion II follows, but conclusion I does not follow.

35. (d) No bangle is an earring (E) + Some earrings are rings (I) = E + I → O* = Some rings are not bangles. Hence, neither conclusion I nor II follows.

36. (d) $? = \frac{5652 \times 0.5}{24} = 117.75$

37. (c) $? = \frac{4808}{8 \times 5} = \frac{4808}{40} = 120.2$

38. (a) $\frac{65}{100} \times 654 - \frac{?}{100} \times 860 = 210.1$

or, $? = \frac{65 \times 654 - 21010}{860}$

or, $? = \frac{42510 - 21010}{860}$

$\therefore\ ? = \frac{21510}{860} = 25$

39. (a) ? = 35154 – 20465 – 5201 = 35154 – 25666 = 9488

40. (a) $\frac{8}{13} \times \frac{559}{192} = \frac{43}{24} = 1\frac{19}{24}$

41. (b) ? = 243 × 124 – 25340 = 30132 – 25340 = 4792

42. (b) $? = \frac{92}{8 \times 2} = 5.75$

43. (c) $(121)^3 \times 11 \div (1331)^2 = (11)^?$

or, $(11^2)^3 \times \frac{11}{(11^3)^2} = (11)^?$

or, $\frac{11^6 \times 11}{11^6} = (11)^?$

$\therefore\ ? = 1$

44. (a) ? = 283.56 + 142.04 + 661.78 = 1087.38

45. (d) 281.12

46. (d) $390.5 \times \sqrt{?} = 284 \times 22$

or, $\frac{284 \times 22}{390.5} \times \sqrt{?}$

or, $\frac{62480}{390.5} = \sqrt{?}$

or, $16 = \sqrt{?}$

47. (d) ? = 12.5 × 8.4 × 7.6 = 798

48. (d) $? = \frac{4477}{44 \times 5.5} = \frac{4477}{242} = 18.5$

49. (d) $? = \frac{33.5}{100} \times 250$

$= 33.5 \times 2.5 = 83.75$

50. (c) $? = \frac{1}{2} \times \frac{3}{5} \times \frac{4}{9} \times 5820$

$= \frac{69840}{90} = 776$

51. (b) 12 men's one day's work $= \frac{1}{6}$

10 men's one day's work $= \frac{10}{12 \times 6}$

$\therefore$ 10 men can complete the work in $\frac{36}{5}$ days.

10 men and 21 women can complete the work in 3 days.

$\therefore$ 21 Women can complete the work in

$$= \frac{\frac{36}{5} \times 3}{\frac{36}{5} - 3} = \frac{36 \times 3}{21} = \frac{36}{7}$$

21 women's 1 day's work $= \frac{7}{36}$

12 women's 1 day's work

$$= \frac{12 \times 7}{21 \times 36} = \frac{1}{9}$$

Hence 12 women will complete the work in 9 days,

52. (a) Original price of LED TV

$$= 133200 \times \frac{100}{111} = 120000$$

53. (d) Daugther's age

$$= 38 \times \frac{3}{19} = 6 \text{ years}$$

54. (d) $\frac{3}{5} = 0.6, \frac{1}{4} = 0.25, \frac{5}{6}$

$$= 0.83, \frac{7}{9} = 0.78$$

$$\frac{8}{11} = 0.73$$

Ascending order $\frac{1}{4} < \frac{3}{5} < \frac{8}{11} < \frac{7}{9} < \frac{5}{6}$

$\frac{8}{11}$ is the third fraction.

55. (b) The Distance covered by car in 3 hours

= 124 × 3 = 372 km

Distance covered truck

= 372 – 120 = 252 km

Average Speed of Truck

$$= \frac{\text{Distance}}{\text{Time}} = \frac{252}{3} = 84 \text{ km/hr}$$

56. (a) Cost of 4 calculators and 2 stencils = 6200

Cost of 10 calcuators and 5 stencils

= 6200 × 2.5 = 15500.

57. (d) Average

$$= \frac{214 + 351 + 109 + 33 + 752 + 614 + 456 + 547}{8}$$

$$= \frac{3376}{8} = 422$$

58. (b) Average of four numbers is 54

Four numbers are x, (2 + 2), $x + 4$ and $x + 6$,

Then

A	B	C	D
x	$x+2$	$x+4$	$x+6$
51	53	55	57

Product of A and C

= 51 × 55 = 2805

59. (b) 55% of x + 40% of x = 180.5

or, 95% of x = 180.5

or, $\frac{95x}{100} = 180.5$

$\therefore \quad \frac{80x}{100} = \frac{80}{95} \times 180.5 = 152$

60. (c) Number of employees who got promoted

$$= 950 \times \frac{28}{100} = 266$$

61. (c) 25 is the least number to be added to 3000 to make it a perfect square.

$\sqrt{3025} = 55$

62. (d) Compound Interest

$$= P\left[\left(1 + \frac{R}{100}\right)^T - 1\right]$$

$$= 7640\left[\left(1 + \frac{15}{100}\right)^2 - 1\right]$$

$$= 7640\left[\left(1 + \frac{23}{20}\right)^2 - 1\right]$$

$$= 7640\left[\frac{529}{400} - 1\right]$$

$$= \frac{7640 \times 129}{400} = ₹\,2463.9$$

63. (d) Maximum marks

$$= 847 \times \frac{100}{55} = 1540$$

64. (d) Guavas required for 28 days

= 35 dozen

Guavas required for 36 days

$$= \frac{36}{28} \times 35 = 45 \text{ dozen}$$

65. (c) Selling price

$$= 4510 \times \frac{145}{55} = ₹\,11890$$

66. (b) $\frac{(?)^{1.5}}{288} = \frac{6}{(?)^{1.5}}$

$\Rightarrow (?)^3 = 6 \times 288$

$\therefore \quad ? = \sqrt[3]{6 \times 288} = 12$

67. (d) Area = 745.36 cm^2

or, $\pi r^2 = 745.36$

or, $r^2 = 273.16$

$\therefore r = 15.4$

Circumference = 2πr

$$= 2 \times \frac{22}{7} \times 15.4 = 96.8$$

68. (b) The pattern is as follows:

5 × 2 + 5 =15

15 × 2 + 5 = 35

35 × 2 + 5 = 75

75 × 2 + 5 = 155

155 × 2 + 5 = 310 + 5 = 315

69. (a) The pattern is as follows:

3 × 2 = 6

6 × 3 = 18

18 × 4 = 72

72 × 5 = 360

360 × 6 = 2160

70. (d) The pattern is as follows:

$688 - 472 = 216 = 6^3$

$472 - 347 = 125 = 5^3$

$347 - 283 = 64 = 4^3$

$283 - 256 = 27 = 3^3$

$\therefore ? = 256 - 2^3 = 256 - 8 = 248$

7 Practice Set

Reasoning

1. In a certain code language 'TERMINAL' is written as 'NSFUMBOJ' and TOWERS' is written as 'XPUTSF'. How is 'MATE' written in that code?

(a) FUBN (b) UFNB
(c) BNFU (d) ENDS

2. The positions of how many digits in the number 5314687 will remain unchanged after the digits are rearranged in ascending order within the number?

(a) None (b) One
(c) Two (d) Three

3. What should come in place of question mark (?) in the following series?
AC EG IK MO ?

(a) PR (b) QS
(c) OR (d) PS

4. 'ERID' is related to 'DIRE' in the same way as 'RIPE' is related to

(a) EPIR (b) PERI
(c) EPRI (d) PEIR

5. How many meaningful English words can be made with the third, fifth, seventh and ninth letters of the word DOWNGRADED, using each letter only once in each word?

(a) None (b) One
(c) Two (d) Three

Directions (Q. 6-10): *In each question below, a group of digits/symbols is given followed by four combinations of letters numbered* (a), (b), (c) *and* (d). *You have to find out which of the combinations* (a), (b), (c) *and* (d) *correctly represents the group of digits/symbols based on the following coding system and the conditions that follow and mark the number of that combination as your answer.*

Digit/Symbol: 5 9 @ © 3 8 1 $ % 4 2 6 ★ 7 δ #
Letter code: B E P A K D F H Q I R J U M V T

Conditions:

(i) If the first unit in the group is an even digit and the last unit is a symbol, both these are to be coded as the code for the symbol,

(ii) If the first unit in the group is an odd digit and the last unit is an even digit, their codes are to be interchanged.

(iii) If both the first and the last units in the group are symbols both these are to be coded as 'X'.

6. @91$26

(a) JEFHRP (b) PEFHRP
(c) XEFHRX (d) PEFHRJ

7. 387#©9

(a) KMDTAE (b) KDMATE
(c) EDMTAK (d) None of these

8. 4@312δ

(a) VPKFRV (b) VPKFRI
(c) XDMTAK (d) IPKFRV

9. %4187★

(a) QIFDMU (b) UIFDMQ
(c) XIFDMX (d) UIFDMU

10. 9124δ6

(a) EFRIVJ (b) JFRIVE
(c) EFRIVE (d) XFRIVX

Directions (Q. 11-14): *In the following questions, the symbols δ, %, *, S and © are used with the following meaning as illustrated below:*

'P % Q' means 'P is not smaller than Q'.

'P ★ Q' means 'P is neither greater than nor equal to Q'.

'PδQ' means ' Pis neither smaller than nor equal to Q'

'P $ Q' means 'P is neither greater than nor smaller than Q'.

'P © Q' means "P is not greater than Q'.

Now, in each of the following questions assuming the given statements to be true, find which of the two conclusions I and II given below them is/are definitely true.

Given Answers:

(a) if only conclusion I is true.
(b) if only conclusion II is true.
(c) if either conclusion I or II is true,
(d) if neither conclusion I nor II is true.

11. Statements: D$T, T%M, M★J
Conclusions: I. JδD
II. M © D

12. Statements: B★K, K$N, N%R
Conclusions: I. R$K
II. R★K

13. Statements: H%F, F★W, W$E
Conclusions: I. EδF
II. HδW

14. Statements: ZδD, D©K, KδM
Conclusions: I. M★D
II. ZδK

15. In the following question, select the related word pair from the given alternatives
Power : Watt : : ? : ?

(a) Pressure : Newton
(b) Force : Pascal
(c) Resistance : Mho
(d) Work : Joule

Directions (Q. 16-20): *Study the following information carefully and answer the questions given below:*

P, T, V, R, M, D, K and W are sitting around a circular table facing the centre, V is second to the left of T. T is fourth to the right of M. D and P are not immediate neighbours of T. D is third to the right of P. W is not an immediate neighbour of P. P is to the immediate left of K.

16. Who is second to the left of K?
(a) P (b) R
(c) M (d) W

17. Who is on the immediate left of V?
(a) D
(b) M
(c) W
(d) Data inadequate

18. Who is third to the right of V?
(a) T (b) K
(c) P (d) None of these

19. What is R's position with respect to V?
(a) Third to the right
(b) Fifth to the right
(c) Third to the left
(d) Second to the left

20. Four of the following five are alike in a certain way based on their positions in the above seating arrangement and so form a group. Which of the following does not belong to that group?
(a) DW (b) TP
(c) VM (d) RD

Directions (Q. 21-24): *Each of the questions below consists of a question and two statements numbered I and II given below it. You have to decide whether the data provided in the statements are sufficient to answer the question. Read both the statements and give answer*

(a) if the data in statement I alone are sufficient to answer the question, while the data in statement II alone are not sufficient to answer the question.
(b) if the data in statement II alone are sufficient to answer the question, while the data in statement I alone are not sufficient to answer the question.
(c) if the data either in statement I alone or in statement II alone are sufficient to answer the question.
(d) if the data given in both the statements I and II together are not sufficient to answer the question,

21. Towards which direction is Village M from Village T?
I. Village P is to the south of Village M and Village P is to the west of Village T.
II. Village K is to the east of Village M and Village K is to the north of Village T.

22. On which day in July was definitely Mohan's mother's birthday?
I. Mohan correctly remembers that his mother's birthday is before eighteenth but after twelfth July.
II. Mohan's sister correctly remembers that their mother's birthday is after fifteenth but before nineteenth July.

23. How is 'near' written in a code language?
I. 'go near the tree' is written as 'sa na pa ta' in that code language.
II. 'tree is near home' is written as 'ja pa da sa' in that code language.

24. Among A, B, C, D and E, each having scored different marks in an exam, who has scored the lowest marks?
I. D has scored more marks than only three of them.
II. A has scored more marks than only E.

25. In a certain code language, "BAD" is written as "7" and "SAP" is written as "9". How is "BAN" written in that code language?
(a) 8 (b) 3
(c) 4 (d) 6

Directions (Q. 26-30): *Study of the following information carefully and answer the given questions.*

A word and number arrangement machine when given an input line of words and numbers rearranges them following a particular rule in each step. The following is an illustration of input and rearrangement. (All the numbers are two-digit numbers.)

Input: pink for 25 72 white jar 12 96
Step I: 96 pink for 25 72 white jar 12
StepII: 96 for pink 25 72 white jar 12
Step III: 96 for 72 pink 25 white jar 12
Step IV: 96 for 72 jar pink 25 white 12
StepV: 96 for 72 jar 25 pink white 12
Step VI: 96 for 72jar25 pink 12 white

And step VI is the last step of the rearrangement.

As per the rules followed in the above steps, find out in each of the following questions the appropriate step for the given input. (All the numbers are two-digit numbers.)

26. Input: 16 power failure 61 53 new cost 27
How many steps will be required to complete the rearrangement?
(a) Six (b) Seven
(c) Five (d) Four

27. Step II of an Input: 84 ask quit these 39 12old51 Which of the following will definitely be the input?
(a) quit these 39 12 old 84 ask 51
(b) quit these 39 12 old 51 84 ask
(c) quit 84 these ask 39 12 old 51
(d) Cannot be determined

28. Step III of an Input: 63 bed 5 8 never go home 46 28 How many more steps will be required to complete the rearrangement?
(a) Four (b) Three
(c) Five (d) Seven

29. Input: rows 25 columns 39 46 fear star 72
Which of the following steps will be the last but one?
(a) V (b) VI
(c) VII (d) None of these

30. Input: ordinary 47 tablet 36 dry 91 32 handle
Which of the following will be step VI of the rearrangement?
(a) 91 dry 47 handle 36 32 ordinary tablet
(b) 91 dry 47 handle 36 ordinary 32 tablet
(c) 91 dry 47 handle 36 ordinary tablet 32
(d) 91 47 dry handle 32 tablet 36 ordinary

Directions (Q. 31-35): *Study the following information carefully and answer the questions given below:*

A, B, C, D, E, F and G are seven members of a club. Each of them likes one day of the week, viz Monday, Tuesday, Wednesday, Thursday, Friday, Saturday and Sunday, not necessarily in the same order. Each of them owns a different, car, viz Swift, Alto, Figo, Beat, SX4, Estillo and Optra, not necessarily in the same order.

C likes Wednesday and his favourite car is neither SX4 nor Optra. E does not like Monday and his favourite car is Beat. The favourite car of the one who likes Friday is Figo. The one whose favourite car is Estillo likes Tuesday. D likes Saturday and D's favourite car is not SX4. G's favourite car is Alto. F likes Thursday. B does not like Estillo.

31. Who among the following likes Tuesday?
(a) A (b) B
(c) C (d) Data inadequate

32. Whose favourite car is Figo?
(a) A (b) B
(c) E (d) C

33. Who among the following likes Sunday?
(a) A (b) C
(c) F (d) E

34. Whose favourite car is SX4?
(a) B (b) A
(c) F
(d) Data inadequate

35. Which of the following combinations is correct?
(a) F-Thursday-Estillo
(b) C-Wednesday- Alto
(c) D-Saturday-Beat
(d) All are incorrect

Quantitative Aptitude

Directions (Q. 36-50): *What should come in place of question mark (?) in the following questions?*

36. $\frac{5}{8}\times 2\frac{3}{5}\div\frac{4}{9}=?$
(a) $2\frac{13}{27}$ (b) $1\frac{11}{27}$
(c) $2\frac{23}{32}$ (d) $3\frac{21}{32}$

37. $10.8 \times 5.5 \times 8.4 = ?$
(a) 458.69 (b) 489.96
(c) 498.96 (d) 485.69

38. $45 \div 5 - 0.5 = ?$
(a) 10 (b) 12
(c) 9.5 (d) 8.5

39. $3.5 \times (60 \div 2.5) = ?$
(a) 62 (b) 96
(c) 74 (d) None of these

40. $(4 \times 4 \times 4 \times 4 \times 4 \times 4)^5 \times (4 \times 4 \times 4)^8 \div (4)^3 = (64)^?$
(a) 17 (b) 10
(c) 16 (d) 18

41. $5 \times ? = 8484 \div 4$
(a) 444.2 (b) 424.2
(c) 442.2 (d) 422.2

42. $7059 - 2350 + 1936 = ? \times 50$
(a) 123.6 (b) 132.3
(c) 132.6 (d) 132.9

43. 16% of 550 ÷ ?% of 500 = 2.5
(a) 5.64 (b) 8.11
(c) 7.04 (d) 6.08

44. $8648 - 7652 = ? \times 40$
(a) 24.7 (b) 28.9
(c) 27.4 (d) None of these

45. 22% of 364 – ? = 23
(a) 50.02 (b) 57.08
(c) 53.16 (d) 59.14

46. $683.46 - 227.39 - 341.85 = ?$
(a) 114.22 (b) 141.22
(c) 144.22 (d) 112.22

47. $3\frac{2}{3}+2\frac{3}{4}+1\frac{1}{2}=?$
(a) $8\frac{11}{12}$ (b) $10\frac{12}{13}$
(c) $7\frac{11}{12}$ (d) $9\frac{11}{13}$

48. $\sqrt{?} - 5 = \sqrt{2209}$
(a) $\sqrt{2704}$ (b) $(52)^2$
(c) $\sqrt{52}$ (d) 52

49. 14.5% of 608 = ?
(a) 88.16 (b) 86.18
(c) 81.68 (d) 86.88

50. $840 \div 40 \div 0.5 = ?$
(a) 8.5 (b) 21
(c) 10.5 (d) 42

Directions (Q. 51-55): *What approximate value should come in place of question mark (?) in the following questions? (Note: You are not expected to calculate the exact value.)*

51. $750.0003 \div 19.999 = ?$
(a) 49 (b) 22
(c) 45 (d) 38

52. $6888.009 - 487.999 - 87.989 = ?$
(a) 6000 (b) 6570
(c) 6430 (d) 6310

53. $(9.5)^2 = ?$
(a) 75 (b) 90
(c) 125 (d) 110

54. $19.003 \times 22.998 - 280.010 = ?$
(a) 220 (b) 110
(c) 160 (d) 90

55. $5454 \div 54 \div 5 = ?$
(a) 25 (b) 15
(c) 30 (d) 20

Directions (Q. 56-60): *What should come in place of question mark (?) in the following number series?*

56. 10000 2000 400 80 16 3.2 ?
(a) 0.45 (b) 0.38
(c) 0.64 (d) 0.54

57. 2 10 42 170 ? 2730 10922
(a) 588 (b) 658
(c) 596 (d) 682

58. 600 519 ? 406 370 345 329
(a) 435 (b) 455
(c) 425 (d) 445

59. 5 ? 15 75 525 4725 51975
(a) 6 (b) 10
(c) 8 (d) 4725

60. 3 6 12 24 48 96 ?
(a) 192 (b) 182
(c) 186 (d) 198

61. Three women and 18 children together take two days to complete a piece of work. How many days will nine children alone take to complete the piece of work if six women alone can complete the piece of work in three days?

(a) Nine (b) 8
(c) Five (d) six

62. What will come in place of both question marks (?) in the following question?

$$\frac{(?)^{1.8}}{32} = \frac{16}{(?)^{1.2}}$$

(a) 16 (b) 64
(c) 2 (d) 8

63. Out of the fractions $\frac{5}{7}, \frac{4}{9}, \frac{6}{11}, \frac{2}{5}$ and $\frac{3}{7}$, what is the difference between the largest and the smallest fraction?

(a) $\frac{6}{13}$ (b) $\frac{11}{18}$
(c) $\frac{7}{18}$ (d) $\frac{7}{20}$

64. The average weight of 21 boys was recorded as 64 kg. If the weight of the teacher was added, the average increased by one kg. What was the teacher's weight?

(a) 86 kg (b) 74 kg
(c) 72 kg (d) 98 kg

65. The perimetre of a square is twice the perimetre of a rectangle. If the perimetre of the square is 72 cm and the length of the rectangle is 12 cm, what is the difference between the breadth of the rectangle and the side of the square?

(a) 9 cm (b) 12 cm
(c) 18 cm (d) 3 cm

**66. Find the average of the following set of scores.
253, 124, 255, 534, 836, 375, 101, 443, 760**

(a) 427 (b) 413
(c) 441 (d) 409

67. Raj sold an item for ₹ 6,384 and incurred a loss of 30%. At what price should he have sold the item to have gained a profit of 30%?

(a) ₹ 14,656 (b) ₹11,856
(c) ₹ 13,544 (d) None of these

68. What would be the simple interest accrued in four years on a principle of ₹ 18,440 at the rate of 15 pcpa?

(a) ₹ 1,075 (b) ₹ 12,250
(c) ₹ 11,500 (d) None of these

69. A truck covers a distance of 640 km in 10 hr. A car covers the same distance in 8 hr. What is the ratio of the speed of the truck to that of the car?

(a) 3 : 4 (b) 1 : 2
(c) 5 : 6 (d) 4 : 5

70. The ratio of Sita's, Riya's and Kunal's monthly income is 84 :76 : 89. If Riya's annual income is ₹ 4,56,000, what is the sum of Sita's and Kunal's annual incomes? (In some cases monthly income is used while in others annual income is used.)

(a) ₹ 11,95,000 (b) ₹ 9,83,500
(c) ₹ 11,30,000 (d) ₹ 10,38,000

English Language

Directions (Q. 71-75): *In each of these questions, two sentences (I) and (II) are given. Each sentence has a blank in it. Four words (a), (b), (c) and (d) are suggested. Out of these, only one fits at both the places in the context of each sentence. Number of that word is the answer.*

71. I. Boats take more time going against the _____ of the river.
II. She keeps herself abreast of ______ events.

(a) low (b) latest
(c) water (d) current

72. I. While trying to open the door, the _____ broke.
II. It is not difficult to _____ tricky situations.

(a) handle (b) knob
(c) bracket (d) overcome

73. I. This course teaches you not to _____ to temptations.
II. We hope to increase our ______ of rice this year.

(a) succumb (b) produce
(c) yield (d) share

74. I. When you play your radio at high ______ it disturbs others.
II. We have just received a latest _____ of this encyclopedia.

(a) edition (b) volume
(c) channel (d) frequency

75. I. It helps to rinse one's mouth early morning with a _____ of salt and water.
II. You can always refer to this reference material to find the _____ to these problems.

(a) mixture (b) answers
(c) liquid (d) solution

Directions (Q. 76-80): *In each question below a sentence with four words printed in bold type is given. These are numbered as* (a), (b), (c) *and* (d). *One of these four words printed in bold may be either wrongly spelt or inappropriate in the context of the sentence. Find out the word which is wrongly spelt or inappropriate, if any. The number of that word is your answer.*

76. Solving the energy **challenge /a)** requires **behaviour/(b)** changeand new **technological/(c) approaches./d)**

77. The first thing that catches your **eye /(a)** in this **building/(b)** is the **flour/(c)** with laser **lights./(d)**

78. The **services/(a)** sector has **contributed/(b) significantly/(c)** to the economic **grow./(d)**

79. IT Companies **have**/(a) been allotted **landing/(b)** in this area to **develop/ (c)**and start their **operations./(d)**

80. Other **then/(a)** the regular **incentives /(b),** the **government/(c)** is offering land sites at **concessional** rates. **/(d)**

Directions (Q. 81-85): *Which of the phrases* **(a), (b), (c)** *and* **(d)** *given below should replace the phrase given in bold in the following sentence to make the sentence grammatically correct.*

81. **In terms with** seating capacity, it is the third largest stadium in India.
(a) On terms with
(b) As far as
(c) In respective to terms with
(d) In terms of

82. That actor can double for the star **if needed be**
(a) if need
(b) if need be
(c) while it is needed
(d) whenever needed be

83. The 1982 Asian Games **brought about** a major change in India.
(a) brought after
(b) bring after
(c) best resulted
(d) No correction required

84. Tourism surely has suffered **given the huge** social unrest in the country.
(a) giving the huge
(b) because to
(c) as the huge
(d) No correction required

85. **Combining the** ongoing crisis in Europe, the data does make a case for a pause in rate hike.
(a) Together
(b) Apart with
(c) Combined with
(d) Combination of

Directions (Q. 86-90): *Read the following passage to answer the given questions based on it. Some words/phrases are printed in bold to help you locate them while answering some of the questions.*

The e-waste (Management and Handling) Rules, 2011, notified by the Ministry of Environment and Forests, have the **potential** to **turn** a growing problem into a developmental opportunity. With almost half-a-year to go before the rules take effect, there is enough time to create the necessary infrastructure for collection, dismantling and recycling of electronic waste. The focus must be on sincere and efficient implementation. Only decisive action can reduce the pollution and health costs associated with India's hazardous waste recycling industry. If India can achieve a transformation, it will be creating a whole new employment sector that provides good wages and working conditions for tens of thousands. The legacy response of the States to even the basic law on urban waste, the Municipal Solid Wastes (Management and Handling) Rules has been one of **indifference**; many cities continue to simply burn the garbage or dump it in lakes. With the emphasis now on segregation of waste at source and recovery of materials, it should be **feasible** to implement **both sets of rules** efficiently. A welcome feature of the new e-waste rules is the emphasis on extended producer responsibility. In other words, producers must take responsibility for the disposal of end-of-life products. For this provision to work, they must ensure that consumers who sell scrap get some form of financial incentive.

The e-waste rules, which derive from those pertaining to hazardous waste, are scheduled to come into force on May 1, 2012. Sound as they are, the task of scientifically disposing a few hundred thousand tonnes of trash electronics annually depends heavily on a system of oversight by State Pollutions Control Boards (PCBs). Unfortunately, most PCBs remain unaccountable and often lack the resources for active enforcement. It must be pointed out that, although agencies handling e-waste must obtain environmental **clearances** and be authorised and registered by the PCBs even under the Hazardous Wastes (Management, Handling and Transboundary Movement) Rules 2008, there has been little practical impact. Over 95 per cent of electronic waste is collected and recycled by the informal sector. The way forward is for the PCBs to be made accountable for enforcement of the e-waste rules and the levy of penalties under environmental laws. Clearly, the first order priority is to create a system that will absorb the 80,000-strong workforce in the informal sector into the proposed scheme for scientific recycling. Facilities must be created to upgrade the skills of these workers through training and their occupational health must be ensured.

Recycling of e-waste is one of the biggest challenges today. In such a time, when globalisation and information technology are growing at a pace **which could only be imagined few years back**, e-waste and its hazards have become more prominent over a period of time and should be given immediate attention.

86. **What, according to the passage, is important now for e-waste management?**
(a) Making rules
(b) Reviewing rules
(c) Implementing rules
(d) Notifying rules

87. **Which of the following can be one of the by-products of effective e-waste management?**
(a) India can guide other countries in doing so.
(b) It will promote international understanding.
(c) It will promote national integration.
(d) It will create a new employment sector.

88. **Which of the following rules has not been indicated in the passage?**
(a) e-waste Rules 2011
(b) Pollution Check Rules
(c) Hazardous Wastes Rules, 2009
(d) Municipal Solid Wastes Rules

89. **"Both sets of rules" is being referred to which of the following?**
(a) Solid wastes and hazardous wastes
(b) e-waste and hazardous waste
(c) Solid waste and e-waste
(d) Solid waste and recycling waste

90. **e-waste rules have been derived from those pertaining to**
(a) Hazardous waste
(b) PC waste
(c) Computer waste
(d) Municipal solid waste

91. **Which of the following will help implement "both sets of rules"?**
(a) Employment opportunities
(b) International collaboration
(c) Financial incentive
(d) Segregation of waste at source

92. **e-waste Rules came / come into force from**
(a) 2008 (b) 2009
(c) 2010 (d) 2012

93. **Which of die following best explains the meaning of the phrase "which could only be imagined few years back" as used in the passage?**
(a) It was doomed.
(b) It took us few years.
(c) It took us back by few years.
(d) None of these

94. **Which of the following is true in the context of the passage?**
(a) No city dumps its waste in lakes.
(b) Some cities burn garbage.
(c) PCBs have adequate resources for active enforcement.
(d) e-waste was a much bigger challenge in the past.

95. **Which of the following is not true in the context of the passage?**
(a) Some form of financial incentive is recommended for the producers.
(b) Some financial incentive is recommended for the consumers.
(c) e-waste will be a few hundred thousand tonnes.
(d) The agencies handling e-waste have to obtain environmental clearances.

Directions (Q. 96-98): *Choose the word which is most nearly the same in meaning of the word printed in **bold**, as used in the passage.*

96. **Clearance**
(a) Cleaning (b) Permission
(c) Sale (d) Remedy

97. **Turn**
(a) Throw (b) Chance
(c) Send (d) Transform

98. **Potential**
(a) Intelligence
(b) Aptitude
(c) Possibility
(d) Portion

Directions (Q. 99-100): *Choose the word which is most opposite in meaning of the word printed in **bold** as used in the passage.*

99. **Feasible**
(a) Unattended
(b) Physical
(c) Practical
(d) Unviabie

100. **Indifference**
(a) Interest (b) Difference
(c) Ignorance (d) Rule-bound

Answer Sheet

1.(c)	2.(c)	3.(b)	4.(a)	5.(b)	6.(d)	7.(d)	8.(a)	9.(c)	10.(b)
11.(b)	12.(c)	13.(a)	14.(d)	15.(d)	16.(b)	17.(a)	18.(d)	19.(a)	20.(d)
21.(c)	22.(d)	23.(d)	24.(b)	25.(a)	26.(a)	27.(d)	28.(a)	29.(d)	30.(b)
31.(a)	32.(b)	33.(d)	34.(c)	35.(d)	36.(d)	37.(b)	38.(d)	39.(d)	40.(a)
41.(b)	42.(d)	43.(c)	44.(d)	45.(b)	46.(a)	47.(c)	48.(b)	49.(a)	50.(d)
51.(d)	52.(d)	53.(b)	54.(c)	55.(d)	56.(c)	57.(d)	58.(b)	59.(d)	60.(a)
61.(d)	62.(d)	63.(d)	64.(a)	65.(b)	66.(d)	67.(b)	68.(d)	69.(d)	70.(d)
71.(d)	72.(a)	73.(c)	74.(b)	75.(d)	76.(a)	77.(c)	78.(d)	79.(b)	80.(a)
81.(d)	82.(b)	83.(d)	84.(d)	85.(c)	86.(c)	87.(d)	88.(b)	89.(d)	90.(a)
91.(d)	92.(d)	93.(d)	94.(b)	95.(a)	96.(b)	97.(d)	98.(b)	99.(d)	100.(a)

Solutions

1. **(c)** As,

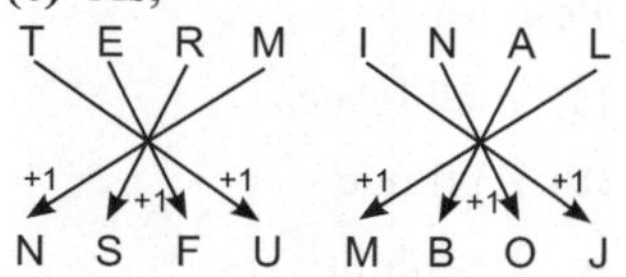

and

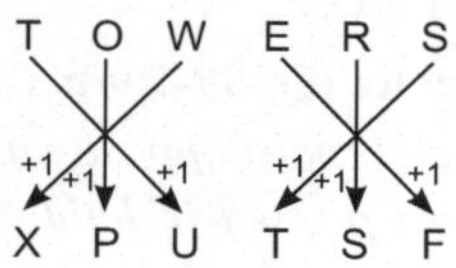

Similarly,

So,

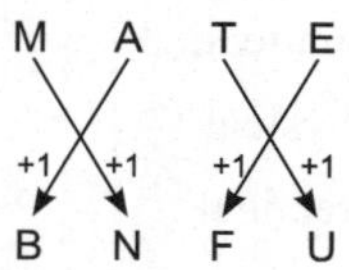

2. **(c)** 5 [3] 1 4 [6] 8 7
1 [3] 4 5 [6] 7 8

So, position of two digits, ie 3 and 6, remains unchanged after the digits are rearranged in ascending order within the number.

3. **(b)**

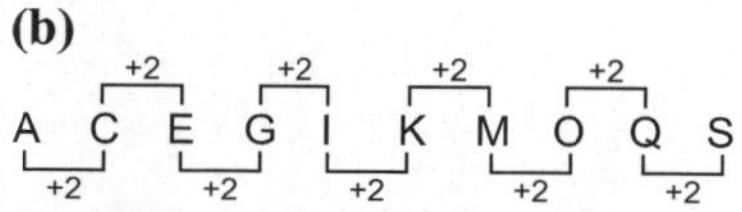

So, Q S should come in the place of question mark.

4. **(a)** ERID → DIRE. Alphabets are written in reverse order Thus, RIPE → EPIR

5. **(b)** The third, fifth, seventh and ninth letters are W, G, A and E respectively.

Only one meaningful word can be formed using these letters which is WAGE

6. **(d)** @ 9 1 \$ 2 6
↓ ↓ ↓ ↓ ↓ ↓
P E F H R J

7. **(d)** 5 3 8 7 # © 9
↓ ↓ ↓ ↓ ↓ ↓
K D M T P E

8. **(a)** 1 4 @ 3 1 2 δ
↓ ↓ ↓ ↓ ↓ ↓
V P K F R V
(Condition (i) applies.)

9. **(c)** % 4 1 8 7 ★
↓ ↓ ↓ ↓ ↓ ↓
X I F D M X
(Condition (iii) applies.)

10. **(b)** 9 1 2 4 δ 6
↓ ↓ ↓ ↓ ↓ ↓
J F R I V E
(Condition (ii) applies.)

11. **(b)** $D = T$....(i); $T \geq M$ ...(ii)
$M < J$ ...(iii)
Combining all the three, we have,,$D = T \geq M < J \Rightarrow$ No relationship between D and J can be established. Hence conclusion I is not true. Again, combining (i) and (ii), we get, $D = T \geq M \Rightarrow D \geq M \Rightarrow M \leq D$. Therefore, conclusion II is not true.

12. **(c)** $B < K$ ...(i); $K = N$ ...(ii) $N \geq R$ ...(iii)
Combining (ii) and (iii), we get $K = N \geq R \Rightarrow R \geq K$. Therefore neither conclusion I nor conclusion II is true. But both are exhaustive. Hence either conclusion I ($R = K$) or conclusion II ($R < K$) is true.

13. **(a)** $H \geq F$ ...(i); $F < W$....(ii); $W = E$ ...(iii)
Combining (ii) and (iii). we get $F < W = E \Rightarrow F < E \Rightarrow E > F$. Hence conclusion I is true Again, combining (i) and (ii), we have, $H \geq F < W \Rightarrow$ No relationship between H and W can be determined. Therefore conclusion II is not true.

14. **(d)** $Z > D$ ...(i); $D \leq K$ ...(ii); $K > M$ ...(iii)
Combining (ii) and (iii), we have $D \leq K > M \Rightarrow$ No relationship between D and M can be determined Hence conclusion I does not follow. Again, combining (i) and (ii), we get, $Z > D \leq K \Rightarrow$ No relationship between Z and K can be determined. Therefore conclusion II is not true

15. **(d)** 'Watt' is the unit of 'power' similarly, 'Joule' is the unit of 'work'.

Hints for (16-20):

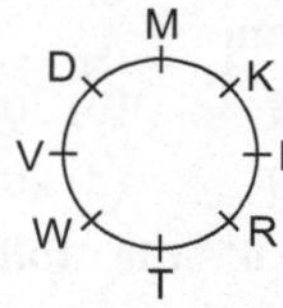

16. **(b)** **17.** **(a)** **18.(d)** R **19.** **(a)** **20.(d)**

Hints for (21-25):

21. **(c)** From I. M
PT
Thus, it can be found that M is to the north-west of T So, I alone is sufficient to answer the question.
From II. M K
T
Thus, it can be deduced that M is to the north-west of T. So, II alone is also sufficient to answer the question Thus, the answer can be found by using either of the statements alone.

22. **(d)** **From I.** Possible dates of birthday of Mohan's mother are 13th, 14th, 15th, 16th or 17th of July Thus, 1 alone is not sufficient to answer the question.
From II. Possible dates of birthday of Mohan s mother are 16th, 17th or 18th of July.
Thus, II alone is also not sufficient to answer the question. Now, even after combining 1 and II, it is found that Mohan's mother's birthday is either on 16th or 17th July.
Thus, the answer cannot be found even after combining both the statements. Hence, option (d) follows.

23. **(d)** **From I.** go near the tree → sa na pa ta
Thus, code for 'near' cannot be found
From II. tree is near home → ja pa da sa
Again, code for 'near' cannot be found
After combining I and II, it is found that the code for 'near' can be either 'sa' or 'pa'.

Thus, the answer cannot be found even after combining both the statements

24. **(b) From I.** – > D > – – – is obtained if all of them are arranged in descending order of the marks scored.
But we cannot say who among them scored the lowest marks
From II. It is clear that E has scored the lowest marks Thus, II alone is sufficient to answer to the question

25. **(a)** BAD ⇒ 7, 2 + 1+ 4 = 7
SAP ⇒ 9, 19 + 1 + 16 = 36
or 3 + 6 = 9
BAN ⇒ 17 or 1 +7 = 8
In Cooding language BAN will be written as 8.

(26-30): In the first step, the largest number goes to the left most position, pushing the rest of the line rightward In the next step, the word that comes first in the alphabetical order occupies the second position from the left, pushing the rest of the line rightward Thus the numbers and words gets arranged alternately till all the numbers are placed in the descending order and the words in the alphaoeticai order.

26. **(a) Input:** 16 power failure 61 53 new cost 27
Step I: 61 16 power failure 53 new cost 27
Step II: 61 cost 16 power failure 53 new 27
Step III: 61 cost 53 16 power failure new 27
Step IV: 61 cost 53 failure 16 power new 27
Step V: 61 cost 53 failure 27 16 power new
Step VI: 61 cost 53 failure 27 new 16 power

27. **(d)** We cannot move backwards

28. **(a) Step III:** 63 bed 58 never go home 46 28
Step IV: 63 bed 58 go never home 46.28
Step V: 63 bed 58 go 46 never home 28
Step VI: 63 bed 58 to 46 home never 28
Step VII: 63 bed 58 go 46 home 28 never
This is the final step. Thus, four more steps are required to complete the rearrangement.

29. **(d)** Step IV will be the last but one step.
Input: rows 25 columns 39 46 fear star 72
Step I: 72 rows 25 columns 39 46 fear star
Step II: 72 columns rows 25 39 46 fear star
Step III: 72 columns 46 rows 25 39 fear star
Step IV: 72 columns 46 fear rows 25 3.9 star
Step V: 72 columns 46 fear 39 rows 25 star
This is the final step.

30. **(b)** Input: ordinary 47 tablet 36 dry 91 32 handle
Step I: 91 ordinary 47 tablet 36 dry 32 handle
Step II: 91 dry ordinary 47 tablet 36 32 handle
Step III: 91 dry 47 ordinary tablet 36 32 handle
Step IV: 91 dry 47 handle ordinary tablet 36 32
Step V: 91 dry 47 handle 36 ordinary tablet 32
Step VI: 91 dry 47 handle 36 ordinary 32 tablet

Hints for (31-35): On the basis of information given in the question, we can have the following table:

Member	Day	Car
A	Tuesday	Estillo
B	Friday	Figo
C	Wednesday	Swifl
D	Saturday	Optra
E	Sunday	Beat
F	Thursday	SX4
G	Monday	Alto

31. **(a)** 32.**(b)** 33.**(d)** 34.**(c)** 35.**(d)**

36. **(d)** $\frac{5}{8}\times\frac{13}{5}\times\frac{9}{4}=\frac{117}{32}=3\frac{21}{32}$

37. **(b)** ? = 10.8 × 5.5 × 8.4 = 498.96

38. **(d)** $? = \frac{45}{5} - 0.5 = 9 - 0.5 = 8.5$

39. **(d)** ? = 3.5 × 24 = 84

40. **(a)** $(64 \times 64)^5 \times (4 \times 4 \times 4)^8 \div (64)^1 = (64)^?$
Or, $64^5 \times 64^5 \times 64^8 \div (64) = (64)^?$
Or, $64^{5+5+8-1} = 64^?$
? = = 17

41. **(b)** $? = \frac{8484}{4\times5} = 424.2$

42. **(d)** $? = \frac{6645}{50} = 132.9$

43. **(c)** 88 ÷ ?% of 500 = 2.5
or, 88 = 2.5 × ?% o f 500
or, $\frac{88}{2.5} = ?\%$ of 500
or, $35.2 = \frac{500}{100}$
or, $? = \frac{35.2\times100}{500} = 7.04$

44. **(d)** $? = \frac{996}{40} = 24.9$

45. **(b)** ? = 80.08 – 23 = 57.08

46. **(a)**

47. **(c)** $(3+2+1)+\left(\frac{2}{3}+\frac{3}{4}+\frac{1}{2}\right)$
$= 6+\frac{8+9+6}{12} = 6+\frac{23}{12} = 7\frac{11}{12}$

48. **(b)** $\sqrt{?} = 47 + 5 = 52$
or, $? = (52)^2 = 2704$

49. **(a)** ? = 14.5% of 608 = 88.16

50. **(d)** $? = \frac{840}{40\times0.5} = 42$

51. **(d)** $? = \frac{750}{20} = 37.5$

56. **(c)** The pattern of the series is as follows:
10000 ÷ 5 = 2000
2000 ÷ 5 = 400
400 ÷ 5 = 80
80 ÷ 5 = 16
16 ÷ 5 = 3.2
3.2 ÷ 5 = 0.64

57. **(d)** The pattern of the series is as follows:
2 × 4 + 2 = 10
10 × 4 + 2 = 42
42 × 4 + 2= 170
170 × 4 + 2 = 682

58. **(b)** The pattern of the series is as follows:

$600 - 9^2 = 600 - 81 = 519$

$519 - 8^2 = 519 - 64 = 455$

$455 - 7^2 = 455 - 49 = 406$

$406 - 6^2 = 406 - 36 = 370$

59. **(d)** The pattern of the series is as follows:

$5 \times 1 = 5$

$5 \times 3 = 15$

$15 \times 5 = 75$

$75 \times 7 = 525$

$525 \times 9 = 4725$

60. **(a)** The pattern of the series is as follows:

$3 \times 2 = 6$

$6 \times 2 = 12$

$12 \times 2 = 24$

$24 \times 2 = 48$

$48 \times 2 = 96$

$96 \times 2 = 192$

61. **(d)** Six women alone can complete the work in three days. Then, three \women alone can complete the work in six days

3 women and 18 children together can complete the work in 2 days.

3 women can complete the work in 6 days.

18 children can complete the work in $\frac{6 \times 2}{6-2}$ days $= 3$ days. So, 9 children will complete the work in 6 days.

62. **(d)** $?^{1.8} \times ?^{1.2} = 32 \times 16$

or, $?^{1.8+1.2} = 512$

or, $?^3 = 512 = 8^3$

$\therefore\ ? = 8$

63. **(d)** $\frac{5}{7} = 0.71; \frac{4}{9} = 0.44; \frac{6}{11}$

$= 0.545; \frac{2}{5} = 0.4; \frac{3}{4} = 0.75$

Largest fraction $= \frac{3}{4}$

Smallest fraction $= \frac{2}{5}$

Difference $= \frac{3}{4} - \frac{2}{5} = \frac{15-8}{20} = \frac{7}{20}$

64. **(a)** Total weight of 21 boys

$= (64 \times 21 =)\ 1344$ kg

Total weight along with the teacher $= (65 \times 22) = 1430$ kg

Teacher's weight

$= (1430 - 1344) = 86$ kg

65. **(b)** Perimetre of square = 72 cm

Perimetre of rectangle

$= \left(\frac{72}{2}\right) = 36$ cm

$\therefore$ Side of the square $= \frac{72}{4} = 18$ cm

Perimeter of rectangle $= 2(1 + b)$

or, $2(12 + b) = 36$

or, $b = 18 - 12 = 6$ cm

Difference $= (18 - 6) = 12$ cm

66. **(d)** Average

$$= \frac{253 + 124 + 255 + 534 + 836 + 375 + 101 + 443 + 760}{9}$$

$= \frac{3681}{9} = 409$

67. **(b)** Cost price of the item

$= 6384 \times \frac{100}{70}$

SP of item with 30% profit

$= 6384 \times \frac{100}{70} \times \frac{130}{100} = ₹11856$

68. **(d)** SI

$= \frac{P \times r \times t}{100} = \frac{18440 \times 15 \times 4}{100} = ₹11064$

69. **(d)** Speed of the truck

$= \frac{640}{10} = 64$ km/hr

Speed of the car $= \frac{640}{8} = 80$ km/hr

Ratio $= \frac{64}{80} = \frac{4}{5} = 4:5$

70. **(d)** Ratio of monthly income and ratio of annual income will be the same,

i.e., 84 : 76 : 89

$\therefore$ Sum of Sita's and Kunal's annual income

$= \frac{4560000}{76} \times (84 + 89) = ₹1038000$

8 Practice Set

Reasoning

1. **Four of the following five are alike in a certain way and hence form a group. Which of the following does not belong to that group?**
(a) Walk (b) Cry
(c) Play (d) Alive

2. **How many such pairs of letters are there in the word 'VIRTUAL', each of which has as many letters between them in the word (in both forward and backward directions) as they have between them in the English alphabetical series ?**
(a) None (b) One
(c) Two (d) Three

3. **How many meaningful English words can be formed with the letters 'ILP' using all the letters only once in each word?**
(a) None (b) One
(c) Two (d) Three

4. **If each alternate letter in the word 'FLIPPER' starting with F is changed to the next letter in the English alphabetical series and each of the remaining letters is changed to the previous letters in the English alphabetical series, then how many letters will appear more than once in the new arrangement?**
(a) None (b) One
(c) Two (d) Three

5. **Pointing to a girl, Mr Arun said, "She is the daughter of 'my mother's only child". How is the girl related to Mr A run ?**
(a) Sister (b) Mother
(c) Cousin (d) Daughter

6. **In a certain code language, 'LISP' is coded as 'MJTQ', similarly 'PLAN' is coded as 'QMBO'. How will 'FORT' be coded in the same code language?**
(a) ENSQ (b) GPUS
(c) ENQS (d) GPSU

7. **'Artificial' is related to 'Natural' in the same way as 'Private' is related to ______.**
(a) Future (b) Personal
(c) Public (d) Closed

8. **Four of the following five are alike on the basis of being divisible by a particular number and hence form a group. Which of the following does not belong to that group ?**
(a) 21 (b) 91
(c) 65 (d) 77

9. **In a class of 25 students, Lata's rank is 13th from the top and Parul's rank is 19th from the bottom. If Vishal's rank is exactly between Lata's and Parul's rank what is Vishal's rank from the top ?**
(a) 10th (b) 8th
(c) 9th (d) 7th

10. **What should come next in the number series given below?**
1 1 2 1 2 3 1 2 3 4 1 2 3 4 5 1 2 3 4 5 6 1 2 3 4 5 6
(a) 5 (b) 2
(c) 8 (d) None of these

Directions (Q. 11-15): Study the following information to answer the given questions:

Eight friends A, B, C; D, E, F, G and H are sitting around a circle facing the centre, not necessarily in the same order. F sits fourth to the left of B. A and H are immediate neighbours of F. C sits third to the left of A. G sits third to the right of E.

11. **What is D's position with respect to B ?**
(a) Immediate left
(b) Sixth to the right
(c) Second to the left
(d) Seventh to the left

12. **What are the immediate neighbours of G ?**
(a) F and H (b) A and F
(c) C and H (d) B and C

13. **If C is related to E in a certain way and similarly F is related B in the same way, to whom is A related to?**
(a) H (b) D
(c) G (d) C

14. **Four of the following five are alike in a certain way based on their seating positions in the above arrangement and so form a group. Which is the one that does not belong to the group ?**
(a) FE (b) HA
(c) DG (d) BE

15. **If all the eight friends are made to sit alphabetically in the clockwise direction starting from A, positions of how many will remain unchanged (excluding A)?**
(a) None (b) One
(c) Two (d) Three

Directions (Q. 16-20): In each question below arc two statements followed by two conclusions numbered I and II. You have to take the two given statements to be true even if they seem to be at variance from commonly known facts and then decide which of the given conclusions logically follows from the given statements disregarding commonly known facts.

Given answer

(a) if only conclusion I follows.

(b) if only conclusion II follows.

(c) if either conclusion I or conclusion II follows.

(d) if neither conclusion I nor conclusion II follows.

16. Statements: Some windows are grills.
All glasses are grills.
Conclusion: I. All grills are windows,
II. At least some grills are glasses.

17. Statements: Some painters are artists.
Some dancers are painters.
Conclusions: I. All artists are dancers.
II. All painters are dancers.

18. Statements: All cabins are rooms.
All rooms are buildings.
Conclusions: I. All rooms are buildings.
II. All cabins are buildings

19. Statements: All rings are necklaces.
No necklace is a bracelet.
Conclusions: I. No rings is a bracelet.
II. All necklaces are rings.

20. Statements: All hands are arms.
Some hands are muscles.
Conclusions: I. Some muscles are arms.
II. All muscles are arms.

Directions (Q. 21-25): Study the following information to answer the given questions:

Seven friends — L, M, N, O, P, Q and R are sitting in a straight line facing North, not necessarily in the same order. M sits fifth to the right of O. P sits third to the right of L. Both L and P do not sit at the extreme ends of the line. Q and R are immediate neighbours of each other. N sits third to the left of Q.

21. What is O's position with respect of R ?

(a) Second to the right
(b) Third to the left
(c) Second to the left
(d) Third to the right

22. Which of the following represents the friends sitting at the extreme ends of the line?

(a) O, M (b) Q, O
(c) N, M (d) O, N

23. If all the seven friends are made to sit in alphabetical order from left to right, the positions of how many will remain unchanged?

(a) Four (b) Three
(c) One (d) None

24. Who sits exactly in the middle of the row ?

(a) P (b) L
(c) Q (d) R

25. Four of the following five are alike in a certain way based on their seating positions in the above arrangement and so form a group. Which is the one that docs not belong to the group ?

(a) M P (b) R Q
(c) O N (d) L N

Directions (Q. 26-28) : In each question below is given a group of numbers/symbols followed by four combinations of letter codes numbered (a), (b), (c) and (d). You have to find out which of the combinations correctly represents the group of numbers/symbols based on the following coding system and the conditions and mark the number of that combination as your answer.

Number/ Symbols	9	4	&	5	%	3	#	7	6	@	8	+	2	$
Letter Codes	X	P	J	H	B	D	K	F	S	T	N	G	R	L

Conditions:

(i) If the first element is a symbol and the last element is a number then the codes for both are to be interchanged,

(ii) If both the first and last elements are symbols, then the last element is to be coded as the code for the first element,

(iii) If the group of elements contains only one symbol, then that symbols is to be coded as A.

26. 28% 956

(a) RNBXHS (b) RNAXSH
(c) RNBXSH (d) RNAXHS

27. @62 + 74

(a) PSRGFT (b) TSRFGP
(c) PSRFGT (d) PRSGFT

28. + 5963%

(a) GHXSDG (b) GSIIXDB
(c) GHXDSG (d) GHSXDB

Directions (Q. 29-32): In these questions, relationships between different elements is shown in the statements. These statements are followed by two conclusions. Give answer

(a) if only conclusion I follows.

(b) if only conclusion II follows.

(c) if either conclusion 1 or conclusion II follows.

(d) if both conclusions I and II follow.

29. Statement: $A < L < T < R \leq H > K$
Conclusions: I. $H > L$
II. $K > T$

30. Statement: $P = N > D \geq G < B = J$
Conclusions: I. $G < P$
II. $G < J$

31. Statement: $F \leq C \geq V = Z < X = U$
Conclusions: I. $V < U$
II. $Z < F$

32. **Statement:** $Q \le E = I > N \ge R \ge S$
Conclusions: I. $E = S$
II. $S \le N$

Directions (Q. 33-35): Study the following arrangement of consonants, vowels, numbers and symbols carefully and answer the questions given below:

H @ F ! 3 U 6 % G I T * P L 8 $ ^ 9 S 2 7 & A M K + J © D 4 # 5 & E

33. **Which of the following is ninth to the right of the twentieth from the right end of the above arrangement?**
(a) K (b) M
(c) U (d) A

34. **How many such consonants are there in the above arrangement, each of which is immediately preceded by a symbol and also immediately followed by a symbol?**
(a) None (b) One
(c) Two (d) Three

35. **If all the symbols are dropped from the arrangement, which of the following will be the twelfth from the left end?**
(a) 9 (b) 2
(c) S (d) 7

Quantitative Aptitude

Directions (Q. 36-45): What will come in place of the question mark (?) in the following questions?

36. **$(3325 \div 25) \times (152 \div 16) = ?$**
(a) 1269.4 (b) 1264.9
(c) 1265.3 (d) 1263.5

37. $\sqrt{3136} - \sqrt{1764} = \sqrt{?}$
(a) 14 (b) $(196)^2$
(c) –14 (d) None of these

38. $5\frac{1}{5} + 2\frac{2}{15} + 3\frac{2}{3} = ?$
(a) 15 (b) 13
(c) $\frac{11}{15}$ (d) None of these

39. **$-15 - 27 - 88 - 63 + 255 = ?$**
(a) 55 (b) 74
(c) 62 (d) 59

40. **$(2525 \times 0.25 \div 5) \times 7 = ?$**
(a) 889.43 (b) 883.75
(c) 886.45 (d) 881.75

41. $\frac{14}{19} \times \frac{57}{70} \times \frac{20}{21} = ?$
(a) $\frac{2}{7}$ (b) $\frac{4}{7}$
(c) $\frac{2}{9}$ (d) $\frac{3}{7}$

42. **32% of 500 + 162% of 50 = ?**
(a) 231 (b) 245
(c) 237 (d) None of these

43. **45316 + 52131 – 65229 = ? + 15151**
(a) 17063 (b) 17073
(c) 17076 (d) 17067

44. $\sqrt{25 - 12 + 155 + 1} = ?$
(a) 13 (b) 14
(c) 17 (d) 16

45. $\frac{184 \times 4}{23\% \text{ of } 400} = ?$
(a) 7 (b) 9
(c) 8 (d) 5

46. **What will come in place of both the question marks (?) in the following question ?**
$$\frac{(?)^{4/3}}{32} = \frac{128}{(?)^{5/3}}$$
(a) 16 (b) 12
(c) 18 (d) 14

47. **The speed of a man is $\frac{3}{4}$th the speed of a bicycle. The bicycle covers 192 m in 8 seconds. How much time will the man take to cover 54 m?**
(a) 3 seconds (b) 4 seconds
(c) 7 seconds (d) 5 seconds

48. **If the following fractions are arranged in a descending order (from left to right), which of them will be second from the right end ?**
$$\frac{4}{9}, \frac{6}{13}, \frac{5}{11}, \frac{13}{16}, \frac{7}{12}$$
(a) $\frac{16}{13}$ (b) $\frac{4}{9}$
(c) $\frac{13}{16}$ (d) $\frac{5}{11}$

49. **A factory produces 1515 items in 3 days. How many items will they produce in a week?**
(a) 3530 (b) 3553
(c) 3533 (d) 3535

50. **What is the least number that can be added to 4800 to make it a perfect square?**
(a) 110 (b) 81
(c) 25 (d) None of these

51. **Which of the following words can be written in 120 different ways?**
(a) STABLE (b) STILL
(c) WATER (d) NOD

52. **What would be the compound interest obtained on an amount of ₹ 1,210 at the rate of 6. p.c.p.a. after a year?**
(a) ₹ 70.5 (b) ₹ 74.6
(c) ₹ 73.8 (d) ₹ 72.6

53. **The cost of 5 pens and 8 pencils is ₹ 31. What would be the cost of 15 pens and 24 pencils?**
(a) ₹ 93 (b) ₹ 99
(c) ₹ 96 (d) None of these

54. **Find the average of the following set of scores:**
432, 623, 209, 378, 908, 168
(a) 456 (b) 455
(c) 453 (d) 458

55. **If the numerator of a fraction is increased by 300% and the denominator is increased by 200%, the resultant fraction is $\frac{4}{15}$. What is the original fraction?**
(a) $\frac{3}{5}$ (b) $\frac{4}{5}$
(c) $\frac{2}{5}$ (d) $\frac{1}{5}$

56. Joel purchased 40 notebooks at the rate of ₹ 18 per notebook and 55 pencils at the rate of ₹ 8 per pencil. What is the total amount that he paid to the shopkeeper?
(a) ₹ 1,165 (b) ₹ 1,160
(c) ₹ 1,166 (d) ₹ 1,161

57. The sum of five consecutive odd numbers is 265. What is the sum of the largest number and twice the smallest number?
(a) 156 (b) 153
(c) 155 (d) 151

58. The average of five numbers is 34.4. The average of the first and the second number is 46.5. The average of the fourth and the fifth number is 18. What is the third number?
(a) 45 (b) 46
(c) 42 (d) None of these

59. One of the angles of a parallelogram is 45°. What will be the sum of the larger angle and twice the smaller angle of the parallelogram ?
(a) 228° (b) 224°
(c) 225° (d) 222°

60. 9 women can complete a piece of work in 19 days. I low many days will 18 women take to complete the same piece of work?
(a) 12 days (b) 6.5 days
(c) 9 days (d) None of these

61. If $(11)^3$ is subtracted from $(46)^2$, what will be the remainder?
(a) 787 (b) 785
(c) 781 (d) 783

62. The ratio between Gloria's and Sara's present ages is 4 : 7 respectively. Two years ago the ratio between their ages was 1 : 2 respectively. What will be Sara's age three years hence ?
(a) 17 years (b) 14 years
(c) 11 years (d) 8 years

Directions (Q. 63-65): What should come in place of the question.mark (?) in the following number series?

63. 800 400 200 100 50 ?
(a) 20 (b) 30
(c) 25 (d) 35

64. 213 35 68 112 ?
(a) 173 (b) 178
(c) 163 (d) 167

65. 650 601 565 540 524 ?
(a) 512 (b) 514
(c) 511 (d) 515

66. A plot of 1800 sq ft is available at the rate of ₹ 630 per sq ft. If 45% of the total cost of the plot is to be paid at the time of booking it, how much is the booking amount?
(a) ₹ 11,34,0007 (b) ₹ 5,10,3007
(c) ₹ 6.03,0007 (d) ₹ 6,00,300

67. A, B and C are three consecutive even integers such that four times A is equal to three times C. What is the value of B?
(a) 12 (b) 10
(c) 16 (d) 14

68. A bus covers 572 km in 13 hours. What is the speed of the bus?
(a) 40 km/hr (b) 44 km/hr
(c) 43 km/hr (d) 47 km/hr

69. The sum of the squares of two odd numbers is 11570. The square of the smaller number is 5329. What is the other number?
(a) 73 (b) 75
(c) 78 (d) 79

70. What is the difference between the simple and compound interest earned from a sum of ₹ 13033 at a rate of 13 per cent per annum for a period of 3 years (rounded off to 2 digits after decimal) ?
(a) ₹ 5,082.87 (b) ₹ 689.41
(c) ₹ 5,772.28 (d) None of these

English Language

Directions (Q. 71-75): In each of the following sentences, an idiomatic expression or a proverb is highlighted. Select the alternative which best describes its use in the sentence.

71. The stunt that I, recently attempted was a **piece of cake.**
(a) The stunt that I recently attempted was enjoyable to watch
(b) The stunt that I recently attempted was very challenging
(c) The stunt that I recently attempted was celebrated by all
(d) The stunt that I recently attempted was a simple task

72. The boy broke the window and **took to his heels.**
(a) The boy broke the window and fell on his heels
(b) The boy broke the window and ran away
(c) The boy broke the window with his heels
(d) The boy ran into the window

73. I pledged myself to serve the king faithfully.
(a) I made a mistake by promising to serve the king faithfully
(b) I made a fool of myself in order to serve the king
(c) I boasted about serving the king faithfully
(d) I made a solemn and formal promise to serve the king faithfully

74. There is a **crying need** for improvements to our public transport system.
(a) There is an obvious need for improvements to our public transport system
(b) There is a well documented need for improvements to our public transport system.
(c) There is a minor need for improvements to our public transport system.
(d) There is a serious need for improvements to our public transport system.

75. In an old bookshop I happened to **light upon** a volume that belonged to my grandfather.
(a) In an old bookshop I happened to discard a volume that belonged to my grandfather.
(b) In an old bookshop I happened to purchase a volume that belonged to my grandfather.
(c) In an old bookshop I happened to look for a volume that belonged to my grandfather.
(d) In an old bookshop I happened to discover by chance a volume that belonged to my grandfather.

Directions (Q. 76-80): Pick out the most effective word/ phrases from the given alternatives marked (a), (b), (c) and (d) given below each sentence to fill in the blank to make the sentence meaningful and grammatically correct.

76. By the middle of the 19th Century, the urban population of England ______ the rural population.

(a) have exceed
(b) exceeded
(c) was to exceed
(d) exceeds

77. The house that the actress lives in is beautiful, but the surroundings are ________unpleasant.

(a) quite
(b) more and more
(c) a little quite
(d) very little

78. My friend and I decided to watch a play, however ______enjoyed it.

(a) hardly of us
(b) some few of us
(c) we scarcely only
(d) neither of us

79. It is difficult to speak a language fluently unless _______ regularly.

(a) it is in practice
(b) it is by practising
(c) it will be practised
(d) it is practised

80. By the time he was eighteen years old, Peter ______ to make a living and support his family.

(a) begins
(b) began
(c) started beginning
(d) would begin

Directions (Q. 81-90): Read the following passage carefully and answer the questions given below it. Certain words are printed in bold to help you to locate them while answering some of the questions.

Lumbini is a beautiful place in the southern part of Nepal. About 2,500 years ago, a baby boy was born to the king and queen. The baby was named Siddharth. His mother, died when he was five days old. The baby boy grew into a **handsome** prince. His father tried to keep him happy. The little prince had everything he needed - fine clothes, the best food and good toys. But he was not interested in them. He wanted to be alone and was always found in deep thought. Later, he was married to a beautiful princess. She was called Yashodhara. They had a son and named him Rahul. The king hoped that Siddharth would become a great ruler.

One day Siddharth was driving through the street in his chariot, He saw an old man and then a sick man. The oldman could **hardly** walk. The sick man groaned in pain. Then he saw some people carrying a dead body, others were wailing and weeping at the loss of a dear one. Siddharth was very upset to see so much suffering and unhappiness. He was shocked. Then he saw an entirely different sight. A man in yellow robes was walking along the street. There was no trace of sadness on his **radiant** face, instead it shone with peace. He was a monk who had given up the world to escape the misery of life.

Siddharth wanted to find out why there was so much suffering in the world. He wanted to find out how men could be free of misery. He could find neither peace nor happiness in the life he was leading at the palace. One night Siddharth left his home, his wife and his little son. He went into the forest. He wanted to search for a way out of suffering and sorrow for all mankind. He meditated and got enlightenment. He became Lord Buddha, the enlightened one. Truth **was revealed** to him and he learnt all the secrets of life and the world.

He found out that the world was full of sorrow and unhappiness. The reason for it was greed and selfishness. To be free from suffering, we must be free from greed and desire. Desire is the **root** cause of all human suffering. He advocated the Middle Path and asked his followers to avoid the two extremes.

81. Which of the following sentences is true according to the passage ?

(a) Lord Buddha was born in Lumbini.
(b) The little boy was very happy with fine clothes, good food and toys.
(c) Siddharth divorced his first wife.
(d) Siddharth and Yashodhara had no children and so they were very unhappy

82. What was Siddharth interested in as a child ?

(a) He was interested in making new friends as he did not have any siblings.
(b) His interests were largely in studying and reading books.
(c) He was interested in the best of clothes and good toys .
(d) In spending time alone in deep thought.

83. Which of the following can be inferred about Siddharth ?

(A) Siddharth was different from other princes his age.
(B) Siddharth was a spoilt child.
(C) Siddharth was lonely because he did not have a mother.

(a) Only (A)
(b) Only (B)
(c) Only (C)
(d) Only (B) and (C)

84. What did the King wish for his son, Siddharth ?

(a) He wanted Siddharth to become a great ruler.
(b) He wished that Siddharth would not marry Yashodhara.
(c) He wished that Siddharth's son would take over his kingdom
(d) He wished that Siddharth would behave like the other princes.

85. What incident changed Siddharth's life forever ?

(a) His mother's death.

(b) The incident where he saw a monk free from the misery of life.

(c) The birth of his son

(d) His marriage to Yashodhara.

86. Why did Siddharth leave his home?

(a) He wanted to run away from his wife and son

(b) He did not want to become heir to his father's throne

(c) He was in search of a bigger kingdom

(d) He wanted to search for a way out of suffering and spend time in meditation.

87. According to Siddharth what was the reason for suffering and unhappiness in the world?

(a) The increased mumber of deaths

(b) The advocacy of the Middle Path.

(c) Human greed and selfishness

(d) People were unaware of the benefits of meditation.

88. What according to passage is the root cause for all human suffering ?

(A)Desire (B) Happiness

(C)Meditation

(a) Only (A)

(b) Only (B) and (C)

(c) Only (B)

(d) Only (C)

89. Why was Siddharth called the enlightened one ?

(a) He was smarter than all the princes of his age.,

(b) He was the King's son.

(c) Truth was revealed to him through meditation.

(d) He had a great ability to resist temptation

90. Why did Lord Buddha advocate the Middle Path ?

(a) He believed that it was the only way to eliminate poverty.

(b) He believed that it was the only way of obtaining true happiness.

(c) He was a staunch believer of living an extreme life.

(d) He did not have a happy life being a prince.

Directions (Q. 91-93): Choose the word which is most nearly the SAME in meaning as the word printed in bold as used in the passage.

91. Root

(a) Secondary (b) Common

(c) Burning (d) Main

92. Hardly

(a) Easily (b) Barely

(c) Suddenly (d) Carefully

93. Radiant

(a) Full (b) Happy

(c) Burning (d) Sober

Directions (Q. 94-95): Choose the word which is most OPPOSITE in meaning to the word printed in bold as used in the passage.

94. Revealed to

(a) Hidden from

(b) Exposed to

(c) Presented to

(d) Manifested from

95. Handsome

(a) Dear (b) Ugly

(c) Precious (d) Spoilt

Directions (Q. 96-100): Read each sentence to find out whether there is any grammatical error in it. The error, if any, will be in one part of the sentence. The number of that part is the answer.

96. If tomorrow is (a)/declared a holiday, (b)/we shall go (c)/to a picnic. (d)

97. My grandfather used (a)/ to goes (b)1 for a walk (c)/every morning. (d)

98. The blast from (a)/the explosion (b)/ knocked the factory worker (c)/to unconsciousness. (d)

99. Raju found it difficult 1)/to explain (b)/his final exam marks (c)/to his parents. (d)

100. My friend become (a)/terribly upset (b)/after losing her purse (c) /at the supermarket. (d)

Answer sheet

1.(d)	2.(b)	3.(b)	4.(a)	5.(d)	6.(d)	7.(c)	8.(c)	9.(a)	10.(d)
11.(a)	12.(d)	13.(c)	14.(d)	15.(a)	16.(b)	17.(d)	18.(b)	19.(a)	20.(a)
21.(b)	22.(c)	23.(d)	24.(c)	25.(d)	26.(d)	27.(a)	28.(a)	29.(a)	30.(d)
31.(a)	32.(b)	33.(b)	34.(c)	35.(a)	36.(d)	37.(d)	38.(d)	39.(c)	40.(b)
41.(b)	42.(d)	43.(d)	44.(a)	45.(c)	46.(a)	47.(a)	48.(d)	49.(d)	50.(d)
51.(c)	52.(d)	53.(a)	54.(c)	55.(d)	56.(b)	57.(c)	58.(d)	59.(c)	60.(d)
61.(b)	62.(a)	63.(c)	64.(d)	65.(d)	66.(b)	67.(d)	68.(b)	69.(d)	70.(d)
71.(d)	72.(b)	73.(d)	74.(d)	75.(d)	76.(b)	77.(a)	78.(d)	79.(d)	80.(b)
81.(a)	82.(d)	83.(a)	84.(a)	85.(b)	86.(d)	87.(c)	88.(a)	89.(c)	90.(b)
91.(d)	92.(b)	93.(b)	94.(a)	95.(b)	96.(d)	97.(b)	98.(a)	99.(b)	100.(a)

Solutions

1. **(d)** 'Alive' is different from the other given words. *Walk', 'Cry', 'Play'* and *'Study'* are various actions of human beings. *'Alive'* means *'living'; 'not dead'; 'in existence'; 'continuing'* etc.

2. **(b)** V I R T U A L

3. **(b)** Meaningful word : LIP

4. **(a)**

F L I P P E R

+1 –1 +1 –1 +1 –1 +1

G K J O Q D S

5. **(d)** The only child of Arun's mother means Arun himself. Therefore, the girl is the daughter cf Arun.

6. **(d)** As,

L I S P and P L A N

+1 +1 +1 +1   +1 +1 +1 +1

M J T Q   Q M B O

Therefore, F O R T

+1 +1 +1 +1

G P S U

7. **(c)** 'Artificial' is antonym of 'Natural'. Similarly, 'Private' is antonym of 'Public'.

8. **(c)** All other numbers are multiple of 7, but 65 is not.

$21 = 7 \times 3 : 91 = 7 \times 13;$

$77 = 7 \times 11 : 35 = 7 \times 5;$

But, $65 = 7 \times 9.28$

9. **(a)** Parul's rank is 19th from the bottom that means Parul's rank is (25 – 19 + 1 = 7th from the top. And Lata's rank is 13th from the top given).

+6

• Parul (7th)

–

–

• Vishal (10th)

–

–

• Lata (13th)

+12

10. **(d)** 1, 12, 123, 1234, 12345, 123456, 1234567

Hints for (11-15):

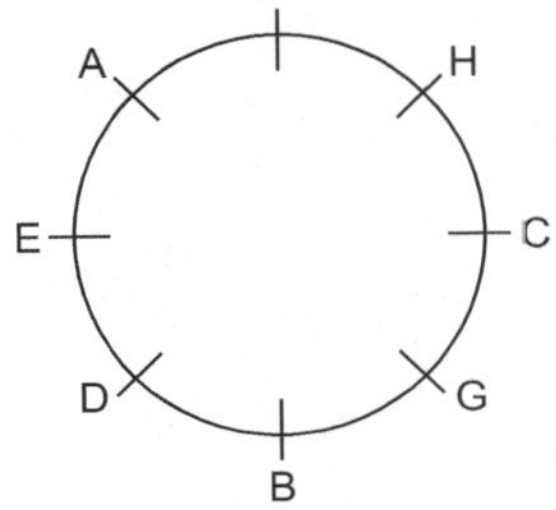

11. **(a)** D is to the immediate left of B.

12. **(d)** B and C are immediate neighbours of G.

13. **(c)** C is sitting just opposite to E. F is sitting just opposite to B. Similarly, A is sitting just opposite to G.

14. **(d)** Except in the pair BE, in all other pairs the first person is second to the left of the second person. B is second to the right of E.

15. **(a)**

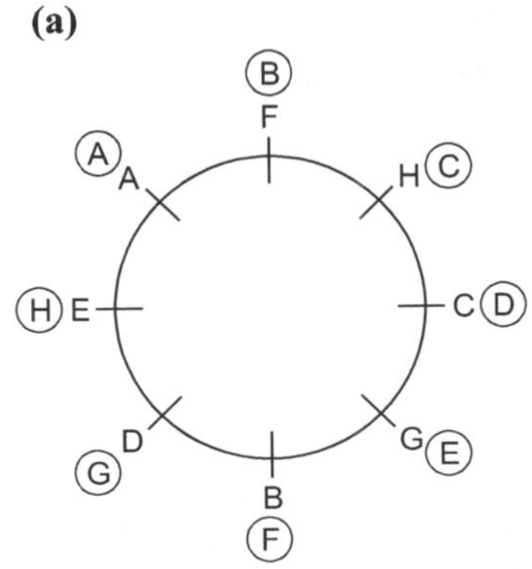

Hints for (16-20):

16. **(b)** All glasses are grills (A) → conversion → Some grills are glasses (I). Therefore, conclusion

II (At least some grills are glasses) follows.

17. **(d)** Both the premises are particular affirmative. No conclusion follows from the two particular premisses.

18. **(b)** All cabins are rooms + All rooms are buildings = A + A = A = All cabins are buildings. Therefore, conclusion II follows.

19. **(a)** All rings are necklaces + No necklace is a bracelet = A + E = E = No ring is a bracelet. Therefore, conclusion I follows.

20. **(a)** Some hands are muscles (I) → conversion → Some muscles are hands (I) + All hands are arms (A) = I + A = I = Some muscles are arms. Therefore, conclusion II follows.

Hints for (21-25):

Left → N O L Q R P M ← Right

21. **(b)** O is third to the left of R.

22. **(c)** N and M are sitting at the extreme ends of the line.

23. **(d)**

Left → N O L Q R P M ← Right

L M N O P Q R

24. **(c)** Q is sitting exactly in the middle of the row.

25. **(d)** Except LN, in all others the first person is to immediate right of the second person. L is second to the right of N.

26. **(d)**

2	8	%	9	5	6
↓	↓	↓	↓	↓	↓
R	N	A	X	H	S

Condition (iii) is applicable.

27. **(a)**

@	6	2	+	7	4
↓	↓	↓	↓	↓	↓
P	S	R	G	F	T

Condition (i) is applicable.

28. **(a)**

+	5	9	6	3	%
↓	↓	↓	↓	↓	↓
G	H	X	S	D	G

Condition (ii) is applicable.

29. **(a)** $A < L < T < R \leq H > K$

Conclusions:

I. H > L: True

II. K > T: Note True

30. **(d)** $P = N > D \geq G < B = J$

Conclusions:

I. G < P: True

II. G < J: True

31. **(a)** $F £ C \geq V = Z < X = U$

Conclusions:

I. V < U: True

II. Z < F: Note True

32. **(b)** $Q \leq E = I > N \geq R \geq S$

Conclusions:

I. E = S: Not True

II. S ≤ N:True

33. **(b)** Ninth to the right of the 20th from the right means (20 – 9) = 11th from the right, i.e., M.

34. **(c)** Such combination are @ F ! and + J ©

35. **(a)** As per the question, twelfth element from the left end is 9.

36. **(d)**

$$? = \frac{3325}{25} \times \frac{152}{16} = 133 \times 9.5 = 1263.5$$

37. **(d)** $\sqrt{3136} - \sqrt{1763} = \sqrt{?}$

$\Rightarrow$ $56 - 42 = \sqrt{?}$

$\Rightarrow$ $\sqrt{?} - 14$

$\therefore$? = 14 × 14 = 196

38. **(d)** $? = 5 + \frac{1}{5} + 2 + \frac{2}{15} + 3 + \frac{2}{3}$

$$= 10 + \frac{1}{5} + \frac{2}{15} + \frac{2}{3}$$

$$= 10 + \frac{3+2+10}{15} = 10 + \frac{15}{15}$$

$$= 10 + 1 = 11$$

39. **(c)** ? = –15 – 27 – 88 – 63 + 266 – 193 + 255 = 62

40. **(b)** $? = \frac{2525 \times 0.25 \times 7}{5} = 883.75$

41. **(b)** $? = \frac{14}{19} \times \frac{57}{70} \times \frac{20}{21} = \frac{4}{7}$

42. **(d)** $? = \frac{500 \times 32}{100} + \frac{50 \times 162}{100}$

$$= 160 + 81 = 241$$

43. **(d)** 45316 + 52131 – 65229 = ? + 15151

$\Rightarrow$ 32218 = ? + 15151

$\therefore$? = 32218 – 15151 = 17067

44. **(a)** $\sqrt{25 - 12 + 155 + 1} = \sqrt{169} = 13$

45. **(c)** $? = \dfrac{\frac{184 \times 4}{400 \times 23}}{100} = \frac{184 \times 4}{4 \times 23} = 8$

46. **(a)** $?^{4/3} \times ?^{5/3} = 32 \times 128$

$\Rightarrow$ $?^3 = 2^5 \times 2^7 = 2^{12}$

$\therefore$ $? = (212)^{1/2} = 2^4 = 16$

47. **(a)** Speed of bicyle

$= \frac{Distance}{Time} = \left(\frac{192}{8}\right)$

= 24 metres/ second

$\therefore$ Speed of man

$= \left(24 \times \frac{3}{4}\right)$ = 18 metres/second

$\therefore$ Required time

$= \frac{\text{Distance}}{\text{Speed}} = \left(\frac{54}{18}\right)$ = 3 seconds

48. **(d)** $\frac{4}{9} = 0.44; \frac{16}{13} = 0.46; \frac{5}{11}$

$= 0.45; \frac{13}{16} = 0.8125$

$\frac{7}{12} = 0.583$,

$\therefore$ Clearly, $\frac{13}{16} > \frac{7}{12} > \frac{6}{13} > \frac{5}{11} > \frac{4}{9}$

49. **(d)** Required number of items

$= \frac{1515 \times 7}{3} = 3535$

50. **(d)** 4800 < 4900

$\sqrt{4900} = 70$

51. **(c)** (a) The word STABLE has six distinct letters.

$\therefore$ Number of arrangements

$= {}^6P_6 = 6!$

= 6 × 5 × 4 × 3 × 2 × 1 = 720

(b) The word STILL has five

letters in which letter 'L'comes twice.

Number of arrangements

$= \frac{5!}{2} = 60$

(c) The word WATER has five distinct letters.

∴ Number of arrangements

$= 5! = 120$

(d) The word NOD has three distinct letters.

∴ Number of arrangements

$= 3! = 6$

(e) The word DARE has four distinct letters

∴ Number of arrangements

$= 4! = 24$

52. **(d)** CI for one year

$= \frac{\text{Principle} \times \text{Rate} \times \text{Time}}{100}$

$= \frac{1210 \times 6 \times 1}{100} = ₹\,72.6$

53. **(a)** 5pens + 8pencils = 31

On multiplying by 3, we have,

15 pens + 24 pencils

= 3 × 31 = Rs 93

54. **(c)** Required average

$= \frac{432 + 623 + 209 + 378 + 908 + 168}{6}$

$= \frac{2718}{6} = 453$

55. **(d)** Let the original fraction be $\frac{x}{y}$.

Now, according to the question,

$\frac{x \times 400}{y \times 300} = \frac{4}{15} \Leftrightarrow \frac{x}{y} = \frac{4}{15} \times \frac{3}{4} = \frac{1}{5}$

56. **(b)** Amount paid

= ₹ (40 × 18 + 55 × 8)

= ₹ (720 + 440) = ₹ 1160

57. **(c)** Third number $= \frac{265}{5} = 53$

∴ Smallest number = 49

Largest number = 57

∴ Required value

= 57 + 2 × 4 = 57 × 98 = 155

58. **(d)** Third number

= 5 × 34.4 – 2 × 46.5 – 2 × 18

= 172 – 93 – 36 = 43

59. **(c)** Second angle of parallelogram

= 180° – 45° = 135°

∴ Required value

= 135 + 2 × 45 = 135 + 90 = 225°

60. **(d)** Quicker Method:

$M_1D_1 = M_2D_2$

$\Rightarrow 9 \times 19 = 18 \times D_2$

$\Rightarrow D_2 = \frac{9 \times 19}{18} = 9.5$ days

61. **(b)** Required remainder

$= (46)^2 - (11)^3$

= 2116 – 1331 = 785

62. **(a)** Let Gloria's and Sara's present ages be $4x$ and $7x$ years respectively.

Two years ago,

$\frac{4x - 2}{7x - 2} = \frac{1}{2}$

∴ Sara's age three years hence

$= 7x + 3$

= 7 × 2 + 3 = 14 + 3 = 17 years

63. **(c)** The pattern of the number series is as given below:

800 ÷ 2 = 400

400 ÷ 2 = 200

200 ÷ 2 = 100

100 ÷ 2 = 50

50 ÷ 2 = 25

64. **(d)** The pattern of the number series is as given below:

2 + 1 × 11 = 2 + 11 = 13

13 + 2 × 11 = 13 + 22 = 35

35 + 3 × 11 = 35 + 33 = 68

68 + 4 × 11 = 68 + 44 = 112

112 + 5 × 11 = 112 + 55 =167

65. **(d)** The pattern of the number series is as given below:

$650 - 7^2 = 650 - 49 = 601$

$601 - 6^2 = 601 - 36 = 565$

$565 - 5^2 = 565 - 25 = 540$

$540 - 4^2 = 540 - 16 = 524$

$524 - 3^2 = 524 - 9 = 515$

66. **(b)** Total cost of plot

= ₹ 630 × 1800

∴ Booking amount

$= \frac{630 \times 1800 \times 45}{100} = ₹\,510300$

67. **(d)** Let the three consecutive even numbers A, B and C be x, $x + 2$ and $x + 4$ respectively. Now, according to the question,

$4x = 3(x + 4)$

$\Rightarrow 4x - 3x = 12$

$\Rightarrow x = 12$

$\therefore B = x + 2 = 12 + 2 = 14$

68. **(b)** Speed of bus

$= \frac{\text{Distance}}{\text{Time}} = \left(\frac{572}{13}\right) = 44$ kmph

69. **(d)** $(\text{Larger number})^2$

= 11570 – 5329 = 6241

∴ Larger number $= \sqrt{6241} = 79$

70. **(d)** $\text{SI} = \frac{13033 \times 13 \times 3}{100} = ₹\,5082.87$

$\text{CI} = 13033\left[\left(1 + \frac{13}{100}\right)^3 - 1\right]$

$= 13033 \times 0.44 = ₹\,5772.28$

∴ Difference

= ₹ (5772.28 – 5082.87) = ₹ 689.41

9 Practice Set

Reasoning

1. In a certain code, 'can you read this' is written as 'can @ read # this ★ you $' and 'how are you today' is written as are @ how # today ★ you $. How will 'can be true or' be written in the same code?

(a) or @ true # can ★ be $
(b) be S can ★ or # true @
(c) be @ can ★ or # true $
(d) be @ can # or ★ true $

2. Four of the following five are alike in a certain way and hence form a group. Which of the following does not belong to that group?

(a) 49 (b) 36
(c) 16 (d) 27

3. Which of the following will come in place of question mark (?) in the following series based on the English alphabetical order?

ZX US QO ? HF CA

(a) LJ (b) MK
(c) NL (d) KI

4. The positions of the first and the fourth letters of the word 'ABSENT' are interchanged. Similarly, the positions of the second and fifth letters and the third and sixth letters are interchanged. In the new arrangement thus formed, how many letters are there between the letter which is third from the right and the letter which is first from the left, in the English alphabetical series?

(a) Two (b) Four
(c) Five (d) Three

5. 'Bricks' are related to 'Walls' in the same way as 'Trees' are related to

(a) Roots (b) Branches
(c) Forest (d) Plants

6. How many meaningful English words can be formed with the letters 'OLBT' using all the letters but each letter only once in each word?

(a) One (b) Two
(c) Three (d) Four

Directions (Q. 7-8): *Read the following information carefully and answer the questions given below:*

Among J, K, L, M and N, each with a different weight, J is heavier than L but lighter than K. M is lighter than L. K is lighter than N.

7. Who among the following is the heaviest?

(a) N (b) K
(c) L (d) M

8. Who among the following is the second lightest?

(a) N (b) K
(c) L (d) M

9. If each vowel in the word BROUGHT is replaced by the next letter in the English alphabetical series and each consonant is replaced by the. previous letter in the English alphabetical series, and then the alphabets so formed are arranged in alphabetical order from left to right, which of the following will be the fourth from the left?

(a) V (b) P
(c) G (d) Q

10. How many such pairs of letters are there in the word DECAYS, each of which has as many letters between them in the word (in both forward and backward directions) as they have between them in the English alphabetical series?

(a) One (b) Two
(c) Three (d) None

Directions (Q. 11-15): *In each of the questions below, two statements are given followed by two conclusions numbered I and II. You have to take the two statements to be true even if they seem to be at variance with commonly known facts and then decide which of the given conclusions logically follows from the given statements disregarding commonly known facts. Give answer*

(a) if only conclusion I follows.
(b) if only conclusion II follows.
(c) if both conclusions I and II follow.
(d) if neither conclusion I nor conclusion II follows.

11. Statements: All animals are birds.
All birds are crows.

Conclusions:

I. All animals are crows.
II. All crows are birds.

12. Statements: Some tricks are magic.
All magics are true.

Conclusions:

I. There is a possibility that all tricks are true.
II. There is a possibility that all magics are tricks.

13. Statements: All e-mails are messages.
Some messages are letters.

Conclusions:

I. Atleast some letters are e-mails,

II. Some messages are not e-mails.

14. Statements: Some threads are cottons.

Some cottons are nylons.

Conclusions:

I. All nylons are threads.

II. Atleast some nylons are threads.

15. Statements: Some clocks are watches.

No clock is a wall.

Conclusions:

I. All walls are watches.

II. There is a possibility that all watches are clocks.

Directions (Q. 16-20): *The following questions are based on the following three-digit numbers given below:*

437 254 829 147 563

16. If all the digits of each of the numbers are arranged in ascending order within the number which number will be the second highest?

(a) 254 (b) 437

(c) 563 (d) 147

17. If all the three digits of each of the numbers are added, the total of which of the following numbers will be the second lowest?

(a) 437 (b) 829

(c) 147 (d) 254

18. If one is subtracted from the third digit of each of the numbers, how many numbers thus formed will be divisible by three?

(a) One (b) Two

(c) Three (d) None of these

19. Which of the following is the product of the third digit of the lowest number and the second digit of the second highest number?

(a) 42 (b) 21

(c) 35 (d) 24

20. If one is added to the second digit of each of the numbers, how many numbers will have more than one even digit (same or different)?

(a) One (b) Two

(c) Three (d) None of these

Directions (Q. 21-25): *Read the given information carefully and answer the given questions:*

J, K, L, M, N and O are sitting in a straight line facing North, not necessarily in the same order. J is sitting fourth to the left of O and O is not sitting at the extreme end of the line. M is sitting third to the right of N. K is not an immediate neighbour of J.

21. If all the persons are made to sit in alphabetical order from left to right, the positions of how many will remain unchanged as compared to their original seating position?

(a) One (b) Two

(c) Three (d) None of these

22. What is the position of N with respect to J?

(a) Second to the left

(b) Third to the right

(c) Second to the right

(d) Immediate right

23. How many people are sitting between L and O?

(a) One (b) Two

(c) Three (d) None of these

24. Which of the pairs represents the people sitting at the extreme ends of the line?

(a) JL (b) KJ

(c) ML (d) MJ

25. Four of the following five are alike in a certain way based on their seating positions in the above arrangement and so form a group. Which one does not belong to that group?

(a) LJ (b) OM

(c) KN (d) NJ

Directions (Q. 26-30): *Read the following arrangement carefully and answer the questions given below:*

T H A J K R B T A E M D G S O J K U M B D L U H Y A C M

26. How many such vowels are there in the above arrangement which are immediately preceded as well as immediately followed by a consonant?

(a) One

(b) Two

(c) Three

(d) More than four

27. If all the vowels are deleted from the above arrangement, which of the following will be thirteenth from the right end?

(a) K (b) G

(c) M (d) D

28. How many letters are there between the letter that is twentieth from the left and the letter that is sixteenth from the right end in the English alphabetical series?

(a) Five (b) Four

(c) Six (d) Three

29. Which of the following is fifth to the right of the seventeenth from the left end of the above arrangement?

(a) L (b) U

(c) H (d) D

30. If all the vowels are replaced by the next letter in the English alphabetical series, how many Bs will be there in the above arrangement?

(a) Three (b) Two

(c) Four (d) Five

Directions (Q. 31-35): *Read the given information carefully and answer the given questions*

A, B, C, D, E, F, G and H and sitting around a circular table facing the centre. G is sitting third to the right of F. H is not an immediate neighbour of F and G. A is sitting second to the right of H. B is sitting third to the right of C and C is not an immediate neighbour of G. D is not an immediate neighbour of H or C.

31. **Who is sitting exactly between H and A?**
(a) B (b) G
(c) C (d) E

32. **Four of the following five are alike in a certain way based on their seating positions in the above arrangement and so form a group. Which one does not belong to the group?**
(a) FD (b) HG
(c) FC (d) EA

33. **What will come in place of question mark (?) based upon the given seating arrangement?**
AF DG CA ?
(a) HC (b) DG
(c) GE (d) BD

34. **How many persons are sitting between B and E starting from B in anticlockwise direction?**
(a) Onc (b) Two
(c) Three (d) Four

35. **What is the position of E with respect to A?**
(a) Third to the left
(b) Third to the right
(c) Second to the left
(d) Second to the right

Quantitative Aptitude

Directions (Q. 36-50): *What should come in place of question mark (?) in the following questions ?*

36. **54671 – 14456 – 33466 = ?**
(a) 6794 (b) 6745
(c) 6748 (d) None of these

37. **5220 ÷ ? × 15 = 2175**
(a) 36 (b) 32
(c) 34 (d) 38

38. **7777 ÷ 35 = ?**
(a) 242.2 (b) 225.2
(c) 228.2 (d) 222.2

39. $\sqrt{1764}+22=\sqrt{?}$
(a) 8 (b) 4096
(c) 64 (d) $\sqrt{64}$

40. **12.5 × 3.2 × 8.8 = ?**
(a) 358 (b) 355
(c) 354 (d) None of these

41. $(16)^3 \times 4^3 \div 1024 = (4)^?$
(a) 3 (b) 4
(c) 5 (d) 6

42. **84 ÷ 12 ÷ 0.8 = ?**
(a) 7.75 (b) 9.85
(c) 8.75 (d) 10.15

43. **22% of 7 + 166.64 = 340**
(a) 782 (b) 786
(c) 784 (d) None of these

44. **5670 ÷ (28 × 13.5) = ?**
(a) 12 (b) 15
(c) 18 (d) 14

45. **(26.3 × 12 × 20) ÷ 3 + 125 = ?**
(a) 2229 (b) 2292
(c) 2223 (d) 2227

46. $? \times \sqrt{144} = 311 \times 24$
(a) 622 (b) 624
(c) 633 (d) 634

47. **45% of 816 – 23% of ? = 240.7**
(a) 525 (b) 540
(c) 550 (d) 560

48. **18.2% of 890 = ?**
(a) 168.91 (b) 163.98
(c) 165.91 (d) 161.98

49. **122 × 252 – 12234 = ?**
(a) 18150 (b) 18510
(c) 18520 (d) 18501

50. $\frac{3}{4}$ **of** $\frac{1}{2}$ **of** $\frac{2}{5}$ **of 5020 = ?**
(a) 758 (b) 752
(c) 757 (d) 753

51. **A carbon-copy centre requires 18 bundles of paper for 5 days. How many bundles will it require for 65 days?**
(a) 233 (b) 236
(c) 238 (d) 234

52. **The average age of Nitika and Kruti is 21 years. The ratio of their ages is 4 : 3. What is Kruti's age?**
(a) 18 years (b) 24 years
(c) 26 years (d) 16 years

53. **Sunil sold an antique flower vase to Vinay at 12% more than the cost price. If Vinay paid ₹ 17,696 for the vase, what was its original cost price?**
(a) ₹ 15,500 (b) ₹ 15,820
(c) ₹ 15,800 (d) ₹ 15,520

54. **If the fractions** $\frac{4}{9}, \frac{7}{12}, \frac{3}{7}, \frac{12}{17}$ **and** $\frac{1}{2}$ **are arranged in descending order of their values, which one will be the third?**
(a) $\frac{7}{12}$ (b) $\frac{3}{7}$
(c) $\frac{4}{9}$ (d) $\frac{1}{2}$

55. **Find the average of the following set of scores:**
34, 89, 37, 144, 78, 240, 128, 98
(a) 106 (b) 108
(c) 104 (d) 102

56. **What would be the compound interest obtained on an amount of ₹ 8,800 at the rate of 16 percent after 2 years?**
(a) ₹ 3,041.25 (b) ₹ 3,014.28
(c) ₹ 3,044.69 (d) ₹ 3,041.28

57. **The sum of 3 5% of a number and 12% of the same number is 3055. What is the value of 72% of that number?**
(a) 4685 (b) 4680
(c) 4675 (d) 4670

58. **What is the least number that can be added to 3500 to make it a perfect square?**
(a) 200 (b) 169
(c) 100 (d) 25

59. **12 women alone can complete a piece of work in 5 days. whereas 3 women and 9 children together can complete the same piece of work in 10 days. In how many days can 36 children complete the same piece of work?**
(a) 10 days (b) 2 days
(c) 5 days (d) 8 days

60. **The cost of 5 sharpeners and 14 pencils is ₹ 56. What would be**

the cost of 15 sharpeners and 42 pencils?

(a) ₹ 112 (b) ₹ 224
(c) ₹ 186 (d) None of these

61. The average of four consecutive even numbers P. Q, R and S is 55. What is the product of Q and S?

(a) 3123 (b) 3135
(c) 3132 (d) 3125

62. A truck covers a distance of 420 km in a certain amount of time at a speed of 70 km/hr. What is the average speed of a bike that travels a distance of 36 km less than the truck in the same time?

(a) 62 km/hr (b) 64 km/hr
(c) 66 km/hr (d) 68 km/hr

63. What is the area of the circle whose circumference is 264 cm?

(a) 5544 sq cm (b) 5454 sq cm
(c) 5540 sq cm (d) 5548 sq cm

64. Kiran sold an item for ₹ 8,160 and incurred a loss of 15%. At what price should she have sold the item to have a profit of 25%?

(a) ₹ 12,200
(b) ₹ 12,300
(c) ₹ 13,000
(d) None of these

65. What will come in place of both question marks (?) in the following question?

$$\frac{(?)^{1.3}}{45} = \frac{75}{(?)^{1.7}}$$

(a) 25 (b) –15
(c) –25 (d) None of these

66. There are 360 students in a class, out of which 35% are day scholars. How many day scholars are there in the class?

(a) 128 (b) 122
(c) 124 (d) 126

67. In an examination it is required to obtain 55% of the aggregate marks to pass.. A student got 340 marks and was declared failed by 5% marks. What is the maximum aggregate marks a student can get?

(a) 650 (b) 660
(c) 680 (d) None of these

Directions (Q. 68-70): *What should come in place of question mark(?) in the following number series?*

68. 9 41 57 65 69 ?

(a) 73 (b) 75
(c) 72 (d) None of these

69. 7 10 16 25 37 ?

(a) 55 (b) 52
(c) 51 (d) 57

70. 430 422 395 331 ?

(a) 208 (b) 210
(c) 209 (d) 206

English Language

Directions (Q. 71-85): *Read the following carefully and answer the questions given below it. Certain words are printed in bold to help you locate them while answering some of the questions.*

Amrutananda was a well-known and rich landlord in his village. He and his wife were both **cunning** and extremely sly. They made a lot of money by cheating and ill-treating their labcurers who worked in their fields.

One day, a young man named Manikya canu- to Amrutananda, asking for work. Amrutananda was pleasantly surprised. No one ever wanted to work for him because of his reputation, and here was someone walking right into his house! Manikya's next few words made him even happier. Manikya said, 'I will work for you for free. You need not pay me a salary, only give me a place to sleep, two sets of clothes and two meals a day.' Amrutananda was filled with joy when he heard this and was about to agree when Manikya added. 'I have only one condition: I will tell you the truth always, but one day of the year I will lie to you.'

Amrutananda, who lied happily every day of the year, agreed to this odd condition. So Manikya joined him. He was a wonderful worker — hard working and trustworthy. He was very honest and soon became Amrutananda's right hand man. A year went by, and because of Manikya's hard work. Amrutananda had an excellent harvest. He and his wife Mandakini decided to have a big feast to celebrate. They invited all their relatives and friends, who came from across the village and outside to participate in this celebration. Everyone was looking forward to the delicious feast being planned. On the morning of the feast, Amrutananda decided he would also give away some gifts to his relatives, just so that he could show off. So he set off for the market in his cart. As soon as he was out of sight, Manikya went running to his mistress, Mandakini. He wept loudly and beat his chest. Then he fell on the floor sobbing, and announced. The master is dead. The cart **overturned** on the road. Our master has been flattened like a chapatti.' As soon as Amrutananda's wife and relatives heard this, they started wailing. Manikya rushed nut saying he would bring back the body, while everyone started preparing loriiie last rites.

Manikya now went running to his master and said "Master! Your wife is dead. My kind, loving mistress is dead. A cobra bit her and she fell to the ground, as blue as the spring sky." Amrutananda was stunned. His beloved Mandakini, his partner in all his schemes, was dead! He couldn't believe it. He rushed back home shouting her name.

Mandakini was weeping loudly, sitting in the courtyard. When she saw her husband run in, she stopped mid-wail, and Amrutananda too stood open-mouthed and speechless. Then they fell into each other's arms, unable to believe their eyes,

At once they turned to Manikya, "What is the meaning of this, Manikya?' his master demanded in a stern voice. Manikya smiled, "Remember my condition, that I would lie only once in a year? Well, I choose today. You see what lies can do? They nearly destroyed your life. Now think about what happens to the people you lie to everyday." Saying this he walked out. leaving behind a stunned and ashamed landlord.

71. Why didn't anyone want to work for Amrutananda?

(a) He always ill-treated and cheated his labourers.
(b) He wanted people to work for him for free.
(c) He never paid their dues on time.
(d) He hardly made them work.

72. Why did Manikya volunteer to work for Amrutananda for free?

(a) His food and shelter would be taken care of.
(b) He was fond of Amrutananda.
(c) He had heard many stories of Amrutananda's generosity.
(d) He wanted to teach Amrutananda a lesson.

73. What was Manikya's intention behind lying to his master?

A. He wanted to draw some attention to himself.
B. He was jealous of his master.
C. He wanted to cause trouble during the celebration.

(a) Only A (b) Only B and C
(c) Only C (d) None of these

74. What could be the moral of this story?

(a) Lying destroys lives
(b) Never employ anyone for free
(c) Always think before you cry
(d) Never show off your wealth

75. Which of the following statements is false as inferred from the passage?

(a) Amrutananda's wife was bitten by a cobra snake.
(b) Manikya was a very hardworking and trustworthy servant.
(c) Amrutananda was known for his shrewdness.
(d) Manikya chose to work for Amrutananda for free.

76. On what condition did Manikya agree to stay and work for Amrutananda?

(a) He would be treated like a family member.
(b) He would be allowed to lie on any one day in the year.
(c) He would leave the day his master, Amrutananda, lied to him.
(d) He would not accept any salary, either in kind or in cash from Amrutananda.

77. What important lesson did Amrutananda learn from Manikya?

(a) To never hire anyone for free
(b) That hard work is the only key to success
(c) To never show off his wealth
(d) None of these

78. Why did Amrutananda and his wife, Mandakini, wish to have a celebration?

(a) They wanted to treat Manikya to a feast for his effort in the successful harvest.
(b) They wanted to give Manikya a farewell.
(c) They received a rich harvest and so wanted to have a feast.
(d) They had abundant food and did not know what to do with it.

79. Why was Amrutananda's wife crying in the house?

(a) Nothing was going right during the feast.
(b) Her relatives could not make it for the celebration.
(c) Her best servant, Manikya, announced that he was quitting.
(d) She received news that her husband was dead.

80. Which of the following could be an appropriate title for the story?

(a) The Unfortunate Landlord
(b) Manikya the Wise Labourer
(c) The Evil Labourer
(d) The Glorious Feast

Directions Q. 81-83): *Choose the word which is most nearly the SAME in meaning as the word printed in bold as used in the passage.*

81. Overturned

(a) Slipped (b) Rotated
(c) Inverted (d) Accident

82. Odd

(a) Acceptable (b) Normal
(c) Favourable (d) Strange

83. Stunned

(a) Shocked (b) Confused
(c) Doubtful (d) Hesitant

Directions (Q. 84-85): *Choose the word which is most OPPOSITE in meaning of the word printed in bold as used in the passage.*

84. Cunning

(a) Pure (b) Sly
(c) Innocent (d) Harsh

85. Ashamed

(a) Happy (b) Proud
(c) Grateful (d) Peaceful

Directions (Q. 86-90): *Read each sentence to find out whether there is any grammatical error in it. The error, if any, will be in one part of the sentence. The number of that is the answer.*

86. (a) I noticed
(b) several reporters
(c) hovering around
(d) outside of the courtroom.

87. (a) My colleague had
(b) a hard time juggling
(c) the needs of her family
(d) with the demands of her job.

88. (a) Despite all
(b) the media hype,
(c) I found the film as
(d) very disappointing.

89. (a) Given that
(b) there was so less time,
(c) I think the students
(d) done a good job.

90. (a) The winner of
(b) the 'journalist of the year' award was not other than
(c) the editor's
(d) daughter.

Directions (Q. 91-95): *In each of the following sentences, an idiomatic expression or a proverb is highlighted. Select the alternative which best describes its use in the sentence.*

91. In the last budget, the government brought forward a new scheme of taxation.
(a) prioritised (b) displayed
(c) notified (d) introduced

92. The sales of the company are increasing by leaps and bounds.
(a) as proposed
(b) in calculated ways
(c) with extreme rapidity
(d) very slowly

93. The police made considerable headway in sorting the papers.
(a) progress (b) movement
(c) action (d) recognition

94. The kind old woman received the stranger with open arms.
(a) with her arms free
(b) with warmth
(c) with restraint
(d) with gratitude

95. My friend ran off helter-skelter down the slope.
(a) unknowingly
(b) with minimum speed
(c) purposefully
(d) hurriedly and in confusion

Directions (Q. 96-100): *Pick out the most effective word/words from the given words to fill in the blanks to make the sentence meaningfully complete in the context of the sentence.*

96. I have given myself _____ the end of September to finish my research.
(a) between (b) until
(c) to (d) for

97. It is _____ that John did not hurt himself when he fell off his motorbike.
(a) luckily
(b) fortunate
(c) understanding
(d) found

98. You must not look directly at the sun _____ the eclipse.
(a) during (b) in
(c) on (d) to

99. The mist was so thick, it was like walking _____ a cloud.
(a) beyond (b) by
(c) along (d) through

100. I told my friend that he could not catch a big fish _____ a small rod like the one he was carrying, but he insisted _____ trying.
(a) with, on (b) by, about
(c) with, about (d) by, on

Answer sheet

1.(d)	2.(d)	3.(a)	4.(d)	5.(c)	6.(a)	7.(a)	8.(c)	9.(b)	10.(b)
11.(a)	12.(d)	13.(c)	14.(d)	15.(d)	16.(b)	17.(c)	18.(a)	19.(a)	20.(b)
21.(a)	22.(c)	23.(b)	24.(d)	25.(d)	26.(d)	27.(d)	28.(b)	29.(a)	30.(d)
31.(c)	32.(d)	33.(c)	34.(b)	35.(a)	36.(d)	37.(a)	38.(d)	39.(b)	40.(d)
41.(b)	42.(c)	43.(d)	44.(b)	45.(a)	46.(a)	47.(c)	48.(d)	49.(b)	50.(d)
51.(d)	52.(a)	53.(c)	54.(d)	55.(a)	56.(d)	57.(b)	58.(c)	59.(c)	60.(d)
61.(c)	62.(b)	63.(a)	64.(d)	65.(d)	66.(d)	67.(c)	68.(d)	69.(b)	70.(d)
71.(a)	72.(d)	73.(d)	74.(a)	75.(c)	76.(b)	77.(d)	78.(c)	79.(a)	80.(b)
81.(c)	82.(d)	83.(a)	84.(c)	85.(b)	86.(d)	87.(c)	88.(c)	89.(b)	90.(c)
91.(d)	92.(c)	93.(a)	94.(b)	95.(d)	96.(b)	97.(b)	98.(a)	99.(d)	100.(a)

Solutions

1. **(d)** Words are arranged alphabetically and after each word a symbol is placed in this specific order @#★$ as given below: As, can you read this ⇒ are @ read # this ★ you $ and how are you today ⇒ are @ how # today ★ you $ Similarly, can be true or ⇒ be @ can # or ★ true $

2. **(d)** Except 27 all other numbers are squares of integers. $49 = 7^2$; $36 = 6^2$; $16 = 4^2$; $25 = 5^2$

But, $27 = 3^3$

3. **(a)** The series is going in reverse alphabetical order. In every pair there is a gap of one letter. Then after following rule follows between the consecutive pairs of letters:

$Z \xrightarrow{-5} U \xrightarrow{-5} Q \xrightarrow{-5}$

$L \xrightarrow{-4} H \xrightarrow{-5} C$

$X \xrightarrow{-5} S \xrightarrow{-4} O \xrightarrow{-5}$

$J \xrightarrow{-4} F \xrightarrow{-5} A$

4. **(d)** The new arrangement is as: ENTABS.

Third from right is A and first from left is E. There are three letters between A and E in the English alphabetical order.

5. **(c)** The first is a constituent of the second one.

6. **(a)** Bolt

(7-8): According to weight

N > K > J > L > M

7. **(a)** N is the heaviest.

8. **(c)** L is the second lightest.

9. **(b)**

B	R	O	U	G	H	T
↓	↓	↓	↓	↓	↓	↓
A	Q	P	V	F	G	S

Alphabetically → A F G P Q S V

Fourth from the left is P.

10. **(b)** D E C A Y S

11. **(a)** All animal are birds + All birds are crows = A + A = A = All animals are cows. Hence conclusion I follows. Again, All birds are crows (A) → conversion → Some crows are birds (I). Hence conclusion II does not follow.

12. **(d)** Some tricks are magic + All magics are true = I + A = I = Some tricks are true. Hence conclusion I does not follow. Clearly, neither conclusion I nor conclusion II follows.

13. **(c)** All e-mails are messages+Some messages are letters = A + I = No conclusion.

14. **(d)** Both the given premises are particular affirmative (I-type). We know that I-type of statements cannot be combined. Hence, no conclusion follows from the two particular premises.

15. **(d)** Some clocks are watches (I) → conversion → Some watches are clocks (I) + No clock is a wall (E) = I + E = O = Some watches are not walls.

16. **(b)** After rearrangement the numbers will become

347 245 289 147 356

The second highest is 347, ie 437

17. **(c)** Some of digits of the numbers are

14 11 19 12 14

Second lowest total is 12, which is of 147.

18. **(a)** After subtracting I from the third digit of each number.

436 253 828 146 562

Only 828 is divisible by 3.

19. **(a)** Lowest number is 147.

It's third digit is 7

Second highest number is 563

Its second digit is 6.

Their product is 7 × 6 = 42

20. **(b)** After adding 1 to the second digit of each

447 264 839 157 573

447 and 264 have more than one even digit.

Hints for (21-25):

Left → J L N K O M ← Right

21. **(a)** Original Position → J L N K O M

Position in alphabetical order → J K L M N O

Position of J remains unchanged.

22. **(c)** N is second to the right of J.

23. **(b)** N and K

24. **(d)** J and M

25. **(d)** All others are seated consecutively

26. **(d)** A, O, U, U and A

27. **(d)** T H J K R B T M D G S J K M B D L H Y C M

28. **(b)** Twentieth from the left end is B.

Sixteenth from the right end is G. Four letters C, D, E and F are there between them in the English alphabetical series.

29. **(a)** 5th to the right of 17th from left =(17 + 5) = 22nd from left There are 28 elements in the given series. Hence the required lettler = (28 – 22 + 1) = 7th from the right, ie L.

30. **(d)** Count As and Bs in the above series. There are three As and two Bs.

Hints for (31-35):

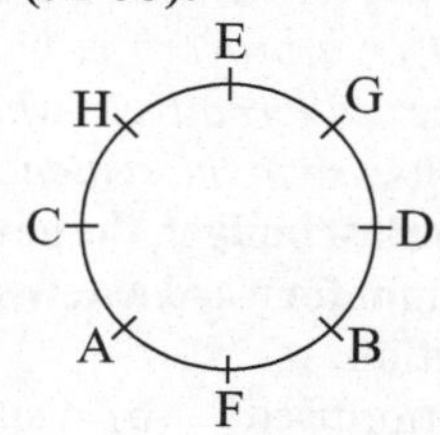

31. **(c)** C is sitting exactly between H and A

32. **(d)** Except in EA, in all others only one person is sitting between the two persons

33. **(c)** $A \xrightarrow{+3} D \xrightarrow{+4} C \xrightarrow{+5} G$

$F \xrightarrow{+3} G \xrightarrow{+4} A \xrightarrow{+5} E$

34. **(b)** Two persons – D and C – are sitting between B and E when we count in anticlockwise direction from B.

35. **(a)** E is third to the left of A.

36. **(d)** 54671 – (14456 + 33466)

54671 – 47922 = 6749

37. **(a)** $\frac{5220 \times 15}{?} = 2175$

$\therefore \; ? = \frac{5220 \times 15}{2175} = 36$

38. **(d)** 7777 ÷ 35 = 222.2

39. **(b)** $\sqrt{1764} + 22 = \sqrt{?}$

$42 + 22 = \sqrt{?}$

$? = 64^2 = 4096$

40. **(d)** 12.5 × 3.2 × 8.8 = 352

41. **(b)** $16^3 \times 4^3 \div 1024 = (4)^?$

$\frac{16 \times 16 \times 16 \times 4 \times 4 \times 4}{1024} = (4)^?$

$4 \times 4 \times 4 \times 4 = (4)^?$

$(4)^4 = 4^?$

42. **(c)** 84 ÷ 12 ÷ 0.8

$= \frac{84}{12} \div 0.8 = ?$

$= \frac{7}{8} = \frac{70}{8} = 8.75$

43. (d) 22% of ? + 166.64 = 340

or 0.22 × ? + 166.64 = 340

or 0.22 × ? = 340 – 166.64

or 0.22 × ? = 173.66

$\therefore\ ? = \frac{173.66}{0.22} = 788$

44. (b) 5670 ÷ (28 × 13.5)

= 5670 ÷ 378 = 15

45. (a) (26.3 × 12 × 20) ÷ 3 + 125

$= \frac{6312}{3} + 125 = 2229$

46. (a) $? \times \sqrt{144} = 311 \times 24$

or, ? × 12 = 311 × 24

$\therefore\ ? = 311 \times \frac{24}{12} = 622$

47. (c) 45% of 816 – 23% of ? = 240.7

0.45 × 816 – 0.23 × ? = 240.7

367.2 – 0.23 × ? = 240.7

or, 0.23 × ? = 367.2 – 240.7

$\therefore\ ? = \frac{126.5}{23} = 550$

48. (d) $\frac{18.2}{100} \times 890 = 161.98$

49. (b) 122 × 252 – 12234

or, 30744 – 12234 = 18510

50. (d) $\frac{3}{4} \times \frac{1}{2} \times \frac{2}{5} \times 5020 = 753$

51. (d) Bundles required for 5 days

= 18

Bundles required for 65 days

$= \frac{18}{5} \times 65 = 234$

52. (a) Sum of the ages of Nitika and Kruti

= 21 × 2 = 42 years

Ratio of Nitika : Kruti = 4 : 3

Kruti's age $= \frac{3}{7} \times 42 = 18$

53. (c) Let the original cost price be ₹ x.

Selling Price

$= x\left(\frac{100+12}{100}\right) = \frac{112}{100}x = 1.12x$

Now, according to the question

$1.12x = 17696$

$\therefore\ x = \frac{17696}{1.12} = 15800$

54. (d) Fractions in descending order are

$\left[\frac{4}{9} = 0.44; \frac{7}{12} = 0.58; \frac{3}{7} = 0.42; \frac{12}{17} = 0.70; \frac{1}{2} = 0.50\right]$

55. (a) Sum of scores = 848

No. of score = 8

Average $= \frac{848}{8} = 106$

56. (d) Amount after 2 years at 16 p.c.p.a. on ₹ 8800 compounded annually

= 8800 × 1.16 × 1.16 = 11841.28

Compound interest = 11841.28 – 8800 = 3041.28

57. (b) Let the number be x.

35% of x + 12% of x – 3055

or 47% of x = 3055

$\therefore$ 72% of $x = \frac{3055}{47} \times 72 = 4680$

58. (c) $\sqrt{3500}$

Hence, the next perfect square will be the square of 60 ie, 3600. add 100 to 3500 to make it perfect square.

59. (c) 12 women complete the work in 5 days.

So, 1 woman in 1 day works

$= \frac{1}{5 \times 12} = \frac{1}{60}$

3 women in 10 days work $= \frac{3 \times 10}{60} = \frac{1}{2}$

So, 9 children complete $\frac{1}{2}$ work in 10 days.

1 child in 1 day $= \frac{1}{2 \times 10 \times 9}$

36 children in 1 day $= \frac{36}{2 \times 10 \times 9} = \frac{1}{5}$

So, 36 children will complete the work in 5 days.

60. (d) Let the cost of 1 sharpener be S and that of 1 pencil be P.

Now, according to the question,

5S + 14P = 56

Multiplying the equation by 3, we get

15S + 42P = 168

61. (c) Average of consecutive even numbers is 55.

Let the even numbers be x, $x + 2$, $x + 4$ and $x + 6$

Now, according to the question,

$\frac{x + x + 2 + x + 4 + x + 6}{4} = 55$

or, $\frac{4x + 12}{4} = 55$

or, $4x + 12 = 4 \times 55 = 220$

or, $4x = 220 - 12 = 208$

or, $x = \frac{208}{4} = 52$

so, P, Q, R and S would be 52, 54, 56 and 58 respectively.

Now, Q × S = 54 × 58 = 3132

66. (d) Required number of day scholars = 35% of 360 = 126

67. (c) The student was declared failed by 5% marks. It means he got 50% marks in aggregate.

5.0% of total marks = 340

Total marks = 680

68. (d)

9 41 57 65 69 71

+32 +16 +8 +4 +2

69. (b)

7 10 16 25 37 52

+3 +6 +9 +12 +15

70. (d) 430 422 395 331 206

$-(2)^3$ $-(3)^3$ $-(4)^3$ $-(5)^3$

10 Practice Set

Reasoning

1. **Ramesh correctly remembers that his friend Raju started working after April but before September. Vinod correctly remembers that Raju did not have a job before May. Madan correctly remembers that the month Raju started working had 30 days. In which month of the year did Raju definitely start working?**
(a) July
(b) August
(c) September
(d) June

2. **If it is possible to make only one meaningful word from the fourth, sixth, ninth and eleventh letters of the word CONTAMINATE, then the second letter from the left is your answer. If no such word can be formed then your answer is X and if more than one such word can be formed your answer is Y.**
(a) X (b) T
(c) M (d) Y

3. **Starting from Point X, Joy walked 15 metres towards West. He turned left and walked 20 metres. He again turned left and walked 15 metres. After which he turned right and walked for another 12 metres. How far is Joy from point X if he is facing North at present?**
(a) 27 m (b) 35 m
(c) 32 m (d) 42 m

4. **'2' is subtracted from each odd digit and ' 1' is added to each even digit in the number 7652348. Which of the following will be the sum of the second digit from the right and the third digit from the left of the new number thus formed?**
(a) 10 (b) 8
(c) 4 (d) 6

5. **Which of the following will come in place of the question mark?**
ZX YV WS ? PJ
(a) TO (b) TN
(c) UO (d) SO

6. **In a class of 40 children, Saurabh's rank is eighth from the top. Mamta is five ranks below Saurabh. What is Mamta's rank from the bottom?**
(a) 27th (b) 29th
(c) 28th (d) 26th

7. **Four of the following five are alike in a certain way and so form a group. Which is the one that does not belong to the group?**
(a) Iron (b) Copper
(c) Ceramic (d) Silver

8. **In a certain code 'RAISE' is coded as 'SBJTF' and 'LEASE' is coded as 'MFBTF'. How will 'FLOWN' be coded in the same code?**
(a) PXMGO (b) GXMPO
(c) GMPXO (d) PXOGM

9. **How many such pairs of letters are there in the word PRODUCTION, each of which has as many letters between them in the word (in both forward and backward directions) as they have between them in the English alphabetical series?**
(a) None (b) One
(c) Two (d) Three

10. **How many meaningful English words can be formed with the letters ABKC using each letter only once in each word? (All the four letters are to be used in the word.)**
(a) None (b) One
(c) Two (d) Three

Directions (Q. 11-15): *Read the following information carefully and answer the questions given below:*

A, B, C, D, P, Q, R and S are sitting around a circle facing the centre. P is third to the left of A and R is second to the right of A. Q is not an immediate neighbour of either P or R. C sits third to the right of B and S sits exactly between C and R.

11. **Who is sitting on the immediate right of A?**
(a) Q (b) R
(c) D (d) B

12. **What is S's position with respect to D?**
(a) Third to the left
(b) Third to the right
(c) Second to the left
(d) Immediate right

13. **Four of the following five are similar in a certain way based on their positions in the seating arrangement and so form a group. Which of the following does not belong to that group?**
(a) QD (b) CS
(c) AB (d) SR

14. **Who sits between P and S?**
(a) D (b) R
(c) Q (d) C

15. **How many persons sit between A and P when counted in anticlockwise direction from A?**
(a) One (b) Two
(c) Three (d) Four

Directions (16-20): *Read the following arrangement carefully and answer the questions given below*

2 4 8 5 6 β 1 3 @ 6 4 5 2 # 9 7 1 © 3 €

16. How many pairs of numbers are there in the series highlighted in bold in the above arrangement each of which has as many numbers between them (in both forward and backward directions) as they have between them in the numerical series?
(a) One (b) Two
(c) Three (d) Four

17. If all the symbols are dropped from the above arrangement, which of the following will be the twelfth from the right end of the above arrangement?
(a) 2 (b) 5
(c) 3 (d) 7

18. Which of the following digit/ symbol is second to the right of the tenth from the left end?
(a) @ (b) 4
(c) 3 (d) 5

19. How many symbols are there in the above arrangement, each of which is immediately followed by a perfect square? (1 is also a perfect square.)
(a) One (b) Two
(c) Three (d) Four

20. How many perfect squares are there in the above arrangement, each of which is immediately preceded by an even number? (1 is also a perfect square.)
(a) None (b) One
(c) Two (d) Three

Directions (Q. 21-25): *In each of the questions below are given three statements followed by two conclusions numbered I and II. You have to take the three given statements to be true even if they seem to be at variance with commonly known facts and then decide which of the given conclusions logically follows from the three statements disregarding commonly known facts.* Give answer

(a) if only conclusion I follows.
(b) if only conclusion II follows.
(c) if either conclusion I or conclusion II follows.
(d) if neither conclusion I nor conclusion II follows

21. Statements: Some black are blue.
No blue are white.
Some white which are black are grey.

Conclusions:
I. Some grey are blue.
II. Some white are not black.

22. Statements: Some actors are dancers.
All dancers are musicians.
No musicians are painters.

Conclusions:
I. Some painters are actors.
II. No painters are dancers.

23. Statements: All villages are cities.
All cities are countries.
All countries are towns.

Conclusions:
I. All towns are villages.
II. Some cities are not towns.

24. Statements: Some books are poetry.
All poetry is philosophy.
Some philosophy is psychology.

Conclusions:
I. Some books are philosophy.
II Some psychology is not philosophy.

25. Statements: All children are students.
Some students are adults.
All adults are workers.

Conclusions:
I. Some students are workers.
II. All children are adults.

Directions (Q. 26-30): *The following questions are based on the five three-digit numbers given below:*

374 659 821 945 247

26. In each number. 2 is added to the middle digit and then the first 2 digits are interchanged. Which number will be the largest?
(a) 659 (b) 945
(c) 374 (d) 247

27. If 1 is subtracted from the last digit of each of the numbers, how many numbers thus formed will be divisible by two?
(a) None (b) One
(c) Two (d) Four

28. If in each number, the first and the second digits are interchanged, which of the following will be the third lowest number?
(a) 374 (b) 659
(c) 821 (d) 945

29. If in each number, all the three digits are arranged in ascending order within the number, which of the following will be the second highest number?
(a) 374 (b) 659
(c) 821 (d) 945

30. If one is subtracted from the last digit of each of the numbers, in how many numbers thus formed will the last digit be a perfect square? (1 is a also a perfect square.)
(a) None (b) One
(c) Two (d) Three

Directions (Q. 31-35): *Study the information carefully and answer the given questions:*

A, D, E, F, H, J and K are sitting in a straight line facing North, not necessarily in the same order.

(a) D sits fourth to the right of A.
(b) E is at the extreme left end of the line. There are five persons between E and K.
(c) J sits third to the left of K, F is not an immediate neighbour of D.

31. How many persons sit between A and H?
(a) One (b) Two
(c) Three (d) Four

32. Which of the following represents the person sitting exactly in the middle of the line?
(a) J (b) F
(c) H (d) A

33. Four of the following are alike in a certain way based on their

seating positions in the above arrangement and so form a group. Which pair does not belong to that group?

(a) AF (b) JH
(c) EA (d) FH

34. What is the position of F with respect to H?

(a) Second to the right
(b) Immediatly to the right
(c) Immediatly to the left
(d) Second to the left

35. If the seating arrangement (from left to right) is taken as English alphabets, how many such pairs of letters are there in the arrangement each of which has as many letters between them (in both forward and backward directions) in the arrangement as they have between them in the English alphabetical series?

(a) None (b) One
(c) Two (d) Three

Quantitative Aptitude

Directions (Q. 36-51): *What should come in place of question mark(?) in the following questions?*

36. $45 \times 24 \div 12 - 35 = ? - 153$

(a) 208 (b) 218
(c) 145 (d) 155

37. $(213 - 345) \div 8 = ? \div (-4)$

(a) 25 (b) –66
(c) –4.125 (d) 66

38. $34.36 - 45.67 + 86.56 = ? + 37.96$

(a) 31.29 (b) 32.29
(c) 38.49 (d) None of these

39. $\frac{11}{17} - \frac{9}{34} + \frac{7}{17} = ?$

(a) $\frac{15}{17}$ (b) $\frac{25}{34}$
(c) $\frac{27}{34}$ (d) $\frac{12}{17}$

40. $\sqrt{12 \times 145 \div 6 + 34} = ?$

(a) –18 (b) $(324)^2$
(c) 18 (d) $\sqrt{18}$

41. $(5 \times 6)^2 \times (9 \times 6) \div (4 \times 6) = ?$

(a) 2055 (b) 2505
(c) 2205 (d) 2025

42. $431.44 - 44.63 = ? - 62.65$

(a) 450.46 (b) 468.56
(c) 449.46 (d) 439.56

43. $\frac{3}{11}$ of 77% of 800 = ?

(a) 148 (b) 168
(c) 218 (d) 228

44. $(13)^2 - (5)^2 - \sqrt{676} + 7 = (?)^2$

(a) 10 (b) 20
(c) $\sqrt{5}$ (d) $5\sqrt{5}$

45. ?% of $350 - (6)^2 = 48$

(a) 12 (b) 24
(c) 42 (d) 54

46. $1\frac{2}{7} + 1\frac{1}{14} - 1\frac{3}{28} = ?$

(a) $1\frac{1}{4}$ (b) $1\frac{2}{7}$
(c) $1\frac{1}{7}$ (d) $1\frac{3}{4}$

47. $3353 - 7855 + 9498 = ? + 2233$

(a) 2673 (b) 2763
(c) 3534 (d) 3453

48. $(54.4 \times 5 \times 8) \div 16 + 8 = (?)^2$

(a) $(12)^2$ (b) $\sqrt{12}$
(c) $2\sqrt{12}$ (d) 12

49. $\frac{7}{15}$ of $\frac{5}{12}$ of 540 = ?

(a) 160 (b) 150
(c) 210 (d) 105

50. $95 \times 5 \div 10 + 3 = (?)^2$

(a) $\sqrt{7}$ (b) –7
(c) 28 (d) $(49)^2$

51. $2\frac{1}{3}$ of $1\frac{1}{4}$ of (?) = 280

(a) 116 (b) 124
(c) 48 (d) 96

52. The average speed of a tractor is two-fifths the average speed of a car. The car covers 450 km in 6 hours. How much distance will the tractor cover in 8 hours?

(a) 210 km (b) 240 km
(c) 420 km (d) 480 km

53. The area of a square is four times the area of a rectangle. The length of the rectangle is 25 cm and its breadth is one cm less than one-fifth of its length. What is the perimeter of the square?

(a) 40 cm (b) 60 cm
(c) 160 cm (d) None of these

54. What value will be obtained if the square of 22 is subtracted from the cube of 12?

(a) 1244 (b) 1344
(c) 1454 (d) 1354

55. The marks of six boys in a group are 48,59,87,37,78 and 57. What are the average marks of all six boys?

(a) 62 (b) 64
(c) 61 (d) 63

56. The ratio of the present ages of Tarun and Varun is 3 : 7. After 4 years Varun's age will be 39 years. What was Tarun's age 4 years ago?

(a) 12 years (b) 13 years
(c) 19 years (d) None of these

57. The sum of five consecutive even numbers is equal to 170. What is the sum of the second largest number and the square of the smallest number amongst them together?

(a) 940 (b) 932
(c) 938 (d) None of these

58. How many sacks are required for filling 1026 kg rice if each sack is filled with 114 kg of rice?

(a) 19 (b) 15
(c) 7 (d) 9

59. Ravi consistently runs 350 metres every day except on Tuesdays when he runs 500 metres. How many kilometres will he run in two weeks? (In this question the week starts from Monday.)

(a) 4.5 km (b) 4.8 km
(c) 5.2 km (d) 5.4 km

60. The simple interest accrued in 3 years on a principal of ₹ 25,000 is three-twentieths the principal. What is the rate of simple interest pcpa?

(a) 5 (b) 4
(c) 6 (d) 3

61. **Sumit purchased an item for ₹ 6,500 and sold it at a gain of 24%. From that amount he purchased another item and sold it at a loss of 20%. What is his overall gain/loss?**
(a) Lossof ₹ 42
(b) Gain of ₹ 42
(c) Loss of ₹ 52
(d) Neither gain nor loss

62. **What will come in place of both question marks (?) in the following questions?**

$$\frac{(?)^{3/5}}{33} = \frac{3}{(?)^{2/5}}$$

(a) $(99)^2$ (b) $\sqrt{93}$
(c) $3\sqrt{11}$ (d) 99

63. **What is seventy-four per cent of five-eighths of 1200?**
(a) 555 (b) 565
(c) 445 (d) 455

64. **Mani's monthly income is three-fourths of Rakhi's monthly income. Rakhi's monthly income is ₹ 38,000. What is Mani's annual income?**
(a) ₹ 4.32 lakh (b) ₹ 3.42 lakh
(c) ₹ 3.22 lakh (d) ₹ 4.22 lakh

65. **The length of a rectangle is 24 cm, which is 10 cm more than the diameter of a circle. What is the area of the circle?**
(a) 210 sq cm (b) 176 sq cm
(c) 132 sq cm (d) 154 sq cm

66. **Sohan got 54 marks in Hindi, 65 marks in Science, 89 marks in Maths, 69 marks in Social Science and 68 marks in English. The maximum marks of each subject is 100. How much overall percentage of marks did he get?**
(a) 74 (b) 69
(c) 68 (d) 72

67. **8 women can complete a piece of work in 15 hours. In how many hours will 12 women complete the same piece of work ?**
(a) 12 (b) 6
(c) 8 (d) 10

Directions (Q. 68-70): *What will come in place of question mark (?) in the following number series?*

68. **23 32 45 62 83 (?)**
(a) 116 (b) 106
(c) 102 (d) None of these

69. **9 20 42 75 119 (?)**
(a) 174 (b) 170
(c) 168 (d) 180

70. **17 23 35 59 107 (?)**
(a) 217 (b) 223
(c) 203 (d) 227

English Language

Directions (Q. 71-80): *Read the following passage carefully and answer the questions given below it. Certain words are printed in bold to help you locate them while answering some of the questions.*

The Sun, while going on his daily rounds, saw a princess and fell in love with her. Whenever he could slip away from the heavens he would take human form and go down to the princess to spend some time with her. The princess too became quite fond of him and would wait for him to come. One day the Sun decided to send her a blood-red ruby as a **token** of his love for her. He put the gem in a silk bag, and calling a crow that was flying past, asked the. bird to deliver the gem to his beloved. Crows had milky white feathers in those days and it was considered **auspicious** if a crow came anywhere near you. So the Sun was pleased that he had found a crow to deliver the gem. As the crow sped through the sky with the silken bag, the aroma of food lured him. Looking down, the crow saw that a wedding feast was in progress, and immediately it was distracted from its mission. Food was one thing it could never resist.

Alighting on a tree nearby, it hung the bag on a twig and went off to find some food. While the crow was feasting, a merchant passing by saw the bag on the tree, and knocked it down with a pole. When he opened the bag and saw its contents he almost swooned in joy. Quickly pocketing the ruby, he filled the bag with dry cow dung that was lying there, and then **deftly** returned the bag to the branch. It was all done so quickly that the crow missed all the action. After having its fill, it flew up to the tree, and picking up the bag, took it to the person it was intended for. The princess was in the garden. When the crow gave her the bag, she took it eagerly, knowing that it was from the Sun. But when she saw its contents she reeled back in shock and anger. Believing that it was the Sun's way of telling her that he did not care for her, she flung the bag away, rushed to her palace, and never came out again. When the Sun learnt of what had happened he was **furious.** So great was his anger that when he turned his **scorching** gaze on the crow, its feathers were burned black. Its feathers have been black ever since. The ruby did not stay with the man who stole it. It fell out of his pocket and rolled into a deep pit. Men have been trying to dig it out ever since. Many precious stones have been found in the process, making Myanmar one of the richest sources of rubies and sapphires, but the ruby that the Sun sent to the princess is yet to be found.

71. **While on its way to the princess, the crow was distracted by.**
(a) the merchant calling out to him.
(b) the wedding that was taking place below.
(c) the ruby that the Sun sent for the princess.
(d) the temptation of the smell of food.

72. **What led to the discovery of precious stones in Myanmar?**
(a) Humans discovered the stones in their search for the lost ruby.
(b) The crow spread the news of the lost ruby.
(c) The princess went in search of the lost ruby and discovered other precious stones.
(d) The merchant went in search of the ruby that fell off his pocket.

73. Why did the Sun send his gift for the princess along with the crow?
(a) The princess loved crows.
(b) The crow was the only bird available at the time,
(c) The crow was considered to be an auspicious bird.
(d) The crow knew where the princess lived.'

74. What did the Sun send for the princess as a token of his love?
(a) He sent her the crow.
(b) He sent her dry cow dung.
(c) He sent her a red ruby.
(d) He gifted her the city of Myanmar.

75. Why did the princess fling the gift away?
(a) She did not like rubies.
(b) The crow was known to bring bad luck.
(c) She had found cow dung in the bag.
(d) She thought the Sun was playing a cruel joke on her.

76. What message did the princess get after opening the bag?
(a) That the Sun truly loved her
(b) That the crow was an evil bird
(c) That the crow was playing a joke on her
(d) That the Sun did not love her anymore

77. What could be an appropriate title for the story?
(a) The Careless Black Crow
(b) Myanmar and its Mineral Riches
(c) The Sun and the Princess
(d) The Depressed Princess

78. How did the crow get its black colour?
(a) The crow was punished by the Sun for its clumsiness.
(b) The crow was burned black by the scorching gaze of the angry Sun.
(c) The crow was not considered auspicious any more.
(d) The crow was cursed by the merchant.

79. The joy of the merchant on finding the ruby was shortlived because
(a) He did not succeed in stealing the ruby.
(b) The ruby fell out of his pocket.
(c) The crow returned just in time and caught him red-handed.
(d) He soon discovered many more precious stones.

80. What was the crow's mission?
(a) To deliver the gift to the princess
(b) To attend the wedding
(c) To make the Sun angry
(d) To keep the princess in her palace

Directions (Q. 81-83): *Choose the word which is most nearly the SAME in meaning as the word printed in bold as used in the passage.*

81. Auspicious
(a) Religious (b) Lucky
(c) Fulfilling (d) Charming

82. Deftly
(a) Skilfully (b) Blindly
(c) Eagerly (d) Rightfully

83. Token
(a) Symbol (b) Insurance
(c) Slip (d) Assurance

Directions (Q. 84-85): *Choose the word which is most OPPOSITE in meaning of the word printed in bold as used in the passage.*

84. Scorching
(a) Cool (b) Heated
(c) Warm (d) Silent

85. Furious
(a) Beaming (b) Angry
(c) Forgiving (d) Calm

Directions (Q. 86-95): *Read each sentence to find out whether there is any grammatical error in it. The error, if any, will be in one part of the sentence. The number of that part is the answer.*

86. The course is for/(a) anyone when is interested/(b) in learning/(c) about computers./(d)

87. We were/(a) surprised/(b) that she participated/(c) at the performance held at NCPA./(d)

88. The principal/(a) introducing me/(b) to some of her/(c) teaching staff./(d)

89. As soon as/(a) I getting my/(b) first salary/(c) I spent all my money./(d)

90. Poor people/(a) has no money/(b) therefore they cannot/(c) afford/(d) propermedical facilities.

91. When we/(a) reached the shops,/(b) we find that/(c) they were all closed./(d)

92. The Indian government/(a) should make sure that/(b) men and women is/(c) given equal opportunities./(d)

93. By the times/(a) we reached the classroom,/(b) the lecture/(c) had /(d) already begun.

94. The doctors said that/(a) he was making good progress/(b) and would not/(c) need a operation./(d)

95. Instead of/(a) to buy books,/(b) borrow them/(c) from the library./(d)

Directions (Q. 96-100): *Pick out the most effective word from the given words to fill in the blanks to make the sentence meaningfully complete.*

96. The young boy was unhurt ____ for a minor injury to his knee.
(a) less (b) except
(c) also (d) just

97. There is____ chance of seeing her again____ she leaves.
(a) perhaps, when
(b) also, as
(c) little, before
(d) full, therefore

98. I was annoyed ____ John for arriving late.
(a) on (b) about
(c) by (d) with

99. We are ____ the possibility of buying our own house.
(a) judging (b) initiating
(c) threatening (d) considering

100. The student did not pay ____ to the instructions that were given to her in class.
(a) ear (b) awareness
(c) notice (d) attention

Answer Sheet

1.(d)	2.(d)	3.(c)	4.(b)	5.(a)	6.(c)	7.(c)	8.(c)	9.(d)	10.(b)
11.(d)	12.(a)	13.(c)	14.(d)	15.(d)	16.(c)	17.(b)	18.(d)	19.(b)	20.(c)
21.(d)	22.(b)	23.(d)	24.(a)	25.(a)	26.(c)	27.(d)	28.(d)	29.(d)	30.(b)
31.(b)	32.(a)	33.(d)	34.(d)	35.(c)	36.(a)	37.(d)	38.(d)	39.(c)	40.(c)
41.(d)	42.(c)	43.(b)	44.(d)	45.(b)	46.(a)	47.(b)	48.(d)	49.(d)	50.(b)
51.(d)	52.(b)	53.(d)	54.(a)	55.(c)	56.(d)	57.(d)	58.(d)	59.(c)	60.(a)
61.(c)	62.(d)	63.(a)	64.(b)	65.(d)	66.(b)	67.(d)	68.(d)	69.(a)	70.(c)
71.(d)	72.(a)	73.(c)	74.(c)	75.(d)	76.(d)	77.(c)	78.(b)	79.(b)	80.(a)
81.(b)	82.(a)	83.(a)	84.(a)	85.(d)	86.(b)	87.(c)	88.(b)	89.(b)	90.(b)
91.(c)	92.(c)	93.(a)	94.(d)	95.(b)	96.(b)	97.(c)	98.(d)	99.(d)	100.(d)

Solutions

1. **(d)** As per Rajesh ⇒ May, Jun, Jul, Aug ... (i)
   As per Vinod ⇒ May or after ... (ii)
   From (i) and (ii), we get May, Jun. Jul, Aug. Of these, only Jun has 30 days (Madan's criterion).
2. **(d)** TAME, TEAM, MATE
3. **(c)**

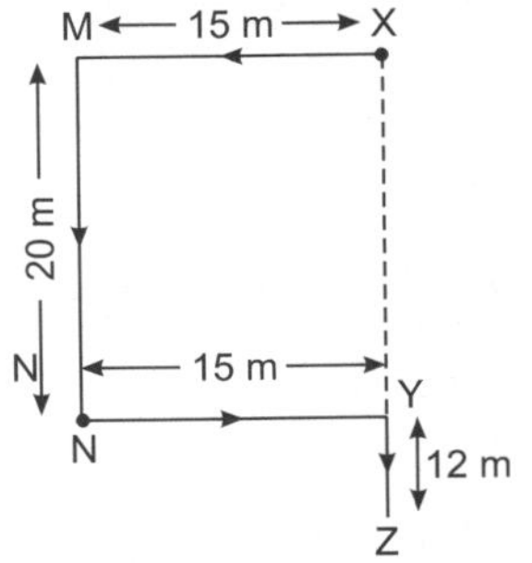

   XZ = XY + YZ = MN + YZ = 20 m + 12 m = 32 m
4. **(b)** 7652348 → 5733159
   Now, 3 + 5 = 8
5. **(a)** The first set of letters follows –1, –2, –3, –4 and the second ones –2, –3, –4, –5.
6. **(c)** Saurabh's rank = 8th from top
   Manila's rank = (8 + 5) = 13th from top
   ∴ Mamta's rank from bottom = 40 – 13 + 1 = 28th
7. **(c)** All others are metals
8. **(c)** Move one letter forward.;
9. **(d)**

   P R O D U C T I O N

10. **(b)**

(11-15):

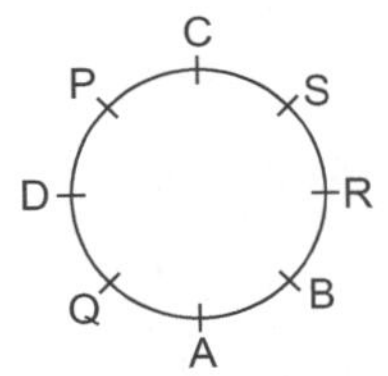

11. **(d)**
12. **(a)**
13. **(c)** In all others, the second person is on the left of the first.
14. **(d)**
15. **(d)** B, R, S and C
16. **(c)** 2 4 8 5 6
17. **(b)** 2 4 8 5 6 1 3 6 4 5 2 9 7 1 3
18. **(d)** 2nd to the right 10th from left = (10 + 2) = 12th from left = 5
19. **(b)** β and #
20. **(c)** 4 and 4
21. **(d)** No blue are white + Some white are grey = E + I = O* = Some grey are not blue. Hence I does not follow. II does not follow from the third statement.
22. **(b)** All dancers are musicians + No musicians are painters = A + E = E = No dancers are painters → conversion → No painters are dancers (E). Hence II follows. Some actors are dancers + No dancers are painters = I + E = O = Some actors are not painters. Hence I does not follow.
23. **(d)** All cities are countries + All countries are towns = A + A = A = All cities'are towns. Hence II does not follow All villages are cites + All cities are towns = A + A = A = All villages are towns → conversion → Some towns are villages (I). Hence I does not follow.
24. **(a)** Some books are poetry + All poetry is philosophy = I + A = I = Some books are philosophy. Hence I follows. Some philosophy is psychology (I) → conversion → Some psychology is philosophy (I). Hence II does not follow.

25. **(a)** Some students are adults + All adults are workers = I + A = 1 = Some students are workers. Hence I follows All children are students + Some students are adults = A + I = No conclusion. Hence II does not follow.

26. **(c)** 374 659 821 945 247

Add 2 to middle digit: 394 679 841965 267

Interchange first two: 934 769 481695 627

Of these, 934 is the largest.

27. **(d)** In other words, find out the odd numbers among the given ones

28. **(d)** 374 659 821 945 247

On interchanging: 734 569 281 495 427

Among these, 495 is the third lowest.

29. **(d)** 374 659 821 945 247

Arranging the digits: 347 569 128 459 247

Of these, 459 is the second highest.

30. **(b)** On subtracting 1, we get 373, 658, 820, 944 and 246. Now, 4 in 944 is a perfect square.

(31-35):

E A F J H D K

31. **(b)** F and J

32. **(a)**

33. **(d)** In all others, the second is on the immediate right of the first.

34. **(d)**

35. **(c)** E A F J H D K

36. **(a)** $45\times\frac{24}{12}-35+153=?$

$\therefore$? = 90 – 35 + 153 = 208

37. **(d)** $\frac{(213-345)}{8}\times(-4)=?$

$\therefore\ ?=\frac{-132}{8}\times-4=66$

38. **(d)** $34.36-45.67+86.56-37.96=?$

$\therefore$? = 37.29

39. **(c)** $\frac{22-9+14}{34}=\frac{27}{34}$

40. **(c)**

41. **(d)** $\frac{(30)^2\times54}{24}=\frac{900\times54}{24}=2025$

42. **(c)**

43. **(b)** $\frac{3}{11}\times77\times8=168$

44. **(d)** $169-25-26+7=(?)^2$

$=125=?^2$

$\Rightarrow\ ?=\sqrt{125}=5\sqrt{5}$

45. **(b)** x% of 350 – 36 = 48

or, $x=\frac{84\times100}{350}=24$

46. **(a)**

$(1+1-1)+\left(\frac{2}{7}+\frac{1}{14}-\frac{3}{28}\right)=\left(1+\frac{8+2-3}{28}\right)$

$=1+\frac{7}{28}=1+\frac{1}{4}=1\frac{1}{4}$

47. **(b)**

48. **(d)**

$\frac{54.4\times5\times8}{16}+8=(?)^2\Rightarrow\ ?=\sqrt{144}=12$

49. **(d)** $\frac{7}{15}\times\frac{5}{12}\times540=105$

50. **(b)** $\frac{92\times5}{10}+3=(?)^2$

or, $46+3=?^2$

or, $?=\sqrt{49}=\pm7$

51. **(d)** $\frac{280\times3\times4}{7\times5}=96$

52. **(b)** Average speed of the car $=\frac{450}{6}=75$ km/h

Average speed of the tractor = $75\times\frac{2}{5}=30$ km/h

Distance covered by the tractor = 30 × 8 = 240 km

53. **(d)** Length of the rectangle = 25 cm

Breadth of the rectangle = $\frac{25}{5}-1=4$ cm

$\therefore$ Area of the rectangle = 25 × 4 = 100 sq cm

$\therefore$ Area of the square = 4 × 100 = 400 sq cm

$\therefore$ Side of the square = 20 cm

$\therefore$ Perimeter of the square = 4 × 20 = 80 cm

54. **(a)** $(12)^3-(22)^2=1728-484=1244$

55. **(c)**

$\frac{48+59+87+37+78+57}{6}=\frac{366}{6}=61$

56. **(d)** Varun's present age = 39 – 4 = 35 years

So, Tarun's present age = 15 years

Tarun's age 4 years ago = 11 years

57. **(d)** Let the numbers be x, $x+2$, $x+4$, $x+6$ and $x+8$.

According to the question,

$x+x+2+x+4+x+6+x+8=170$

or $5x+20=170$

or $x+4=34$

or $x=30$

$\therefore$ Second largest No = 30 + 6 = 36

Square of smallest No. = 900

$\therefore$ Sum of these Nos. = 900 + 36 = 936

58. **(d)**

59. **(c)**

60. **(a)** $I=25000\times\frac{3}{20}=3750$

$r=\frac{3750\times100}{25000\times3}=5\%$

61. **(c)** Second selling price

$=6500\times\frac{124}{100}\times\frac{80}{100}=6448$

Loss = 6500 – 6448 = ₹ 52

62. **(d)**

63. **(a)** $\left(1200\text{ of }\frac{5}{8}\right)$ of 74% = 74% of 750 = 555

64. **(b)**

65. **(d)** $r=\frac{24-10}{2}=\frac{14}{2}=7$

$\therefore$ Area

$=\pi r^2=\frac{22}{7}\times7\times7=154$ sq cm.

66. **(b)**

67. **(d)**

68. **(d)** 23 32 45 62 83 ?
+9 +13 +17 +21 +25

69. **(a)** 9 20 42 75 119 ?
+11 +22 +33 +44 +55

70. **(c)** 17 23 35 59 107 ?
+6 +12 +24 +48 +96